D1035798

UNCERTAIN GLORY

Folklore and the American Revolution

"The Tocsin of Liberty"

Rung by the State House Bell. Independence Hall, Philadelphia, July 4th, 1776.

"Proclaim liberty throughout all the land, unto all the inhabitants thereof." Lev. XXV.10.

UNCERTAIN GLORY

Folklore and the American Revolution

by Tristram Potter Coffin

1971
Folklore Associates
Detroit, Michigan

Library of Congress Catalog Card Number 77-147812

Manufactured in the United States of America

to Fitzgordon (1958-1968)
. . . somewhere a prince

Contents

Illustrations

Acknowledgments

AN AUTHOR ALWAYS HAS acknowledgments to make. These are mine. Let me thank Robert Seager II, who first showed interest in the possibility of a sensible book on folklore and the American Revolution; Walter Clemons, who encouraged me to do the work; and Kenneth Goldstein, who saw the book safely through a "breach birth". Then let me acknowledge the courtesies shown me by the Rosenbach Museum of Philadelphia and by the Historical Societies of Massachusetts, New York, Pennsylvania, and Vermont. Finally, let me thank persons who gave me specific aid along the way: Helen H. Flanders and Henry Glassie for Chapter 3; Horace P. Beck for Chapter 5; William Ferris through his article "William Billings, the Musical Tanner" in *Keystone Folklore Quarterly* (Winter 1967), 261-277 for Chapter 6; Elaine Gropper and Sharon Haynes for Chapter 7; David Winslow, Louis C. Jones, and Mrs. Harold Thompson for Chapter 8; David Cohen for Chapter 11; and Robert S. Stewart. Of course, I don't want to omit my wife and daughters who read the manuscript kindly, and my black setter, Charcoal, who assisted me page by page, revision by revision, by lying on my feet during the composition of most of the book.

As *Uncertain Glory* includes certain songs, tales, and passages that have appeared in print before, let me also express my gratitude for certain permissions: to Edith Fowke and W. J. Gage, Ltd. for "Revolutionary Tea"; to the Duke University Press for "Paul Jones"; to Helen H. Flanders for "The Dying British Sergeant"; to Kenneth S. Goldstein and the American Folklore Society for "Donald Munro" and "Major Androw"; to Alan Lomax for the cover notes from the lp record "All Day Singing from 'The Sacred Harp' "; to Louis C. Jones and the Harold W. Thompson Archive of the New York State Historical Society for the materials obtained from Eleanor Ribley and Helen Roickle concerning Tim Murphy; and to Stephen T. Riley and the Massachusetts Historical Society for the poem by Eb. Stiles entitled "Story of the Battle of Concord, etc."

Acknowledgements

Introduction

1 Folklore's "Perennial Domain"

THERE'S NO POINT IN MY WRITING this book on folklore and the American Revolution unless my readers know what folklore is. And I am certain most of them don't. At least, if my experience at cocktail parties indicates anything, the average "intelligent reader" knows more about his own car than he does about folklore. How many times has a fellow guest asked me what I teach, only to reply when I say folklore, "What kind of folklore? American folklore?"! Alas, it takes me nearly a week of classes to define the word "folklore," much less the phrase "American folklore," to my students at Penn, and even then the tests show that I haven't been particularly successful. I need at least thirty minutes, doing all the talking, and some instinctive comprehension of human nature tells me that people at cocktail parties are summer scholars, sunshine participants, who won't listen that long. It troubles me. There is seldom need for the lawyer, the chemist, or the orthodontist to define his field in public —in social, as it might better be called. Somewhere, somehow by educational osmosis we learn what those professions cover, or we're embarrassed to admit we don't know. But folklore's different. You never meet anyone who has the foggiest idea of what it is really about.

I am pretty well convinced there are less than 200 people in

America who can come up with a decent definition of folklore, and this in the face of the fact the American Folklore Society has about 600 individual members. I consider myself to be among the 200, so let me cite a specific definition I included in an essay for the *South Atlantic Quarterly*[1] a few years back.

> Folklore is, of course, individually created art that a homogeneous group or people who don't, won't, or can't write preserve, vary, and recreate as they pass it along from mouth to ear and ear to mouth. In America, folklore has come to mean myths, legends, tales, songs, proverbs, riddles, superstitions, rhymes, and other forms of literary expression. Related to written literature, and frequently transcribed for one reason or another, it loses its vitality when it is removed from its oral existence. Though folklore may exist in either literate or illiterate societies, its cultural significance is bound to increase when illiteracy is widespread. Someone has described it as "illiterature"—not a bad definition at all.

But a definition like this needs a good bit of explanation, explanation I would recall by means of a mnemonic device pronounced "horc" when I used to "talk for drinks" before ladies' clubs and library associations.

H stands for *homogeneity*. Folklore rises and flourishes in homogeneous groups. In America, these groups are invariably bound together by ethnic, regional, or occupational interests that isolate them from the mainstream of our British-derived, highly educated culture. Homogeneity alone doesn't make a folk group, but I don't see how you are going to have a folk group without it. O stands for *oral transmission*. The literature of the homogeneous group must be passed along by word of mouth, changing, developing variants, as parts are forgotten, details localized, words garbled. R stands for this process of *re-creation*, this ever-becoming new. Thus a song like "Canaday-I-O," adapted by Ephraim Braley in 1854 near Hudson, Maine from an older British piece, "Caledon-i-a," becomes "Michigan-I-O," "Colley's Run-I-O." "The Jolly Lumberman" in the camps of the Great Lakes and Pennsylvania, becomes "The Buffalo

[1] "Harden E. Taliaferro and the Use of Folklore by American Literary Figures," *South Atlantic Quarterly*, Spring 1965, 242.

Skinners," "The Hills of Mexico," "The Boggy Creek" on the western and southwestern plains. C stands for *cultural significance*, and this is my own phrase, to me the *sine qua non* of folklore. If the literature existing in a homogeneous group, even should it be carried orally and thus almost surely subject to re-creation, is not culturally significant to that group, I don't consider it folklore. Thus an assemblage of bearded, socially active hippies sprawling about their pads in San Francisco may well develop a homogeneity that isolates them from conforming citizens, they may sing protest and other "in" songs which they don't write down and which vary over the months, but, basically, when the chips are down, they don't pass their culture on by means of these songs. The hippie, like the rest of us, will send his children to school, to the public library, to the paperback store when he wants them to learn about the problems of a world none of us chose to be born in. "When the vixen teaches the little foxes what it means to be a fox" she turns to those things that I think of as culturally significant.

Therefore, I don't consider that groups such as professional baseball players can be called folk groups or be said to possess folklore. It is true they are homogeneous, with their own traditions, customs, even a few tales or songs. Babe Ruth points a finger at the stands and belts Charlie Root's next pitch where he was pointing— or was he telling how many swings he had left, or was he just wiping sweat from his eye? Buzz Clarkson (or as it Willie McCovey?) paints eyes on his bat so it will see the ball better and break him out of his slump. A rookie wires home from Florida: "Put another cup of water in the soup, Ma, they started throwing curves today." These are anecdotes and beliefs that might become folklore except for two facts. One, the homogeneity of the ballplayer ends when he leaves the stadium or returns from the road-trip and goes home to his literate wife and television set like the milkman, the professor, and the truckdriver. And two, the stories about Ruth and Clarkson and the rookie are merely bric-a-brac in the professional part of the ballplayer's life. They are not the means through which he has found out what it is to be a human being treading the *via dolorosa*, though they may be the means through which he initiates someone into his trade. Thus baseball has a "potential folk literature", a literature that certainly shares many of the characteristics of genuine, culturally significant folk literature, but it is not true folk literature because it is just not *that* important in the overall lives of the participants, who form something one might call a "pseudo-folk group".

The lumbermen of one hundred years ago had a genuine folklore. These men lived for years in the same life pattern with others like themselves, entering the woods in October, staying there in isolation till April or May, coming out, spending all their money on wine, women, and song, shipping as sea-hands for the warm months, spending all their money on wine, women, and song, going back into the woods in October. Unlettered, ignorant, unquestioning, often starting as teen-agers and dying in the cycle, this was their whole life. But today, the lumberman is more like the ballplayer. He is taken in and out of the woods daily, listens to the radio, watches television, and sends his children to the local schools. Thus lumbering no longer seems a folk occupation, though it does still have its heritage from earlier times.

Obviously then as education reaches further and further down into the culture, as mass media outlets flood remote areas, as living standards rise and military drafts upset the population, fewer and fewer genuine folk groups exist. Certainly as Coca-Cola, Keynes, and Mad Ave conquer America and then the World, folklore must die. The ethnically isolated peasant groups, the Mexicans of Los Angeles, the Mexicans of Michoacan, will be acculturated and absorbed, replacing Juan Bobo and Pedro di Urdemales with Cantinflas and Bill Cosby; the regionally isolated mountaineers, the aloof religious sects, the remote occupations (the hill-billies of Arkansas, the Amish of Pennsylvania, the cowhands of Texas) must yield to the call of the city aircraft factory, the high school library, the draft, the movies, and *Life* magazine. All folklorists know this is happening, and many of them, seeing their beloved folklore about to join Latin as a "dead subject" attempt to re-define the discipline, and thus by the magic of semantics to save the day. But they need not worry: for folklore is a phoenix, which can rise full-grown from its own ashes. Should an atomic war, or some such catastrophe, reduce the world to the barbarism it once knew, so that man and woman would have to spend all their time in finding food to eat, in keeping warm, in keeping from being eaten, from the literary culture which is now replacing folklore would be born a new folklore, breeding, like T. S. Eliot's lilacs, "out of the dead land."

Of course, one doesn't have to think about folklore very long before he begins to wonder if folklore among the savage, pre-Columbian American Indians and folklore among the smog-breathing Puerto Ricans of New York City is really the same thing. Both groups are homogeneous, and both groups have a culturally significant lore that is transmitted orally and re-created in the process. But the pre-Columbian American Indians, like the Blacks of Australia and the Bushmen of Africa are a primitive people who have had no or nearly no contact with highly literate, educated societies. Their lore has to be classified a bit differently from that of the New York Puerto Rican (or the medieval peasant or the 19th century Maine lumberman) whose lore may not only borrow from and lend to a literate society that exists by its side, but may actually originate in that literate society. Thus some scholars, most of them anthropologists, distinguish between primitive lore and folklore. It is a technical, if useful, distinction which works better on paper than in actuality. After all cultures are in flux. The Navahoes, once clearly primitives, might well be called folk today.

There is also a distinction that concerns the literature of the folk (the ballads, tales, rimes, etc.) and those traditional things like recipes, barn signs, old ploughshares, and everyday living habits. When I began my career as a folklorist there wasn't any question: in America, folklore meant "folk literature," and my bias toward such a literary approach showed in the definition I wrote in the *South Atlantic Quarterly* and will show again throughout this book. However, Europeans have always interpreted the word more broadly, including arts, crafts, and such under the aegis of "folklore." Recently, definitions similar to the following one by Canadian Marius Barbeau have been gaining vogue in the United States, as the term "folklife" has come to the fore.[2]

[2] This is a portion of one of the definitions printed under the word "folklore" in Maria Leach (editor), *The Standard Dictionary of Folklore, Mythology, and Legend* (New York, 1959), Vol. I, 398.

Whenever sayings, proverbs, fables, noodle-stories, folktales, reminiscences of the fireside are retold;

Whenever, out of habit or inclination, the folk indulge in songs and dances, in ancient games, in merrymaking, to mark the passing of the year or the usual festivities;

Whenever a mother shows her daughter how to sew, knit, spin, weave, embroider, make a coverlet, braid a sash, bake an old-fashioned pie;

Whenever a farmer on the ancestral plot trains his son in the ways long familiar, or shows him how to read the moon and the winds to forecast the weather at sowing or harvest time;

Whenever a village craftsman—carpenter, carver, shoemaker, cooper, blacksmith, builder of wooden ships—trains his apprentice in the use of tools, shows him how to cut a mortise and peg in a tenon, how to raise a frame house or a barn, how to string a snowshoe, how to carve a shovel, how to shoe a horse or shear a sheep;

Whenever in many callings the knowledge, experience, wisdom, skill, the habits and practices of the past are handed down by example or spoken word, by the older to the new generations, without reference to book, print, or schoolteacher;

Then we have folklore in its own perennial domain.

At the University of Pennsylvania the graduate program is now called Folklore and Folklife and courses dealing with museum matters, courses that aren't literary at all, are taught. Many of them have little to do with folklore as I originally thought of it.

By now my reader must be pretty well convinced that folklore would be defined as "a huge bore" in cocktail party small-talk ——— and we have yet to come to the most difficult part of any description of the field, the part where I have to clarify the distinctions between folklore, whether or not it includes primitive lore and folklife, and all that popular literature which Richard M. Dorson has labelled "fakelore,"[3] and which masquerades as the product of oral tradition. Wherever a nation has developed a literary tradition, that is a first-rate literature, it has also developed a popular tradition of trite, formulaic writing fashioned for easy reading by undemanding minds. In modern America, all our promotional material, most of

[3] Dorson coined this word in an article entitled "Folklore and Fakelore" in *American Mercury*, March 1950, 335-343.

our best-sellers, our magazine and newspaper writing, our radio, movie, and television fare ——— in short, what we call our mass media ——— makes up our popular tradition. It would be no problem to understand this sort of material and to dismiss it as a necessary, if inferior, side of our literature were it not for one fact: entrepreneurs, for generations, have recognized that certain types of popular literature will sell better, satisfy better, if they imitate or disguise themselves as folklore. Thus, many songs by commercial hacks such as Stephen Foster, George Gershwin, Irving Berlin, and Bob Dylan are labelled "folksongs"; stories of manufactured heroes like Pecos Bill and Paul Bunyan are peddled as tales told by our ancestors on the frontier; and books advocating quack cures and eccentric potions are sold as treasuries of folk medicine, although the folk, the people who carry their culture orally, never sing "My Old Kentucky Home" or "Summertime," never have heard of Babe, the Blue Ox, know nothing of the powers of honey or vinegar.

Of course "fakelore" gets extremely wide distribution. In a country like ours, even the most remote folk groups are now able to hear Gershwin's songs and learn Paul Bunyan stories. Consequently, we have to face the fact that while popular literature is not genuine folk literature, some of it may become genuine folk literature, if the people who carry their culture orally find it appealing, embrace it, and recreate it. Dan Emmett's minstrel piece, "Old Dan Tucker", a pop tune in its day, is now a genuine folksong known wherever the square dance was danced or the play-party played. It now has hundreds of stanzas, many variants (I even published one about Mrs. Tucker),[4] and is completely re-created. Not too many years ago, I heard a rock and roll singer perform it on the radio, bringing it back from its oral tradition into the popular tradition where it had begun.

It all boils down to this: one has to be an expert to know whether an individual song or tale or custom is folk or phoney. For example, baseball is not a folk game; "Porgy and Bess" is not a folk opera; a performer like Woody Guthrie was once a folk singer, who could sing like a folksinger when he wanted to, but spent much of his career as a writer of propagandistic songs; Davy Crockett was a

[4] See the *Journal of American Folklore (JAF)*, 1960, 156.

folk hero in the 19th century, but he was also the subject of a mass of popular tales composed by urban hacks, as well as being a TV character much like The Lone Ranger and Superman. Confusing as it may be, such has always been the situation in societies that have a literary and sub-literary culture that exist side-by-side with an oral culture. The cultures interchange material continually and indiscriminately, and, believe me, even the scholars aren't clear about what is folklore and what is fakelore in a nation like ours.

However, if you think you have problems dealing with the word "folklore" alone, try adding the word "American" in front of it. For in a nation as recent and culturally diverse as ours, it is risky to insist that a national oral tradition exists or ever has existed. When Hennig Cohen and I published our anthology of folk literature a few years back, we carefully entitled it *Folklore in America*, rather than *American Folklore*, for, as we said in the "Introduction",[5]

Historically, American folk groups have found their homogeneity arising from their occupational, regional, or ethnic identities. As the nation formed and nationalism began to replace localism, folk groups were being subjected to education and communication so intensively that they became sophisticated or sub-literary before they were able to develop a *national* homogeneity. Therefore, in America, one can find a vigorous oral tradition only where he finds a group that is isolated along occupational, regional, or ethnic lines. For example, one cannot collect much folklore from the Germans in New York State, because the Germans in New York have lost their ethnic identity through intermarriage and acculturation and because they have moved up the social and educational ladder. Such people are apt to know more about Paul Bunyan than they do about poltergeists. However, in Pennsylvania, where for religious reasons the Germans have maintained their isolation, one can still collect genuine German folklore, but will also find a certain indifference to America as a nation.

You can see why it frustrates a folklorist to pick up a book called *A Treasury of American Folksong* only to find most of the content popular song, stuff that no folk group has ever sung, stuff that is copyrighted, written by educated music merchants. And

[5] Tristram Potter Coffin and Hennig Cohen (editors), *Folklore in America* (New York, 1966), xvi-xvii.

what does he do when he encounters something entitled *The Folklore of Capitalism?* It's pretty hard to know what such titles mean, if they are supposed to mean anything at all. In brief, folklore is a field of study with its own technical terms, and you bother the devil out of a folklorist when you use them too freely, just as you bother a baseball fan when you don't use phrases like "hot dog" and "mustard" properly. I remember the time Alex Riasanovsky, Pennsylvania's very popular Russian historian, listened to one of my "horc" lectures. He came up to me afterwards, amazed that I felt it appropriate to speak for a full hour on nothing but the definition of my field. "You guys are in real trouble," he said, "having to explain yourselves every time you stand up. I'll bet you never get a chance to talk about the interesting stuff." And that is true.

There is, nonetheless, one interesting matter which I feel I had better bring up at this point: "emotional core." This is my own phrase, and I developed it to describe what happens to a story, in this case a ballad, as it survives in oral tradition.[6] As ballads travel from mouth to mouth they lose details, focus on a climactic part of the plot, and may eventually become so truncated that they seem to be lyric songs with only a little narrative background. Sometimes we haven't the vaguest idea what a ballad is really about unless we can obtain older and more complete versions. I use the phrase "emotional core" to describe what the folk will preserve out of a story. "Mary Hamilton" serves as a good example. The ballad tells of Mary Hamilton, supposedly one of the four maids-in-waiting named Marie who served Mary, Queen of Scots, in the mid-16th century. It tells how the young girl was courted by Lord Darnley, the Queen's consort,

> He courted her in the kitchen,
> He courted her in the hall,
> He courted her on the backstairs,
> And that was the worst of all.

[6] This essay was originally published in *JAF*, 1957, 208-214. So enamoured of it am I, I also included it in *The Critics and the Ballad,* a collection of readings MacEdward Leach and I brought out in 1955 (Carbondale, Ill.) and in my revision of *The British Traditional Ballad in North America* (Philadelphia, 1963).

Pregnant, in real trouble, Mary Hamilton throws her new-born bairn out the window onto the rocks below. But to no avail. The Queen apprehends her, has her tried, and finally executed. This is a good juicy story, with big names, sex, violence, and sentiment. It would make a fine movie. The torrid love affair, the murder of the baby, the confrontation of the Queen and her maid-in-waiting, the trial, the last moments of the pretty girl would keep the audience excited from credits to conclusion. Yet what do the folk treasure in the story?—the lament of the girl as she stands on the gallows about to lose her life, the plaintive lines that tell the world how her rosy cheeks and dimpled chin undid her, that offer a toast to the sailors that sail upon the sea, that recall how

> Little did me mither kin,
> The day she cradled me,
> The paths I was to wander in,
> The death I was to dee.

The folk are obviously most interested by the fact that a young girl is having her life snuffed out long before her time. The sensational parts, the sex, the crime, the trial, are dismissed, as I once put it, "as discreetly as if Mary, Queen of Scots, had written the song herself." And the longer the ballad survives the more of what we would consider the juiciest details vanish. Originally 36 stanzas or so long, with more than 50% of the verses centering on the "emotional core" of the girl who is to die, "Mary Hamilton" usually ends up as a lyric telling nothing but

> Last nicht the Queen had Four Maries,
> This nicht she'll ha' but three.

I make this point to stress that the folk are going to keep exactly what they want in a story, not what we might like or expect them to keep. They are going to preserve what they feel to be the important thing, that "emotional core" that somehow typifies what they feel the world is all about. Thus the folklore of a war such as the American Revolution may tell nothing of Arnold's heroism at Saratoga, give no juicy details of his villainy at West Point, may never mention Lafayette or George Washington, may seem disappointingly similar to the folklore of peace. Yet it will be made up of matter that is significant to the ignorant people who incorporate it into their literature; and no matter how frustrating this may be to us, to our historians, to Madison Avenue, to our politicians and sentimental schoolteachers, it is what makes oral tradition so honest, so essential, so wonderful.

Consequently, I can assure my readers that no one should use folklore as a record of fact. For while folklore may originally record an event with great accuracy ("Casey Jones" still preserves the details of the tragedy on the Illinois Central after 70 years in oral and popular tradition), ultimately the folk concentration on the emotional core, combining with the urge to localize and other forms of variation, will eliminate the specific detail a historian is after. The ballad "Springfield Mountain" offers an excellent case in point. On August 7, 1761, Timothy Myrick (pronounced Merrick), 22 years old and betrothed to Sarah Blake, died of snakebite in Farmington, Connecticut. He was buried in his hometown Wilbraham, once Springfield Mountain, Massachusetts, where his tombstone still stands, and a narrative poem telling of his fate was composed, probably for reading or singing at the funeral. This poem became a folksong and travelled across New England. In and about Springfield, Vermont, it seems to have been localized to fit the death of a member of the Curtis family of Weathersfield, who also probably died of snakebite, and a variant text came into being. Later, the song was adapted by music hall performers for comic purposes in two versions, one with a heroine named Sally, the other with a heroine named Molly. All four of these songs have wandered across America, sometimes intermingling, sometimes maintaining separate identities. The full-length versions of the Myrick ballads, telling how Timothy was bitten, how his father heard his cries but did not heed them, and how the father later discovered the body, may well be accurate historical records of fact. The Curtis texts may not, as the events leading up to young Curtis' death (whatever they were) had to be forced into the context of the already composed Myrick song. The Sally and Molly texts, where Timothy's girl rushes to his aid, attempts to suck the poison from the bite, and dies when the venom enters her bloodstream through a rotten tooth are nonsense. Therefore, a historian might get a fairly accurate record of Myrick's death from the song and he might not. It would depend on which version he found. And in the case of many of the old tales and songs, we simply cannot tell which version survived.

The relationship between the Curtis and Myrick forms of "Springfield Mountain" shows something else about folklore that a lot of historians don't seem to recognize: folklore is essentially formulaic. The simplest way of creating an artistic account of a tragedy or other interesting event is to cast the details into the already established pattern of a song or tale or other art form in one's repertoire. Thus, Wash Saunders, a roundhouse hand, cast the wreck of John Luther Jones' No. 382 into the established mold of a ballad called "Jimmy Jones" dealing with a Pullman porter, and the same pattern has been used for related songs about "Jay Gould's Daughter," a Morman named Zack Black, and a union scab. Any of these revisions may give a pretty accurate historical account of the wreck, as "Casey Jones" does, but they are all risky bets because of the presence of the mold. Zack Black may have "another woman" on the Salt Lake Line because he is a Mormon, but he may also have her because Casey Jones' widow told her children they had "another poppa" there; and Casey Jones' wife may have been blamed for infidelity through the years, not because she was an "easy woman," but because Jimmy Jones had such a mate.

In the same way, Robin Hood, Jesse James, Pretty Boy Floyd, and most the other outlaws have a set pattern into which their lives and escapades fall. Being members of a downtrodden group in time of crisis, they are driven into crime by some tyrannical and completely unreasonable force. Poachers in the forests of rich landowners who can well afford to lose a few deer, ex-guerrillas for the Confederacy fighting Union Yankees after the others have quit; farmers who knock off the very banks that are foreclosing mortgages during drought years, the outlaws are good boys with "the right idea, but the wrong system," as Woody Guthrie remarked about Pretty Boy Floyd.[7] Their hearts are pure; they are sentimental robbers. They take only from the rich, and then, like miniature Lord

[7] This comment was recorded by Alan Lomax from Guthrie and is printed in *Folk Songs of North America* (Garden City, 1960), 427.

Keyneses, distribute it to the less fortunate. They are so courteous to those whom they rob the crime becomes a social occasion; they leave thousand dollar bills under the lunch plates in the homes of impoverished widows who feed them; they join the very posses that search after them. Eventually they have to die, killed by treachery, often for reward by one of their own whom they had no reason to suspect. Over the years they tend to fuse. A historian can't tell one from the other, except for his dress, his language, and his name.

So the folk historian, like the library historian, rewrites what happens as he feels it should have happened, making it appropriate to the formulas of his own particular culture. He may treat the facts with respect; he may not. For one reason or another his account, possibly because of the phrasing, perhaps because of the typical nature of the situation, enters oral tradition. It starts to become folklore. If it is to survive it must pass from person to person, community to community, eventually culture to culture, era to era. To do this, it must lose its uniqueness, assume the time-tested formulas that person after person, group after group, age after age has found satisfactory and catholic. The tale that survives in one area for but a short period of time (the tale of Babe Ruth and his homer) need only suit the tastes of a small, homogeneous group, but a tale that survives for many years in many, many lands (like the one of the outlaw and the widow) must be acceptable to all kinds of tastes and all points of view. The real event may be personal, subjective, unique, but oral tradition is sure to make it general, formulaic, and trite. Thus, it is painfully obvious that we learn more about a recent folk community than we do about the folk of the American Revolution when we in the 20th century collect a ballad about Major André's capture, just as it is painfully obvious we learn more about Victorians than we do about English history when we read Macaulay, more about ourselves than we do about Andrew Jackson when we make a best-selling author of Arthur Schlesinger, Jr.

And so, if you have paid careful attention—and not drifted away toward the bar like a guest at a cocktail party, you are perhaps ready to read a book on folklore and the American Revolution. At least you know what folklore is, or, more important, what it is not—and you know that folklore is formulaic and that it doesn't record historical fact reliably. Refinements in this knowledge should come along the way as we look at the various relationships of this odious occupation and the uncertain glory it can offer.

Uncertain Glory—that's what I have named this book. The phrase comes from Shakespeare's *Two Gentlemen of Verona*, where in Act I, Scene 3 Proteus is made to say,

> O, how this spring of love resembleth
> The uncertain glory of an April day,
> Which now shows all the beauty of the sun,
> And by-and-by a cloud takes all away!

I like this title, not of course because the book is about love, the thing Shakespeare sees as ephemeral and fickle, but because the book is about love's cousin war, the glory of which is also ephemeral and fickle, especially in oral tradition, where old heroes are discarded for new with an insouciance few coquettes could match. I also like the play on words involved. After all, the Revolution did begin on an April day—an "April morning" as Howard Fast called it—and the glory of so many, Warren, Champe, Paulding, Dawes, no longer shows the full beauty of the sun, but has been clouded over, by-and-by. I think it is a good title; it brings into focus what the book is all about.

Originally, I had wanted to use the title *Folklore Goes to War*—my variation on "Lucky Strike Green Has Gone to War," the American Tobacco Company's slogan back in 1942. But even though I have used this first as a working title, then in a sense, to head both halves of the book, I haven't felt free to use it as a full title. For one thing, nobody remembers Lucky Strike Green any longer, and furthermore "Folklore Goes to War" doesn't tell the whole story, for some of the lore never went to war with the troops.

For instance, it is unlikely that Continental soldiers knew of the following, elaborate anecdote about General Washington.[8]

[8] From *The Humorist's Own Book* by the Author of *The Young Man's Own Book* (New York, 1854), 92.

> Washington always kept this useful and scientific officer near his own person; and he not only honoured him with confidence, but with brotherly affection. After the defeat of Gates's army at Camden, General Greene was offered the arduous command of the southern department. The Quaker General, with his usual modesty, replied, "Knox is the man for that difficult undertaking; all obstacles vanish before him; his resources are infinite." "True," answered Washington, "and therefore I cannot part with him."

This is some of that mass of consciously composed material that is made up for propagandistic purposes often long after the war involved is over. Similar anecdotes, equally stuffy, glut the pages of *The Reader's Digest* today. They are safe, commercial, created by the propagandists to picture the hero as he should be and to bring into focus the symbolism of the conflict under concern. Although a small percentage of it may enter oral tradition, most of it is never seen by the folk groups from which so many of the soldiers come. One can rest assured that almost none of the Revolutionary troops gave a hoot for Paul Revere, Betsy Ross, or Patrick Henry whose legends were created, or at least refurbished, by mid-19th century flagwavers.

Soldiers fighting a war, like other occupational groups, are far too parochial to care about images appropriate to national propaganda. They bother themselves only with that which is pertinent to the moment and the place of the war, carrying to their new lives material from all sorts of backgrounds, winnowing from it an occupational lore to fit their needs. A great deal of such lore is re-worked from conventional, time-tested matter brought from home like a picture of a wife or sweetheart. For example, the old American hunting tale of the bent gun has been known to soldiers of most of our wars. Jim Bridger or Kit Carson or Daniel Boone is out hunting. He sees an elk and decides to shoot it. Jim-Kit-Dan never misses a shot, but when he fires at the elk it is neither hurt nor frightened. After a few more shots, the hunter begins to investigate. He discovers the elk is miles away, behind a crystal mountain through which the hunter has seen him. Bending his gun, Jim-Kit-Dan fires around the mountain, killing the elk at once. This old story was told about Revolutionary scout Tim Murphy. Murphy has been out looking for Indians to kill, when a party of redskins suddenly attacks him and chases him. He easily outruns all but a single brave, who pursues him round and round a huge boulder. The Indian has a tomahawk; Tim, a rifle. The sun is setting, so Tim knows that he will soon be at a disadvantage, but he can't seem to hit the Indian for the curve in the boulder makes shooting difficult. Resourcefully, Tim decides to bend the barrel of his rifle to fit the curvature of the rock. He does this with his bare hands, and kills the redskin with one shot. The same story was printed in the *Journal of American Folklore*[9] as collected from an American soldier on a bus in California in the 1940's. The elk or Indian had become a Jap and the rifleman a GI, but the story was still the same. It is just an old hunting lie that has been to battle a number of times.

Nonetheless, wars do create fresh folklore at the folk level. The following local legend surely began with the Revolution and has probably never seen print.[10]

> Simon Girty was a white renegade that used to raid white settlements about the time of the Revolution. He and his cutthroat Indians would sneak up on a lone cabin, scalp the men, and run off with the women and the children. Girty was just plain evil. He and his Indians raided right around Harrisburg and Carlisle. He had an island on the Susquehanna River that he used as a hideout . . . used to bury all the valuables he stole from the cabins there. There's a big rock on the river that they call Girty's Notch. The treasure is still there because Girty was killed on one of his own raids and never got a chance to dig it up.

Collected from an old man in York County, Pennsylvania, it has been localized many miles east of where Girty's deeds were perpetrated. Surely the fear that Pennsylvanians felt over Girty's raids is a genuine part of Revolutionary lore. But today this tale and others like it

[9] See *JAF*, 1949, 176. This tale is numbered 1890E in Antti Aarne and Stith Thompson, *The Types of the Folktale* (A-T) (Helsinki, 1961).

[10] This story was handed in to me by W. E. Hildebrand as part of an assignment given in English 126 (General Folklore) at the University of Pennsylvania in April 1967. The informant was Hub Fissel, then 86, of Dillsburg, York County, Pa.

are not easy to collect, for the events involved are no longer meaningful to the Pennsylvania folk. Even the text above does not concern itself with the War; it concentrates on the cruelty and the mystery associated with the "white Indian," and probably it survives because it explains a place name and offers the lure of locally buried treasure. For when the war is over, and the soldiers return to their previous occupational, ethnic, or regional situation, they either discard or re-adapt the greater part of what they held dear while fighting, preserving only that which seems appropriate to their new needs back at peace.

We must not forget what Barbeau told us: folklore's "perennial domain" is the life of the folk. Thus, if the trooper recalls an anecdote about two of his generals; if one rifleman confounds another with a tale of a bent gun; if a mother frightens her naughty child by telling him of Simon Girty, each will do so only if the tale offers him what our literature offers us—the reaffirmation, ethic, wisdom, and comfort needed by "men born of women." The soldiers who fought in the Revolution knew folklore in this way, not as quaint bric-a-brac, not as charming, inferior stuff, but as a normal part of everyday lives.

Thus there will have to be two parts to *Uncertain Glory*, Part I dealing with folklore as it goes to war; Part II dealing with the fakelore that is able to survive in a highly educated nation like 20th century America. It would be tedious, in fact impossible, to make either Part I or Part II anything near all-encompassing and so the approach in both sections will be selective, illustrative. Chapters 1-3 will describe and analyze the setting, function, content, and historical background of the Revolutionary informant's repertoire: showing how little of the material is actually related to the war, how complex that relationship is when it does occur. I do this by dramatizing what might have been a tale-telling session at Valley Forge, by discussing in great detail the contents of a Revolutionary soldier's songster, and by giving an historical analysis of a single song usually identified with the Revolution, "Yankee Doodle." Chapters 4 and 5 concentrate on the material that is created about the war by highly literate propagandists and that later drifts out into oral tradition to be preserved though the war itself may be forgotten. To illustrate, I have chosen six print shop ballads about Revolutionary heroes and situations which have gradually entered folk repertoires in the last 200 years as well as the hymns of William Billings, hymns which would not have been composed, been widely disseminated, or even influential had it not been for the impetus of the War. The only warning I give the reader on Part I is that he remember that the individual examples used, whether tales, ballads, lyric songs, or hymns, are of little consequence, as is the fact the War is the Revolution. The chapters would say the same things if other genres or another conflict had been the choice.

In Part II the reader is asked to re-focus his mind. Where Part I deals with material that is now circulating or once circulated in oral tradition, Part II is concerned with our own highly literate society and the Revolutionary lore that we educated Americans have created or borrowed and nurtured for own purposes. As the case in point, I have selected legendary history, for nowhere does fakelore reveal its true colors as vividly as it does there. Chapter 6 opens with a seminal idea: that fakelore is winnowed in a highly literate society to serve needs much like those served by folklore in a folk society. It concludes by showing how three legends: one fake, one partly fake, one folk, came into being. Chapters 7-10 then turn to four representative figures: two whose legends have been winnowed or pretty well winnowed from our fakelore; two whose reputations have flourished. These chapters also tell why, stressing three crucial points: one, a legendary figure is not going to survive just because he is a true folk figure; two, all Revolutionary figures are handicapped by the identification of America with its western growth at the time its fakelore was being developed; three, printed publicity is the only way a legendary figure can survive in the teeth of this handicap. The only warning I give the reader on the second half of the book is that he recall accurately the distinctions between folklore and fakelore made "so crystal clear" a few pages back.

And so my Introduction is over. I give it to my reader as he begins his passage through the uncertain realms of traditional glory in the very way Nathaniel Hawthorne presents his reader with a rose to carry through another tale of "human frailty and sorrow."

PART ONE Folklore Goes to War

2 "The Ragged, Lousey, Naked Regiment"

EVERY AMERICAN KNOWS THAT Washington's troops spent the winter of 1777-1778 in cold hardship at Valley Forge. Recently, I read in the paper that some meteorologist had researched the weather for those months and concluded that it wasn't really a bad winter at all, pretty much an average one for the area. But I have lived in Philly, and I still feel sorry for those soldiers up there along the Schuylkill. The Philly climate penetrates; it's clammy and chilly even when the temperature is not too low. And there was snow, plenty of it at times. John J. Stoudt, reconstructing the weather from soldiers' letters and diaries in his book *Ordeal at Valley Forge*,[1] tells us Tuesday, December 23, 1777 was "cold." On Wednesday, there was light snow, "flurries"; and Christmas was white. Four inches fell between Christmas Eve and the 26th, and I would not like to have been the soldier Albigence Waldo describes in his diary entry for December 14, 1777. He must have been miserable ten days later.[2]

[1] John J. Stoudt, *Ordeal at Valley Forge* (Philadelphia, 1963), 37.

[2] See the *Diary of Albigence Waldo* as printed in the *Pennsylvania Magazine of History and Biography*, 1897, xxi, 299-323.

> . . . There comes a soldier, his bare feet seen through his worn-out shoes, his legs nearly naked from the tatter'd remains of an only pair of stockings, his breeches not sufficient to cover his nakedness, his shirt hanging in strings, his hair disheveled, his face meager; his whole appearance pictures a person forsaken and discouraged. He comes, and cries with an air of wretchedness and despair, "I am sick, my feet lame, my legs are sore, my body covered with this tormenting itch—my clothes are worn out, my constitution is broken, my former activity is exhausted by fatigue, hunger, and cold, I fail fast, I shall soon be no more! And all the reward I shall get will be: Poor Will is dead!"

Poor Will! Perhaps he stood in the little square entry of an old farmhouse on Christmas Eve. The snow had begun in earnest—those fine, driving flakes that promise a lot more to come, whispering the ground will be thick in white by morning. The light was fading into darkness. Will was warm where he stood. Behind him, in what had once been the "best room" there burned a fire. As he stood there, knowing it was Christmas Eve, his thoughts drifted back to the farmhouse he had known in York State what seemed a long time ago. He thought of his Episcopalian, English father and his Dutch mother and the Christmases they used to have. Both of them came from stock that made something of Christmas, unlike the Scotch-Irish Presbyterians and the Quakers he had encountered since. He remembered the food, particularly, and how his father insisted on burning a yule-log and using the old wooden trenchers and laurel spoons his grandparents had owned when he was a boy in Virginia. He remembered his mother's disgust at these old utensils on an occasion she thought of as genuinely festive. But she never complained long, as she decorated the rooms with cedar and pine and went about preparing the meals that characterized the season—steaks, roasts, stews, oysters, bear's paws, corn, corn pudding, plums, nuts, squash, with huge amounts of cider, whiskey, and ale. He remembered his mother's reminiscing of her childhood in Albany and her stories of decorating the church with evergreens in the old Dutch way—and his father's attempts to organize wassailing and masquerading as he had known them when a boy. He even thought of his old bedroom, which was really little more than a loft where the main chimney went up, and particularly he thought of the white and blue coverlet and the homespun blankets that he snuggled into as he listened to the men drinking whiskey and telling tales in the "keeping room" below.

As Will was wondering these things and trying to think what Christmas must have been like in the farmhouse now filled with officers behind him, he suddenly became aware of the forms of soldiers passing in the storm, disappearing toward the back of the house where the long slope of the roof went down over what had been the kitchen. Will had no idea where they could be headed in such weather, especially as he knew there was no shelter back there. But after awhile, he heard the crackling of a fire and could see the light of it through the snow. He wondered why they had started a fire on such a night, when it was sure to snow until morning. But there was no doubt they had started it, and it was some fire, too. He could hear the soldiers laughing, and the high-pitched voice of one named Tarbox who had become well-known in camp for his good-humor and tale-telling. It all seemed warmer to him than the doorway, and he wasn't long in heading around back of the house.[3]

Will was a bit surprised when he neared the soldiers and their blaze, because by the sound of their voices he had figured they had built some sort of shelter to keep out of the snow. Instead, there they all were, most of them with blankets or coats over their shoulders, standing around a big open fire with no sign of a shelter anywhere. As he edged in amongst them, he stared at the big logs that were burning. Steam rose from them, and flames flew ten feet into the air. It wasn't so bad to stand there in the driving snow, as long as he was close to the heat. There was something about that fire that made him more contented than he had felt in weeks, that made it seem like Christmas, binding him to the men around him, most of whom were Southern Rhode Islanders whom he knew by sight or not at all.

Tarbox was talking, chirping on and on, and the soldiers around were quiet, except for a few snickers and an exclamation or two.

[3] The following reconstruction of a tale-telling session was suggested by the one described by Will James in Chapter 7 of *Sand* (New York, 1932). There is no question in my mind that James was recreating an actual session that he had observed in cow country.

Will could tell they felt what he felt—and there was no liquor in sight, or food. Just men, a fire, and the snow.

"You boys ever hear of Sam Hyde?" Tarbox asked without waiting for a reply. "Hyde was an Indian, lived somewhere south of Boston—the best shot around. Let me tell you. One day he went out hunting with his brother Joe, and they saw about thirty-five pigeons sitting in a line on a fence. Joe had just shot a rabbit and his gun was empty, but Sam had his gun loaded and he fired quick as a flash. The shot went through the eyes of thirty-four of those birds, when the last one, guessing what was in store for him, flew away. The others just dropped off the fence dead, and they were so fat Sam and Joe couldn't carry but half of them home."[4]

Will glanced around at the soldiers. Not one of them so much as chuckled. They all just stared at the fire, dead-pan. But this didn't faze Tarbox at all. He acted pretty much as if that were the reaction he was expecting and went right on.

"Hyde could drink more liquor and tell more lies than any damned Indian you ever saw. He used to go around begging cider from door to door. One time he was outside of Danversport and cider was hard to come by. But Sam was determined to get some, no matter what. So he went up to this house and when the owner came to the door, Sam said, 'I shot a big buck deer, and if you'll give me a crown I'll tell you where it's at.' The man said he'd give Sam half a crown, and they dickered back and forth for a while. Finally Sam said, 'I'll tell you what. You give me half a crown and a jug of cider, and I'll tell you.' The man agreed and brought Sam the money and the cider, so Sam told him where the deer was. 'You know that half-acre meadow about fifty paces off the road before you get to town?' 'Yes, I know it.' 'Well, there's a big white pine in it, near the brook at the far end. The deer's hidden under some brush right to

[4] This is a variant of "The Lucky Shot" type stories (A-T 1890). A text is printed in "Reminiscences of Danvers in the Forties and Fifties" by William L. Hyde, *The Historical Collections of the Danvers Historical Society* (Danvers, Mass., 1917), V, 8-9. This text was reproduced by Benjamin A. Botkin in *A Treasury of New England Folklore* (New York, 1947), 234. See Botkin's footnote on 549 and the text on 550 to date Sam Hyde and the associated anecdotes.

the left of that tree. You can't miss it.' The man was satisfied, and Sam left. Of course, Sam had never shot a deer, and when the man went to the meadow he realized he had been swindled. He could hardly wait to see the Indian again. And he did meet him about a month later. He ran into him on a corner in Danversport, and stopped him, demanding his money back and threatening him for his dishonesty. But Sam just stood there and asked, 'Wouldn't you be happy if Indians told the truth half the time?' 'I guess so,' replied the man somewhat taken back. 'Well,' says Sam, 'you found the meadow, didn't you? And you found the white pine? Then what do you want—I gave you two truths for one lie?' "[5]

As Tarbox finished a man back in the crowd where Will couldn't see very well began to sing. He might have been drinking earlier, for the words were hard to follow.

> A lovely lass to a friar came
> To confess in the morning early.
> In what my dear was you to blame,
> Now tell to me sincerely.
> I've done a thing I dare not name
> With Sam Hyde who loves me dearly.[6]

The soldiers laughed now, and continued to talk and joke among themselves. The voice of the singer became impossible to follow through the chatter. Eventually, it ceased, but almost at once another took up. Will caught phrases like "damn redskins," "you can laugh at them if you want, but I wouldn't trust one no way," and other curses and expletives. A huge red-headed man was roaring forth a story that he claimed had happened on Nantucket ten years before. He said he knew the Indians involved, having been in the same crew with them on a whaler named *Sally*. It was early fall, and he'd been leaning over the rail, smoking, when a sailor named Ellis started yelling for help, the Indians were killing each other. He ran

[5] A variant of this story was also reproduced in Botkin, 549-550. He took it from Samuel G. Drake, *The Book of Indians* (Boston, 1841), I, 21-22.

[6] For the history of this old song, see Claude M. Simpson, *The British Broadside Ballad and Its Music* (New Brunswick, New Jersey, 1966), 474-475. The earliest printed text known is 1710.

forward, just in time to hear one redskin cry out and die and to find another one, already dead, lying on the planking with a knife wound in his back. Two other Indians he knew only as Quibbey and Charles were standing by holding whale-lances. Quibbey freely admitted killing the two men, and said he would gladly hang for it. With that he threw his knife overboard and let himself be confined. He and Charles were taken on shore and given over to the sheriff. Not long after, they had a quarrel in prison, and Quibbey knifed Charles in the kidneys, killing him. Quibbey was given a trial that was the talk of the Island and was eventually hung in the late part of May the next year. The soldier who was telling the story finished with the comment that "a redskin kills like a weasel, just for the fun of it." Many of the soldiers grunted agreement.[7]

For a while no one spoke, and there was no sound except the hiss of the snow and the crackle of the blaze. But the silence didn't last long. A young fellow began telling a story, a sentimental tale, also meant to be true, and one by one the soldiers were caught up in the new mood, listening carefully and staring at the flames.

"She lived right down the road from our farm, and her father was one of the big men in the area. She fell in love with this Frenchman, a music-teacher, and I guess her father didn't think he was good enough for her. At any rate, they ran off and got married, and the old man wouldn't speak to her or acknowledge her any longer. But finally she got sick and was dying. She wanted to come home, and the old fellow relented. They brought her up along the hills above Pettaquamscutt to a big rock where you can look out across the river and down toward Aquidneck and the Bay. You get a real feel for Narragansett country from up there, so they stopped the litter on which they were carrying her, and she took her last look at the land she was born to. I've heard they carried her on home after that, and she was put to bed. That night a whippoorwill came and sang in the lilac bush under her window, which meant she was going to die. And die she did, with her father by her side weeping and carrying on, cursing himself for his cruelty.

[7] For another, more complete, account of this event, see "Trial and Execution of Nathan Quibbey" by Emil F. Guba in *Historic Nantucket*, October 1967, 12-16. Quibbey was hanged in 1768.

"That's the truth, I guess, but I've always heard she died differently. The way I heard it she got out of the litter up there on the hill and threw herself from the rock, killed herself. I can show you the spot, though the rock never impressed me as big enough to commit suicide from. That's what local folks say really happened, and the family tried to cover it up. I don't know. But I remember about whippoorwills. When I was little, I'd get into bed in my room at the corner of the house scared to death. There was a lilac bush under the window, and I could hear whippoorwills in the laurel beyond the pines. I wondered if one was coming to the lilac to sing to me, you know the way one sang to that Robinson girl."[8]

It was quiet when the youth finished. The fire had gone down a bit, and a few of the soldiers stepped forward to put more fuel on it. Tarbox began to talk again. "Women are like dogs," he said. "They want to know where they stand. There's a fellow I used to know who would have kept that Robinson girl in line, and she'd have been the happier for it. His name was Church, and he lived up there where that stream comes down and widens into a lake just below the hill you were talking about. He got married a few years back, and he and his bride, Abby Congdon, set out with one horse after the wedding to go down to his uncle's place in Matunuck. Abby was riding, and he was walking alongside. Something startled the horse, and he became skittish and shied a little, so Church walked to his head and slapped him on the nose, saying, 'That's once!' They went on. About a mile farther down the road, the horse shied again, this time at a branch waving in the wind. Church picked up a stick, beat the horse on the flank with it, and said, 'That's twice!' But the horse couldn't learn. A few moments later something splashed in the near-by river, and the horse reared on his hind legs, so Church took out a pistol, went over to the horse, and shot him between the eyes, saying, 'That's three times!' Abby was shocked at her new husband's cruelty. She screamed and began berating him, telling him what she thought of him for killing a poor, defenseless horse. Church listened to her for a minute or two, then he walked over to his new bride,

[8] The full story of Hannah Robinson is scattered through Thomas R. Hazard ("Shepherd Tom"), *Recollection of Olden Times* (Newport, 1879). Hannah Robinson, born in 1746, died in 1773.

slapped her gently on the shoulder, and said, 'That's once!' And I'll tell you, they lived happily ever after. I knew one of their sons real well. . . ."[9]

Will recognized this story. It was just like one he'd heard a man in the "keeping room" tell when he lay in bed as a boy. The names and places were different, but it sort of warmed him to hear it, and he had actually begun to feel sleepy when another voice intruded. Will couldn't see the speaker, but the words were very clear.

"If you look south from most anywhere near where that Robinson girl stood, you can see Block Island, at least when the weather's clear. You ever heard of the Palatine Light? The *Palatine* was a German ship full of people coming to this land about fifty or sixty years ago. The natives over there on the Island ran her ashore on purpose to plunder her; put up false lights so the captain sailed her right on the rocks. Everyone was killed, and the wreck set fire to. But she still appears there from time to time, in full sail and burning. Some nights the flames light up the whole sky. Folks around there tell the weather by the *Palatine*. When you see her burn high and clear, you know it's going to be good weather for a spell."

Tarbox's high voice broke in. "I've heard of that ship. My mother used to tell me of an old man who lived out there and went crazy every year on the day the ship was burned. He used to run wild and rave about seeing the *Palatine* being plundered by the Islanders until everything, even the rigging, was gone from her. Then he'd see them put the captain and passengers and crew below deck and burn the whole ship. He'd talk about seeing one fellow leaping from the burning mast and he'd see the spectres of two women whose hands he'd cut off with a cutlass when they tried to cling to the gunwales of his dory as he rowed off from the fire. It seems he had been one of the plunderers and the whole thing was on his conscience."[10]

[9] See A-T 901, *Taming of the Shrew.* Jan H. Brunvand refers to the particular variant used here as "the modern Anglo-American adaption of the old Indo-European narrative traditions of Type 901." See his article "The Taming of the Shrew Tale in the United States" in his handbook *The Study of American Folklore* (New York, 1968), 309. Perhaps the tale was not known to the Colonists in exactly the form used. However, variants of this story were familiar to 18th century Americans.

And so the stories went on. Tarbox seemed to be able to tell them forever. With a little help here and there from one or another of his listeners, he rambled on about the murder of some fellow named Jackson by a Captain Carter who robbed him, about how Point Judith got its name, about Narragansett pacers, about "shift weddings," and a dozen such things. At one point, he got started on the Sweet family of South Kingstown and talked about them for what must have been twenty minutes. It seems the family had originally come from Wales, and there had been a lot of children. One of them, named Benoni, who was a captain in the British service, was "gifted," a natural bone-setter. He lived to be ninety, and called himself Doctor Sweet, although he never did anything but set bones. He died in the early '50s and his son, Job, took over the family business in dislocations. Tarbox claimed he knew Job, and said he set bones for the officers of the troops around Newport, even after the army doctors had given up. Many of the doctors of the time scoffed at Job, and one in Boston even tried to show him up. It seems he pretended to have a dislocated elbow and sent for Dr. Sweet to have it fixed. Job went all the way to Boston and found the city doctor with his arm in a sling, supposedly in great pain. But the minute he touched the limb, Job knew there was nothing wrong with it. He guessed what was going on and purposely dislocated the joint as he pretended to cure it. Then he left, but he hadn't gotten far when the Boston doctor's servant overtook him and implored him to return and restore the now really dislocated limb. Another time he was supposed to have passed a skeleton that had been assembled for display to young doctors, and at one glance seen that a tiny bone in the foot was placed upside down. Tarbox said two of his boys, one named Jonathan and one named Benoni after the grandfather, had the same gift, even though they were just youngsters.[11]

Will couldn't help wondering where all these stories had come from, and he admired Tarbox for the way he told them. And he

---

[10] The story is also told in *Recollections of Olden Times*, 127-129. The "Palatine Ship" was wrecked early in the 18th century.

[11] See *Recollections of Olden Times*, 267 ff. for a complete account of the Sweets as bone-setters. Benoni Sweet, the original immigrant from Wales, died at about 90 c. 1750.

noticed that while the stories were being told the men seemed as happy and contented as if they had been inside under a dry roof. The snow was really heavy now, but the men stood there, their feet wet, the flakes caking on the old coats and blankets that protected them, and listened. It was a bit hard to figure out why, until Will realized what the stories meant to them. These stories identified them, were their earmarks, labelling them as Rhode Islanders, separate from Virginians or Yorkers like him, binding them together regardless of the hardship and isolation this winter had brought.

As he stood there, Will felt a genuine Christmas spirit, although the word was never mentioned. He realized that as the men shared in the story-telling they were reaching out toward each other, reaffirming a unity of which he was not a part, and he felt a little of the strength such identity could bring to otherwise weak, even scared people. And the identity, asserted and symbolized by the stories, made the men tough, so that the worse the conditions this Christmas Eve the more they were able to joke and disregard them. Will recalled seeing these same Rhode Islanders in a rainstorm a few weeks before, waking up at dawn with their clothes sopped, having to put on dripping socks, sticking their heads out into the gray morning and joking about wetting their beds and preferring to sleep in the Schuylkill the next night.

Américo Paredes, discussing modern Mexican-American farmers, has said,

> The regional groups, with their roots in the land, enjoy the feeling of permanence and depth one associates with peasant groups. When their values are challenged, when their coherent world is attacked from the outside by the majority culture, they try to shut out the disturbing elements, making of their lore a stable little tradition to be set against the majority culture.[12]

The soldiers at Valley Forge, or at any other place during the Revolution, must have used their lore in a very similar fashion as insulation against the insecurity and breakdown of the familar world from

[12] Américo Paredes, "Tributaries to the Mainstream: The Ethnic Groups" in Tristram Potter Coffin, *Our Living Traditions* (New York, 1968), 79.

which they had been uprooted and to protect them against the Virginians and Yorkers, who of course were as troubled as they were.

When Colonel Israel Angell wrote to his governor about his Rhode Island regiment at Valley Forge, he described them as "the ragged, lousey, naked regiment,"[13] and I suppose his description would have fit most of the regiments in the Continental Army of late 1777. Yet these men stayed together, or at least a hard core of them did, and eventually went on to fuse their local identities into a real American Army. As Harry E. Wildes says in his book *Valley Forge*,[14]

> Long before the spring was over, Washington's army had been drilled, equipped, and formed into an efficient force. The old practice of shifting at will from one regiment to another had been stopped; the careless granting of furloughs to go home on unrestricted leaves of absence had been ended; the hiring of other soldiers to perform the necessary camp duties had been rigorously forbidden. Steuben had built Washington's disorganized army into an efficient band of trained men quite equal to European professionals.
>
> The spirit of the camp had changed. Instead of being diverse units from rival states, each jealous of the others, and each suspicious that the foreigners would steal away American liberty, the troops were finally bound to the common Continental cause. Virginians who, in February, had refused to take an oath of allegiance to the Continental Congress until they were assured by their political advisers that the oath did not reduce their state to servitude, now stood shoulder to shoulder with the New Englanders whom they once had suspected. Pennsylvanians who had mediated a secession from the other commonwealths now realized that every other former colony was a friend and not an enemy. The army had become, in truth, the "band of brothers" which Washington had sought to form.

What Washington and Von Steuben had to do in order to mould an army out of such disparate peoples was to get them to realize that they had everything in common, that they were really birds of a feather, with mutual respect instead of suspicions. Von Steuben did

[13] As quoted in Harry E. Wildes, *Valley Forge* (New York, 1938), 207.

[14] Wildes, 256-257.

this through discipline, through mutual training, but he had a number of things working with him. For one thing, the very hardship of Valley Forge itself, through which Rhode Islanders, New Yorkers, and Virginians had to pass together did a lot. And going through that hardship and at the same time being subjected to the same discipline aimed at a mutual cause started these men along the road to being "soldiers," not just in name, but from head to toe, heart to brain, a breed who would do as an army what the Rhode Islanders were willing to do as Rhode Islanders around that fire Christmas Eve.

Learning they shared the same tales and kinds of tales had something to do with it. Nothing that Will heard in the snow around the fire was really strange to him or would have been strange to a Virginian or Marylander. Certainly, they would not have known of Hannah Robinson or the Palatine Light, but they would have known similar tales. And variants of the story of Church and his bride, the one Will recognized, as well as variants of those attributed to Sam Hyde were common to all Colonials. But in addition to this literary heritage the Colonists shared two other qualities also very important: one, they were all of them close to the land over which they were fighting; and two, they came from the same general level of society, respecting the same skills in the human being.

I believe "identification with the land" was a greater factor in binding the Colonials into a unit than most historians have realized. Agricultural people, farmers and even townspeople living in areas where the farms come right up to the streets and stores, identify with the land in a way Manhattan cloth salesmen and library scholars no longer understand. In the Civil War, for example, Sherman's march to the sea was actually a rape of the soil, with many of the psychological overtones that are involved in the rape of a Southern belle. Sherman violated land on which a man had been born, on which his ancestors had been born and buried, on which he had worked, seen trees grow and fences rise, on which he expected to be buried. When this land was trespassed upon, something of his intimate self was transgressed. The Colonists of the Revolution, many of whom came from farms that had been "carved out of the wilderness," must have known such feelings and ultimately felt them strongly. Hawthorne, talking about Salem, includes a classic descrip-

"The Edwin M. Abbey Print of Baron von Steuben Drilling the Troops at Valley Forge"

tion of this compulsion in "The Custom House" portion of *The Scarlet Letter.*

> This long connection of a family with one spot, as its place of birth and burial, creates a kindred between the human being and the locality, quite independent of any charm in the scenery or moral circumstances that surround him. It is not love, but instinct. The new inhabitant—who came himself from a foreign land, or whose father or grandfather came—has little claim to be called a Salemite; he has no conception of the oysterlike tenacity with which an old settler, over whom his third century is creeping, clings to the spot where his successive generations have been imbedded. It is no matter that the place is joyless for him; that he is weary of the old wooden houses, the mud and dust, the dead level of site and sentiment, the chill east wind, and the chillest of social atmospheres;—all these, and whatever faults besides he may see or imagine, are nothing to the purpose. The spell survives, and just as powerfully as if the natal spot were an earthly paradise. So has it been in my case. I felt it almost as a density to make Salem my home; so that the mould of features and cast of character which had all along been familiar here—ever, as one representative of the race lay down in his grave, another assuming, as it were, his sentry-march along the main street—might still in my little day be seen and recognized in the old town.

The respect these men could develop for certain qualities in each other was equally as important as their feeling for the land. The best of them were not just laborers or peasants who put in their time the easiest way they could and quit when they felt tired or bored. The best of the soldiers were men who had always taken pride in their craft, whether it was blacksmithing, farming, or being a seahand. Regardless of their other faults and virtues, these men knew their trade, whatever it was, and recognized a "top hand" when they saw him. Being a top hand, that was the highest peak in life most of them could aspire to, and a man who attained that pinnacle was respected as surely as any general or any hero. Of course, some of it was simple respect for skill. A Rhode Island rifleman would automatically respect a Virginian who could shoot as well or better than he. But there was a bit more to it than that. There was an honesty to the rules of the craft and a respect for the ability to take things as they come, to joke at hardship, and look on trouble as a test of skill rather than as a setback. And there was envy too, but a healthy envy that stayed under the surface, driving the Rhode Islander to try to shoot better than the Virginian, driving the South Countyite to take hard knocks with a quicker grin than the Cranstonian.

At first this mutual respect and healthy jealousy worked to bind the local units together. Men, recognizing their identity through tale-telling sessions such as the one described above and using that identity to protect them against the suspicions they harbored toward strangers, saw themselves in the same parochial terms under which they had lived at home. But as time went on, as they saw that the others shared their folklore, their feeling for land, their skills, their reactions to trouble, the suspicions began to vanish and the local attachments flow together, making the groups into a unit, a unit that now had a certain identity that would make it hard to beat, keep it from quitting, not because the soldiers really knew what it was all about, but because something had "got to" them and they weren't about to let that something get away. Those who didn't have it in them to respond this way went home or were outcast. The rest became the "band of brothers" who marched out along the Schuylkill to the tune of "Chester" and "The World Turned Upside Down" in the spring of '78, keepers of an occupational homogeneity that was offering them fresh stability, a stability that would eventually unite the states as well as the troops.

3 "The Green Mountain Songster"

TALE-TELLING SESSIONS LIKE the one Will witnessed at Valley Forge must have been common enough during the Revolution, on both the British and the American sides. Men like Tarbox could go on all night. In their home communities they were looked on as keepers of the culture, and it was a commission that they did not take lightly. Sometimes they were singers, as well as or instead of story-tellers, often with repertoires of hundreds of ballads and lyrics. When such singers went to war, they took their songs with them, where they used them as Tarbox did his tales around campfires and in lodgings to keep up troop morale, relieving homesickness and providing entertainment.

Today, it is virtually impossible to reconstruct the exact repertoire of one of these Revolutionary folksingers. Although we have plenty of printed songsters and city broadsheets, no Walter Scott has left us a collection from the memory of a "battlefield Mrs. Brown." No attic has disgorged a Colonial "ballet book," one of those song treasuries scrawled by some keeper of family traditions. We have only *The Green Mountain Songster* and our imaginations; yet I do believe that between them we can get a pretty good idea of what a typical soldier-singer might have been able to perform.

The Green Mountain Songster, which was originally owned by the late Harold Rugg, a librarian at Dartmouth College, now rests in the Vermont Historical Society at Montpelier. It was published in 1823, almost 40 years after the Revolution was over, with the following cover page and preface.

PREFACE.

WHEREAS, the author of the following collection has for a number of years past been in the habit of singing songs, and being frequently desired to put a collection of them to the press; but at their first proposals, and for a long time since, thought it not worth his while to attempt it. But being frequently urged for so long a time, has concluded to proceed to the gratification of their desires.

Most people are fond of singing. Good moral cheerful songs are useful to cheer the drooping mind. The author has experienced this when called upon to sing where people have been afflicted in their minds, and sinking into melancholy. By hearing a few cheerful songs they have reminded the author of the effect David's harp had upon king Saul.– Some people have a choice for some particular song or songs. With regard to politics, some say sing us a good federal song–some say sing us a good republican song. A song is but a song at any rate. Some seem to side with France and some with England, but France and England are old powers and can take care of themselves–every tub should stand on its own bottom. The author is a clear North American; one of the followers of Gen. GEORGE WASHINGTON. The privations he has undergone has taught him that pure INDEPENDENCE is worth something. Let us subdue all our political animosities, and meet, presenting as one another the OLIVE BRANCH of peace, and unite,

My brethren, unite, with purse and heart and hand.
Divided we shall surely fall, united we shall stand.

SANDGATE, April 8, 1823. THE AUTHOR

When I began to write the present book, I got in touch with Helen H. Flanders to see what she remembered about the discovery of this copy of the *Songster*, which as far as I know is unique. She wrote back as follows:[1]

[1] The entire letter from Helen Hartness Flanders to me, dated April 25, 1967, Smiley Manse, Springfield, Vermont.

THE

GREEN-MOUNTAIN SONGSTER

BEING A COLLECTION OF

SONGS

ON VARIOUS SUBJECTS.

Principally tending to expel melancholy and cheer the drooping mind.

—○○—

BY AN OLD REVOLUTIONARY SOLDIER.

1823

"The Cover Page of *The Green Mountain Songster*"

Dear Tris:

I had known Harold Rugg for many years when Arthur Wallace Peach became chairman of the Committee on Traditions and Ideals for the Vermont Commission on Country Life. Dr. Peach and Harold were working on Vermont prose for one of the books in the series called THE GREEN MOUNTAIN SERIES. I in turn was preparing one of the four volumes; my assignment was VERMONT FOLK-SONGS & BALLADS. Harold brought to me the GREEN MOUNTAIN SONGSTER he discovered in an old bookstore (for $35). Although the manuscript of VERMONT FOLK-SONGS & BALLADS was completed, I was permitted to add a few ballads from his discovery (pp. 240-245 in the VERMONT FOLK-SONGS & BALLADS). I do not remember when Phillips Barry saw the GREEN MOUNTAIN SONGSTER but he was much interested in everything I was finding for VERMONT FOLK-SONGS & BALLADS.

Thinking my letters from him might show about the last days before that book went to press, I have scanned several letters of those early days of the thirties. One paragraph may be a happenstance:

> GREEN MOUNTAIN SONGSTER is the first collection of folk-songs to be printed in America, and on Old World soil, only Percy, Ritson, Scott and Jamieson precede him. . . . I feel rather sure that Mr. Rugg's copy is unique.

Harold let me have photostats made of the entire book before he placed it as a gift to the Vermont Historical Society, of which he was a member of the Board of Directors. I have looked for years when opportunity offered and have never found another copy of the original GREEN MOUNTAIN SONGSTER. Of course I began at Sandgate, Vermont, at the Town Clerk's office. Many of the records were in the attic of the Town Clerk's home. The building where voting took place was originally a Methodist Church, and they talked me into trying to interest people who would give funds for its preservation. It has recently burned, after all these years. But when I was there they would not go with me to the attic to see what could be found. They were unaccustomed to take a stranger there!

I had to forego a trip to Washington and presenting my essay there as a member of the Literary Society. Ralph was not a member but was invited to come and read it. Do give Dr. Leach my greetings. I got two of his collections of Labrador ballads and wrote with enthusiasm to him. Best wishes to your prose-book.

Cordially yours,
Helen Flanders

Later she sent me these two letters from her files.[2]

Dear Mrs. Flanders:

I regret very much that I am unable to help you about the other matters you mentioned in your letter. I have looked up the Heads of Families of the Census of 1790 for the state of Vermont. I do not find any family by the name of Beckwith in Manchester at that time.

I just purchased yesterday a very rare Songster (which I send under separate cover), the only one that I have ever seen. Although you are not using printed material in your collection, you may find one or two songs here which were sung in the early days of Vermont which may be of some interest to you.

Very sincerely yours,
Harold G. Rugg
Assistant Librarian
Dartmouth College
Hanover, N. H.
The College Library

HGR/K
Sorry not to be able to see you Sunday.

Dear Mrs. Flanders:

As far as I am concerned, you may do whatever you wish with the booklet of songs which I sent you. Of course the copyright expired long ago. I have no idea who the author may be.

There is no published history of Sandgate, and I have not had time to look through the Hemenway. Possibly you may be able to find something in that. Curious to relate, this rare pamphlet is not listed in Gilman's Bibliography of Vermont, nor had I heard of it before. I have interleaved my Gilman, and have several hundred titles entered, but this was not among them. It was offered me by a dealer last week, and I immediately snapped it up.

I am glad indeed to know that the books are coming along so well. With kindest regards to Mr. Flanders, I am

Very sincerly yours,
Harold G. Rugg
Assistant Librarian
Dartmouth College
Hanover, N. H.
The College Library

HGR/K

The "rare pamphlet" is, I suspect, a ballet book that was privately printed. The famous ballad scholar, Phillips Barry, discussing it in 1934 in the foreword to Mrs. Flanders' *The New Green Mountain Songster*, wrote,

> To Vermont . . . falls the honor of having its imprint on the title-page of the first collection of traditional folk songs from a folk singer's repertory to be printed in the United States of America.[3]

and it just has to contain a lot of songs the singer knew 40 or 50 years earlier when he was "one of the followers of Gen. George Washington." I know of no other songster that was assembled this early by an American informant rather than by a commercial printer, thus I have to believe it offers the best glass available through which one can see what the troops were actually singing at Bennington, Newport, and Valley Forge.

As with most ballet books, there is no music in *The Green Mountain Songster*, and it is a shame that the Sandgate patriot did not see fit to include the airs. He probably assumed the tunes were well-known, though it would not have been eccentric had he indicated them by common titles. There is no doubt he had tunes. These songs were not recited, and as Barry speculates he "must have sung in the striking *parlando* and *declamando* manner which folk singers in Maine still call the 'old-fashioned way.' "[4]

As we begin to go over *The Green Mountain Songster* in detail, I must make certain that you know the difference between traditional ballads and ballads close to printed sources. Actually, with a little practice, it is not hard to make such distinctions. Oral tradition shapes a text in ways that a reasonably trained reader can recognize with ease. As indicated in the Introduction, there is a tendency in narrative pieces which have survived oral circulation to concentrate on whatever part of the story the folk have selected as

---

[2] These two letters are reproduced in their entirety through the kindness of Mrs. Flanders. They are dated February 12 and 14, 1931, respectively.

[3] Quoted from Helen H. Flanders, et al., *The New Green Mountain Songster* (Hatboro, Pa., 1966), xv. This is a reprint of the original book published with extensive notes by Phillips Barry at New Haven in 1939.

[4] *The New Green Mountain Songster*, xvi.

the climax, to the exclusion of details, motivation, and background. The story proceeds matter-of-factly, with marked understatement and objectivity. Sentimentality, morality, political or patriotic propaganda are modified or eliminated. The language is formulaic and the formulas used again and again so that they have a comfortable familiarity.

Let's look for a moment at "Johny Scott" as it was sung by the Sandgate soldier.[5]

JOHNY SCOTT

Young Johny Scott's a hunting gone,
Into the woods so wild;
The fairest lady in all England,
By Johny Scott's with child.

The news into the kitchen's gone,
The news into the hall,
The news into king Edwar'ds gone,
And that's the worst of all.

King Edward he a letter wrote,
And seal'd it with his hand
And sent away for Johny Scott,
As fast as he could send.

When Johny Scott the letter read,
The tears did flow like sea,
I must unto old England go,
King Edward has sent for me.

Oh, then spoke up his father then,
An aged man was he;
If you unto old England go,
You never'll return to me.

Oh, then spoke up a Scotish knight,
Sat close by Johny's knee,
Three hundred and ten of my life-guard men,
Shall bear his company.

[5] *The Green Mountain Songster* (*GMS*), (Sandgate, Vermont, 1823), 41-43. This text and the texts that follow are reproduced exactly as they appear in the original.

Young Johny on his saddle sat,
Most beautiful and bold,
The hair spread over young Johny's shoulders,
Like the links of gold.

Young Johny call'd his merry men all,
He dress'd them all in white,
And every city that he rode through,
They took him to be some knight.

The last town that he rode into,
He rode it round about,
And there he spi'd his own true love
At a window looking out.

Come down, come down, young Johny said,
And take a walk with me?
I cannot come down my dear, she said,
King Edward has bolted me.

The doors they are all locked fast,
The windows round about,
My feet they are in fetters strong,
And how shall I get out.

Young Johny rode to king Edward's bower,
He knock'd so loud at the ring,
There was none so ready as king Edward himself
To arise and let him in.

Oh, is this the duke of Cumberland,
Or is it George our king,
Or is it my bastard son,
From Flanders new come in.

'Tis not the duke of Cumberland,
Nor is it James your king,
But it's a young Scotish knight
And Johny Scott's by name.

If that your name be Johny Scott,
As I suppose it be,
The fairest lady in all my lands,
Does go with child by thee.

Oh call her down, young Johny said,
To talk a while with me,
I'll make it heir of all my lands,
And her my fair lady.

Oh no, oh no, king Edward cri'd,
No, no, that ne'er shall be,
Before to-morrow by eight o'clock
I'll hang you on a tree.

Oh, then spoke up young Johny's men,
With voices loud and high,
Before we'll see our Captain slain,
We'll fight until we die.

They pick'd him out a battle man,
A very tall man was he,
Betwixt his eye brows measur'd a span—
Betwixt his elbows, three.

The king came down with his merry men all,
Came tripping over the plain,
The queen came down with her merry maids all,
To see young Johny slain.

Young Johny being a nimble man,
A nimble man was he,
Then with the point of his broad sword,
His battle man ended he.

Young Johny with his sword in hand,
Came tripping over the plain;
Is there any more of your English dogs
That you would fain have slain?

Oh, no! oh, no! king Edward cri'd,
I grant your pardon free;
A priest! a priest! young Johny cri'd,
To marry my bride and me.

He clapp'd his horn unto his mouth,
And blew both loud and shrill,
The honour's gone back to fair Scotland,
In spite of England's will.

This is the balladeer's way of telling the story which was printed, supposedly from tradition, by the Reverend Andrew Hall in his *Interesting Roman Antiquities recently discovered from Fife.* About 1679, James Macgill of Lindores had killed Sir Robert Balfour of Denmiln in a duel. Macgill immediately went to London to get a pardon from Charles II, who agreed to give it to him providing he would fight an Italian gladiator (or bully as they were then called). A large stage was erected so that the King and his court could watch. The gladiator, who was a huge man, kept Macgill on the defensive, and eventually began to show off. Once he lept over Macgill, "as if he would swallow him alive." The second time he tried this, Macgill was ready and speared him in mid-air, supposedly calling out, "I have spitted him, let them roast him who will!" Charles is meant to have been so impressed that he knighted Macgill on the spot, in addition to giving him the desired pardon. However, I would take this legend with a grain of salt, at least as far as it goes in describing what actually happened during the fight. Les Aubrays, Lizandré of St. Brieux, is said to have defeated a Moor in similar fashion before the French king.

The Green Mountain Songster text turns the story into a Lochinvar-like, English-Scottish border love tale. Notice how it minimizes the fight. It gives but one stanza to Johny's heroics and doesn't even mention the Italian. Actually, most of the variants of "Johny Scott" are devoted to formulaic action in the best folk fashion. Stanza 2 in the text above tells of the pregnancy of "the fairest lady in all England" in language quite reminiscent of the lines describing Mary Hamilton's indiscretion that I quoted in the Introduction. Stanza 4 is an abbreviation of another cliché. In many versions, the letter sent by the King (sometimes by the girl herself) is read this way.

> The first line of the letter he read,
> His heart was full of joy;
> But he had not read a line past two
> Till the salt tears blind his eye.

Lines almost identical to those that tell how Sir Patrick Spens received the note from his King ordering him to sea and certain death in the winter storms. Also reminiscent of the Spens ballad is the phrase the "Scotish knight, sat close by Johny's knee" in Stanza 6. In Stanza 8, when Johny does set out for England, he proceeds in the same way that Fair Eleanor travels in "Lord Thomas and Fair Annet,"

> She clothed herself in gay attire,
> Her merry men all in green,
> And every town that they road through,
> They took her to be some queen.

When Johny arrives in Stanza 12, "There is none so ready as King Edward himself" to let him in, just as in the ballad "Little Musgrave and Lady Barnard" there is none so ready as the Lady to let Musgrave enter. In brief, there is a set language for set situations that occurs over and over again in these songs, many of which treat similar subjects. These devices help singers recall the stories and act as familiar ground upon which they can rest their memories while performing. After you have been dealing with ballads awhile, you get to know this language, anticipate it, and become genuinely fond of it.

Compare "Johny Scott" with a city piece like "The Female Trooper" which has appeared on numerous British and American broadsides and in many American songsters usually under the title "Polly Oliver." This song circulated widely in printed form and even though it appears in the repertory of the Sandgate soldier and other traditional singers, it clearly has a somewhat different heritage than that of "Johny Scott." Any reader will notice how different the language, the meter, the tone, the whole approach to the story are.[6]

THE FEMALE TROOPER.

> It was down in yonder low lands madam Polly did dwell,
> She was courted by a Captain that lov'd her full well,
> It was her cruel parents did her ruin prove,
> They parted madam Polly and her royal true love.

[6] *GMS*, 7-8. This song is numbered N 14 in G. Malcolm Laws, Jr., *American Balladry from British Broadsides* (Laws, *ABBB*), (Philadelphia, 1957).

Madam Polly was a musing on her down feather bed,
When a comical fancy come into hear head;
Neither father nor mother shall make me false prove,
For I'll dress like a trooper and follow my love.

So early next morning madam Polly arose,
She dress'd herself up in a suit of men's clothes;
It was her coal black hair down her back did hang,
In every degree she look'd like some young man.

Madam Polly was a walking the sandy hill round,
She chanc'd to meet one that she travelling found;
With a brace of bright pistols and a sword by her side,
A valiant grey horse madam Polly did ride.

She rode till she come to the town of renown,
She put up at the tavern at the sign of the crown;
The first that came in was a lord noble prove,
The next that came in was Polly's true love.

What news, said the Captain, what news have you here?
Oh, a letter from Polly, from Polly your dear:
When the letter was open'd ten guineas were found
For you and your soldiers to drink Polly's health round.

When the letter was open'd the money it flew,
For you and your soldiers to drink Polly's health thro';
Madam Polly being weary she hung down her head,
And call'd for a candle to light her to bed.

Here's a bed said the Captain where I lie at my ease,
And you may lie with me kind sir if you please,
Oh, to sleep with a Captain is a very great thing,
I'm a new listed soldier just under our king.

If you'll be my Captain, I'll be under your command,
We'll fight all our enemies by sea and by land;
All this while this brave Captain he never perceives,
Although madam Polly did laugh in her sleeves.

So early next morning the Captain arose,
He dress'd up in a suit of his own clothes,
Crying Polly, O Polly, O Polly my dear,
All this world would I give if I could see Polly.

So early next morning madam Polly arose,
 She dress'd herself up in a suit of her own clothes
The Captain he view'd her from the top to the toe,
 Flew into her arms saying, Polly how do you do?

Madam Polly is married, she lives at her ease,
 She goes when she's a mind and returns when she please,
She has left her cruel parents to lament and to mourn,
 And often times wishing for Polly's return.

In a year or two after a letter they found,
 From the hand of Madam Polly to her parents was bound,
Saying, mourn not for your Polly for she's in good health,
 And lives with her true love and prospers in wealth.

The distinctions in style, meter, tone, and diction that these two texts demonstrate have led scholars to divide British and British-derived ballads (that is, folksongs telling a story) into two rather loose and somewhat inaccurate categories: those of the Child ballad on one side, those of the broadside ballad on the other. Child ballads are those ballads, similar to "Johny Scott," which appeared in the anthology of 305 songs brought out by a meek Harvard professor from 1882 to 1898 under the arrogant title *The English and Scottish Popular Ballads*[7] and which he considered to rise from older folk, rather than city, sources. Child, who knew very little about ballads by today's standards, was a hard worker. Modelling his efforts on those of his acquaintance Svend Grundtvig who was editing a supposedly definitive Danish collection, he grubbed around in archives and old books, wrote letters to anyone he dreamed might help, and came up with an anthology that is truly remarkable for its day. In fact, so awesome was his anthology that scholars all over the world hailed it as canonical. It, of course, was nothing of the sort. The word "folklore" had been coined by William Thoms only a few years before Child began his compilations, the people working in the field were gentlemanly antiquarians, not trained scholars, and many of them were eccentrics to boot. However, it is fair to say

[7] Francis James Child, *The English and Scottish Popular Ballads* (Child), 5 volumes (Boston, 1882-1898).

that from 1898 until the Second World War the Child anthology was considered inviolate by most.[8]

But where the term "Child ballad" is inaccurate because it reflects one man's subjective decisions, the phrase "broadside ballad," referring to songs like "Polly Oliver," is inaccurate because it covers too much. Obviously, all ballads in oral tradition that are not of Child's 305 did not originate on broadsides. Some were written for songsters, some placed in chapbooks, some began life as popular chamber songs of the day, some were once poems, some never saw print but were originated by local singers. Yet a huge number of the non-Child songs did originate on the broadsides, and the term has served as a convenient umbrella.

The broadside itself was a sort of one-page news-sheet, published by printers in towns and cities all over Western Europe and its colonies from about 1500 to the present. These sheets, which have been replaced by newspapers and magazines in our society, were hawked about the streets and carried to rural areas. Any and all kinds of information and entertainment were printed on them: casualty lists, accounts of murders, moral edicts, political speeches, songs, poems, aphorisms, often accompanied by woodcuts that were

[8] Child lists 305 ballads, each with a number. These numbers have been used by all students of traditional balladry since. For example, "Johny Scott" is 99; "Mary Hamilton" is 173; "Sir Patrick Spens" is 53; and so forth. With each ballad is a historical essay, some of them remarkably detailed and still valid; some but a few lines long; others no longer taken seriously. As we look at this anthology today, we realize many of its short-comings. For one thing, Child put into it examples of ballads he felt were old, that he felt had survived in oral tradition for many years. He excluded ballads like "Polly Oliver" that were products of the print shops of recent years. However, as the print shops made no distinction between ballads they published direct from oral tradition and ballads they re-wrote or composed themselves, Child frequently found himself with a print shop text of a ballad that he suspected to be old even though he had no fully traditional text of it. The result was that he was continually involved in subjective decisions, and modern scholars have shown that he made many mistakes, often including songs that are clearly recent (for instance, "The Bailiff's Daughter of Islington," 105, which is very much of the same sort as "Polly Oliver") and left out some ballads that are clearly very old (for instance, "The Bitter Withy" and "The Holy Well"). In addition, Child was unaware that there were

likely to be inappropriate. I haven't got time here to go over the long and fascinating history of the broadside, but perhaps the following quotation from G. Malcolm Laws, Jr.'s book *American Balladry from British Broadsides*[9] will give you the flavor of the business.

James Catnach, along with others of his profession, operated his shop in a region of St. Giles's parish, London, known as Seven Dials from a stone monument displaying seven sun dials, which stood in a circular court at the meeting place of seven streets. Catnach remained in business for 25 years, from 1813 to 1838, and at his retirement turned the firm over to his sister, who was the first of his successors. At least during his early years, his journalistic ethics were not high, and on two occasions his firm was in trouble with the law. In 1818 he was jailed for libel after distributing completely false prose broadsides announcing that local pork butchers were dealing in human flesh. While he was in jail, his mother, who worked with him in the shop, and two sellers of broadsides were reprimanded by a magistrate for circulating an account of a murder which proved to be a pure fabrication. By such means Catnach imposed upon the gullible public when real news was scarce. But his most successful ventures were in the realm of more or less genuine news balladry, which he sometimes composed himself but more frequently bought from the local ballad writers

---

hundreds and hundreds of ballads right under his nose in American oral tradition, more variants of his own 305 than he would have been able to come up with in British oral tradition. Looking at the world from the perspective of Harvard Square, he seems to have thought the ballad pretty well a dead form.

However, during the 20th century collecting in the United States and Canada, analysis, and general catholicism of outlook began to show the error of many of Child's ways. Now everyone, except a few die-hard Harvardians, knows that the Child canon is not a canon. But there isn't a whole lot that can be done about it. Too many scholars have used the Child numbers in too many ways. Treating Child canonically has become too convenient; it is so easy to divide the ballads that have been in oral tradition for a good while from those that have not by simply using Child's decisions. And Child's basic idea is valid, even if his execution of it is sometimes primitive.

Of course, the folk care little for this sort of classification, and it is hard to believe that collectors for years refused to record anything but Child ballads, or, if they took down the others, let them mould in archives without publishing them.

who worked for him and his competitors. It is said that he employed a fiddler who knew the familiar ballad tunes so that any new pieces could be immediately sung to him and to the hawkers who would sell them on the streets.

Especially popular at this time was the type of ballad alleged to have been written by a condemned criminal shortly before his execution, "the criminal being unable, in some instances, to read or write being no obstacle to the composition." Political and sporting events, the deaths of prominent people, and crimes almost without number, these and other items of news or commentaries on the news were Catnach's chief stock in trade. His shop normally employed four men and boys, who worked at four presses of two forms each. From each form 200-300 prints an hour could be pulled, and thus his men could turn out more than twenty thousand broadsides a day. It is reported that on the occasion of a particularly sensational murder, his employees worked night and day for a week and printed some 250,000 copies of the broadside describing it. These prints were sold to and resold by "a ragged, dirty crew of newsmen . . . who assembled by hundreds" at his shop. In addition to the local sale, "every night and morning large bundles were dispatched to the principal towns in the three kingdoms." The murder victim in this case was a man named Weare. Some time after the murder, the trial, and the execution, out of which Catnach made about five hundred pounds, he published a broadside headed "WE ARE ALIVE AGAIN!" "He put so little space between the words 'we' and 'are,' that it looked at first sight like 'WEARE.'

---

[9] Laws, *ABBB*, 38-39. A good general history of the broadside business as it relates to balladry is Leslie Shepard, *The Broadside Ballad* (London, 1962). Of course, American scholars are not likely to use the term "broadside ballad" when referring to native American ballads, most of which derive from the thousands upon thousands of songsters that were circulated in this country. Ballads native to America derive from the late 18th and 19th centuries, for the most part. By then, the popularity of the songsters was so great that these bound volumes were a more prolific source than the simple broadsides in seeding songs in oral tradition. And even though it is perfectly obvious a good many native American ballads did originate on broadsides, and even though there is no marked difference excepting national locale between British and American ballads that originate in printed sources scholars have developed the habit of using the term "broadside ballad" for British songs still close to print and the term "native American ballad" for American songs of the same nature.

Many thousands were bought . . . , but those who did not like the trick called it a 'catch penny,' and this gave rise to this peculiar term, which ever afterwards stuck to the issues of the 'Seven Dials' Press,' though they sold as well as ever." In order to profit indirectly from another brutal murder, Catnach sent two hawkers to Brighton, where for four months they received "almost weekly, fresh supplies of street-papers." Such enterprise apparently paid off, for Catnach's business continued to thrive, despite the competition of many other printers, most of whom seem to have had ethics on a par with his own.

Naturally a lot of Child ballads appeared on such broadsides, and many of the select 305 would not be known today if they had not been used by some printer. However, for every Child ballad there were a thousand or more lyrics, ditties, sentimental pieces produced by the printers themselves or by a hired hack poet. Oliver Goldsmith, for instance, once kept the wolf from the door by writing poems for a print shop. Most broadside poems are stuffy, elaborate, somewhat below artistic mediocrity and set to one of the trite melodies of the day. But like our modern hit tunes, they enjoyed great popularity and frequently print shops saw profit in amassing cheap- or chapbooks and songsters from them. Much of this material, though actually a small percentage of the whole produce, ended up in the repertory of the folksingers of outlying and colonial areas. Ballads that derive from this heritage and that survive in oral tradition are the ones called "broadside ballads."

All this, and the associated problems, fascinate me, and I have made balladry my specialty within folklore. I think some of the excitement and appeal of such matters will come across as we look at the songs recorded by the soldier from Sandgate. Most of the material in his *Songster* is relatively close to print, to the broadsides and more formally published songsters from which the New England singers of that time learned a large bulk of their repertoires. The idea that the Colonial folksinger was illiterate and had to learn his folksongs from the memories of his British ancestors is romantic. And it is not totally incorrect. But it is realistic to accept the fact that the songs that are best known and collected most often have survived because the broadsides and printed songsters preserved them and re-seeded them over and over again in oral tradition. Thus, when we page about in *The Green Mountain Songster* we aren't surprised to find but five Child ballads, all of which smack of the city press: "Lady Margaret and Sweet William" (77); "Johny Scott" (99); "The Shepherd's Son" (112); "Charley's Escape" (209); and "Captain Ward and the Rainbow" (287), plus "The Fair Damsel from London" which American collectors hopefully label 295, although it is clearly a broadside re-writing of the traditional "Brown Girl" which they can't find over here.

Three of the texts are unusual enough to make a ballad scholar sniff the air. One, "The Shepherd's Son," is interesting because it is rarely found in this country any longer.[10]

THE SHEPHERD'S SON.

There was a shepherd's son kept sheep on yonder hill,
And he went forth one merry morning to see what he could
    kill;
He looked east, he looked west, he gave an under look,
And there he spi'd a pretty maid a swimming in the brook.

Kind sir, don't touch my mantua and let my clothes alone,
And I will give you as much fine gold as you can carry home
I will not touch your mantua, I'll let your clothes alone,
But I will take you from the water, my dear you are my own.

Oh, it's fitter for a shepherd's son to keep sheep on yonder
    hill, [swim.
Than to come forth this merry morning to see a maiden
Oh, its fitter for a fair made to say at home and sew her
    silks and seams, [streams.
Than to come forth this merry morning to swim against the

She mounted on a milk-like steed and he upon another,
Away they rode then side by side like sister & like brother;
They came into a meadow, where there were cocks of hay,
A pretty place, said he, my dear for man and maids to play.

Kind sir, don't lay me down for the dew is on the ground,
To rumple my gay clothing which cost me many a pound,
But stay till I come to my daddy's house and to my mam-
    ma's hall, [all.
And there you shall have my portion, my riding-hood and

[10] *GMS,* 51-52.

I will not lay you down for the dew is on the ground,
To rumple your gay clothing which cost you many a pound,
But I'll stay till you come to your daddy's house and to
your mamma's hall,
And there I'll have your portion, your riding-hood and all.

She stepp'd into her daddy's gate and turn'd herself about,
Saying, here's a pretty maid within & there's a fool without;
There is a flower in our garden some call a merrigould,
If young men will not when they may they shall not when
they would.

There is an herb in our garden some call a featherfue,
There's many a girl in our town has made a fool of you;
We have some little roosters that run among the hens,
They often flop their wings and crow, you're just like one
of them.

Pull off your shoes from off your feet and let your feet go
bare, [dare;
And if you meet with a pretty maid then kiss her if you
I will not pull off my shoes nor let my feet go bare,
But if I meet with you again I'll trim you to a hair.

This old story of the girl who avoids rape by tricking her would-be lover is known all over Europe, and usually in much more vigorous and bawdy versions than the one sung (or at least printed) by the Sandgate soldier. In similar tales, the lustful lover may be thrown in the river; tripped into a moat; persuaded by the girl's tears, only to be laughed at; robbed of his horse and money. But dignified as it is, *The Green Mountain Songster* text makes a fine song and stands as the one really complete version that has been uncovered from tradition in the United States. The rarity of the song over here may well be due to the popularity of a ballad on the same general theme, "Kathy Morey." Kathy is tricked by a local sport on the guise that his sister is waiting to pick fruit with them "in yonder bower." She soon finds his sister "knew nothing of the matter" and that "she must quickly comply." She pretends complete willingness, but requests the youth climb a tree till her supposedly approaching father passes. When he is well up in the branches, she mocks him and runs off. The boy, who is at first furious, begins to admire the combination of virtue and ingenuity that Kathy has displayed, and he eventually marries her. This song probably dates from the early 19th century. However, it is not a well-done piece, and when you compare a typical text like the one below from modern Virginia[11] with the Sandgate soldier's "The Shepherd's Son," you realize that bad ballads, like bad money, often drive out good.

KATHY MOREY.

Come all my young and lively lads and listen to my story;
I'll tell you how I fixed a plan to trick young Kathy Morey.

I went down to her father's house, just like a clever fellow;
I said to her the grapes were ripe and very nice and mellow.

I said to her my sister dear was there in yonder bower,
And I could go and get her grapes and spend a pleasing hour.

As Kathy went along I ran and suddenly pursued her,
I met her down in yonders grove thinking I'd delude her.

I told her that my sister dear knew nothing of the matter
And she must quickly comply because I had no time to flatter.

She took my hand and seeming pleased—"There's one thing
I do fear, sir,
If my father comes this way, he'll surely catch us here, sir.

"If you'll but go and climb the tree and wait till he is gone, sir,
We'll safely by the shady brook sport and gayly play, sir."

I went climbing in the tree, not feeling much offended
And Kathy stood and laughed beneath to see how I ascended.

She says: "You look just like an owl and your favors I will
shun, sir,
So you can get down as you got up—and you have had your
fun, sir."

And Kathy ran across the plain, she left me half descended.
I cursed, I swore, I tore my shirt to see how she had fooled me.

[11] As sung by Robert Seager, now Dean of the College, Washington College, Chestertown, Maryland. Seager learned the song in his youth in Covington, Virginia.

That Kathy is a clever wench I'll gladly bet my life, sir,
And before long I sought her out and we are man and wife, sir.

Two, "Lady Margaret and Sweet William," while common enough in America, is not usually found in the form that the *Sandgate soldier* sang it.[12]

LADY MARGARET AND SWEET WILLIAM.

LADY Margaret sat in her own bowery all alone, [groans;
And under her bowry east winder she heard three pitiful
Oh, is it my father dear, she said, or is it my brother John,
Or is it my loving dear Willian from Scotland newly come
home?

It is not your father, he said, nor is it your brother John,
But is your loving dear William from Scotland newly come
home. [brought me any fee,
Oh have you brought me any gold, she said, or have you
Or have you bro't any fine linnen from Scotland home to me?

I have not bro't you any gold, he said nor have I bro't you
any fee, [me;
But I've brought you my winding sheet 'tis rotted off from
Give me my troth Lady Margaret, he said, I'll give thee
thine again, [my pain.
For the longer I tarry and talk with you the sharper'll be

I will not give you your troth she said nor you give mine to
me,
Until you carry me to fair Scotland your bowry for to see.
My bowry 'tis a poor bowry it is both deep and dim;
My bowry 'tis a poor bowry to put a fair lady in.

I will not give you your troth she said nor will I have mine
again,
Until you kiss my merry merry lips or wed me with a ring.
I cannot kiss your merry, merry lips, my breath it is so strong,
My face it is all worm-eaten, I am no living man.

[12] *GMS*, 34-35.

She pulled up her petticoat, almost unto her knee, [she;
And in a cold and winter's night the pale ghost follow'd
Oh who are these, sweet William, she said, are standing at
your head? [refus'd to wed.
They're three pretty maids, Lady Margaret, he said, that I

Oh who are these, sweet William, she said, are standing at
your feet? [fus'd to keep.
They're three children, Lady Margaret, he said, that I re-
Oh who are these, sweet William, she said, are standing by
your side? [ing my soul to guide.
They're three pretty maids, Lady Margaret, he said, wait-

The first is for my drunkenness, the second's for my pride,
The third is for my false swearing and wandering in the
night; [thine again,
Give me my troth, Lady Margaret, he said, I'll give thee
For the longer I tarry and talk with you the sharper'll be
my pain.

She had a handkerchief in her hand she spread it on the
ground, [body down;
Saying, here is your faith and troth William, God lay your
She had a willow in her hand, she laid it across his breast,
Saying, here is your faith and troth, William, I wish your
soul at rest.

So here is your faith and troth William, and give me mine
again,
But if you're dead and gone to hell in hell you must remain.

This is a beautiful text and shows balladry at its best. One can see the old Revolutionary soldier in his kitchen by the fireplace, a few neighbors gathered about him, while his wife prepared tea and food. He might be sitting in a chair, his head tilted back, his eyes closed as he sang. There would be no accompaniment, no noise in the room, as the ballad told the tale of supernatural doings, rural troths, and country customs no longer practiced. Perhaps when he finished, his wife would remark, "The Lord have mercy on their souls," and the neighbors would shake their heads and nod, aware for a moment of the heritage of human woe of which they were all a part.

Today, as a scholar looks at the cold text, he notes that it is a variation of the song printed in Motherwell's manuscript from the recitation of a Mrs. McCormick as learned in Dumbarton about 1795, the Child 77C text. He notes that most other American texts, though similar, show William's parents lying at his head and feet, his hellhounds by his side, seldom mentioning the return of the troth at the end. But he knows also that he is dealing with a laboratory specimen, a butterfly mounted under glass, for ballads such as this one owe their very nature to the singer-listener relationship through which they have flourished over the ages.

The third song, "Charley's Escape" ("Geordie" as it is called in the Child canon) is an exciting ballad, particularly from the scholarly point of view. It is an old Scottish song about a Geordie Gordon who is in prison for political reasons and who is in danger of being hung. He gets a message to his wife, telling her to hasten to Edinburgh, which she does. There she is told that a large sum of money will free her husband. Dramatically, she raises the cash on the spot, pays the charges, and rides off with Geordie. Early scholars figured Geordie to be George Gordon, the fourth Earl of Huntly, who got in trouble with the Queen's Regent in 1554 for failure to execute a commission against a highway robber. Huntly, after threats to banish him, hang him, deprive him of his lands, was finally fined. But even if Huntly is the correct Geordie historically, the name is common enough and the number of men in jail awaiting hanging large enough that the ballad has attached itself to other local situations. In one text Huntly's enemy in the 1554 affair, the Earl of Cassilis, incredibly becomes the Geordie of the song.

Ultimately, this historical Scottish song gave birth to a pair of English broadsides, one on the death of a Northumberland "gentleman" named George Stoole, who was executed for stealing cattle; the other concerning George of Oxford, who stole the King's white steeds and sold them in Bohemia.[13] Most of the American texts derive from the latter song, which dates from the late 17th or early 18th century. In them, the hero, who may also have committed murder, is hanged. As far as I know, there are but four of the hundreds of

[13] See Child, IV, 140-142.

New World texts that have a happy ending with the sweetheart or wife rescuing her lover. Two of these are southern variants of Child's F version, a Scottish piece telling the traditional, happily-ever-after story, which opens deceptively with a couple of stanzas borrowed from "George of Oxford" or a similar broadside.[14] The other two are from Henry W. Shoemaker's *Mountain Minstrelsy* as collected in Pennsylvania in the 1920s by John French[15] and from *The Green Mountain Songster* as printed below.[16] These are unusual because, unlike the ones from North Carolina, they are not traditional, but rather broadside, texts with a happy ending. The original, possibly a songster version, from which they derive, is lost and very likely unique.

CHARLEY'S ESCAPE.

As I walk'd over London bridge, twas on one morning early,
Twas there I spied a gay lady lamenting for her Charley;
Come saddle to me my milk white steed, come bridle to me
so early, [the life of Charley.
That I may go down to my good lord Judge, and plead for

She met the Judge then at his door, she look'd exceding
sorry, [me the life of Charley.
Saying good lord Judge grant me my request, it's but spare
The Judge look'd over his left shoulder, he look'd exceed-
ing sorry, [demned already.
Saying pretty maid you have come too late, for he's con-

The Judge look'd over his left shoulder, he look'd exceed-
ing straightly, [mercy on ye;
Saying young man you must die to-day, and the Lord have
As Charley walk'd through the hall taking his leave of many,
But when he come to his own true love, oh! it grieved him
worse than any.

[14] See my article on the Child F variants, "Traditional Texts of 'Geordie' in America," *Southern Folklore Quarterly*, 1949, 161-168.

[15] Henry W. Shoemaker, *Mountain Minstrelsy* (Philadelphia, 1931), 162.

[16] *GMS*, 33-34.

Charley never rob'd the king's highway, nor yet hath he kill'd any, [at Bohema.
But he stole sixteen of the king's fair dears and sold them
I wish I was on yonder hill, where kisses I've had many,
With a good broadsword all drawn in my hand, I'd fight for the life of Charley.

When Charley sat on the gallows high, with the silken cord about him, [without him.
This fair maid said that she must die for she could not live
The Judge took her by the lilly white hand and led her to the parlor, [to your Charley.
Saying pretty maid he is pardon'd, now go, you're welcome

Such a text attracts a scholar the way a pheasant attracts a setter. You know you won't catch the bird, but trying is irresistable. Is there a natural connection between northern Pennsylvania and Vermont that might offer a clue to the identity of the Sandgate soldier? What broadside or songster tradition do these two variants share—one sung in the 1920s, one dating from a century earlier?

The research necessary to answer such questions can be exhausting. It is staggering to think of the thousands and thousands of pages of unindexed, even uncatalogued, broadsides and songsters housed in archives all about New England and the Middle Atlantic area. You could literally devote your life to the Harris collection at Brown, to the Thomas collection in Worcester, to others like them without hope of finding a single text to serve as an archetype for these unusual versions of "Charley's Escape." Furthermore, you would be working under the awareness that one imaginative singer or one visit by some Vermonter to Pennsylvania might account for everything.

Obviously, it wouldn't be appropriate to get sidetracked by such research here. However, I couldn't resist looking a little into the possibilities, and I wrote to Henry Glassie, then the Pennsylvania State Folklorist of the Ethnic Culture Survey at the Bureau of Archives and History in Harrisburg to learn if there would be reason to suspect Vermont material to have been carried to northern Pennsylvania. His letter came back by return mail.[17]

Dear Tris,

I am glad you received the photo of Dr. Leach. I bothered our printer for awhile about it and when I was south on vacation he finally came through and the picture was sent on to you.

It is historically reasonable that there would be similarities between Vermont and Potter County texts of the same ballads. Potter is in the northern tier of Pennsylvania counties which cleanly fit into the region of the Northeast. Maps which have been presented of dialect, folk housing and communities all agree on this. Perhaps the best statement of that consensus is in Fred Kniffen's "Folk Housing: Key to Diffusion" which appeared in the *Annals of the Association of American Geographers* in, I think, December, 1965. Northern Pennsylvania, like New York and New England, includes an early abandoment of log construction and acceptance of Greek Revival house forms. Two migrations caused this: first it was settled by people from New England and New York in the early nineteenth century and, second, it was a lumbering area and lumbermen moved down from those northern areas in the mid-nineteenth century.

In order to check my generalizations offered above, I looked through Victor L. Beebe, *History of Potter County, Pennsylvania* (Coudersport, Pa.: Potter County Historical Society, 1934). He gives the details, which I didn't know. Settlement began in Potter County in 1807. In the first decade and a half settlers came from New Jersey, New York, Connecticut, New Hampshire and Vermont. He devotes pages 29-32 to the family of Major Isaac Lyman, "the second permanent settler in the county" (p. 29), who was born in 1759 and came from Bolton, Vermont to New York to Tioga Co. Pa. in 1809, and Potter Co. in 1810; Beebe says (p. 31), "I have devoted so much time to Major Lyman's family, because so many of his descendants are among our citizens today, probably more than those of any other man. . . ." He is the only Vermonter I noticed, but the New England connections are many. Chapter VIII is devoted to lumbering; the lumbermen came, apparently, mostly from New York, but at least one (p. 170) came from Oldtown, Maine.

In the 1840's some Germans, Irish and Norwegians showed up in

---

[17] The entire letter from Glassie to me, dated October 11, 1967, Harrisburg, Pennsylvania. The Dr. Leach mentioned is MacEdward Leach, the famous ballad authority who taught both Glassie and me at the University of Pennsylvania and who had died the previous July 11.

Potter County, but these were all direct from the Old World and there seems to be no historic connection between Potter County and German-Scotch-Irish-Quaker southern Pennsylvania: the County's family, commercial and cultural connections were all with the Northeast.

I would certainly think the similarities you've spotted are the results of migration—even if the migrants carried a songster along—from New England to northern Pennsylvania.

Things go well but busily here. It was very good to hear from you.

Best wishes,

Henry Glassie, State Folklorist
Ethnic Culture Survey

HG/mk

Here's what Beebe says about Lyman in direct quotation,[18]

We must now introduce the second permanent settler in the county, Major Isaac Lyman. He was born in 1759, and when we first hear of him, he lived at Bolton, Vermont. He served as ensign in the Revolution, taking part in the battle of Bennington. In the battle of Lake George, his company was betrayed by a traitor, and only 15 men escaped, he being one of the number. He afterwards engaged in the milling business at Hebron, N. Y., a small place near the State line northeast of Albany. He was three times married. The first marriage was to Sallie Edgcomb in 1782. Mr. Milo Lyman tells me that she was a near relative of Jonathan Edgcomb, whom I shall mention later among our early settlers. She died in August, 1791, having borne six children, one of whom, Jonathan, died in childhood. The oldest daughter, Sallie, probably married near the old home; there is no further record of her. The remaining four children, Lydia, Charlotte, Eunice, and John, all eventually came to Pennsylvania, and all settled in Potter except Charlotte, who married Ira Wells, whose residence was in McKean County, according to the Lyman genealogy. Lydia married Thomas Bellows, and Eunice married Cephas Nelson, both being among our early settlers.

Major Lyman married Laura Pierce in 1792, six months after the death of his first wife. The children of this marriage, besides one or two that died in infancy, were Burrell, Laura, Harry, Isaac, and Otis. About 1805 or 1806, Major Lyman's domestic affairs seem to have run

[18] Victor L. Beebe, *History of Potter County, Pennsylvania* (Coudersport, Pa., 1934), 29-30.

afoul of some obstruction that is now forgotten. He gave his wife a written document which he wished her to regard as a divorce, but which had no legal status whatever, and came to Charleston Township, Tioga County, where he lived for about two years. Here, on March 3, 1809, he married Patience Mann Spafford, a widow with one son, Lorenzo D. Spafford, and two daughters, Lucretia and Marietta. Tradition says that Major Lyman frightened the young woman into a marriage post haste, giving her only a moment to accept or reject him. However, that may be, there were married, and the first child of this union, Charles, was born January 13, 1810. The three Spaffords became members of Major Lyman's family.

So there is some smoke here, though how much fire is hard to tell. After all, Lyman fought in the Revolution, he came from Hebron, New York which is just up the road from Sandgate, Vermont, and his life span is exactly contemporary with that of the compiler of *The Green Mountain Songster.* In fact one could almost present him as the "follower of Gen. George Washington," for he would have been 18 or 19 during the winter of Valley Forge and 64 when the ballet book was published.

With this lead, I checked farther to see if there weren't more songs that other informants in Shoemaker shared with the author of *The Songster.* Unfortunately, Shoemaker's collectors worked sporadically and whimsically. However, two such texts do show up. One is "Brave Wolfe"; the other, "Old Granny Wales," both of which we will discuss later. "Brave Wolfe" is not uncommon in the eastern part of America, even today, so its presence in the two repertoires proves little, but "Old Granny Wales" is almost never collected from oral tradition any longer. Thus, the Shoemaker fragment that John French found in Potter County assumes significance. Perhaps, it means only that the Sandgate soldier sang the same sort of songs which the persons who migrated from Vermont to northern Pennsylvania sang. Perhaps, it means more. I'll probably never make the effort to find out, or, if I do, I'll probably end up frustrated. But the fogs of time lift just enough in a case like this to stir the spirit and make one look longingly at the archives.

The other Child ballads in *The Green Mountain Songster* are interesting, but undistinguished and quite literary. Like the rest of the collection, to which we will now turn, they show how vitally folksongs need the regenerative force of print to endure in a relatively literate culture.

"Brave Wolfe" certainly offers no exception, having been a broadside and songster favorite from the end of the 18th century till the middle of the 19th. Even today, it is relatively easy to collect from oral tradition in the northeastern areas. Excepting "Lovewell's Fight," which deals with a rather sordid affair in the King Phillip's War about 1723[19] and "Braddock's Defeat," which G. Malcolm Laws has called a "relic of the French-Indian Wars,"[20] this song reaches farther back into American history than any of our military ballads. The account of Wolfe's demise is not particularly accurate, though like most legendary matter there is a kernel of truth hidden beneath the romanticism.[21]

GENERAL WOLFE.

Cheer up you young men all let nothing fright you,
Although the objection call let it delight you,
Let not your courage fail till after trial,
Nor let your fancy move the first denial.

I went to see my love not to delude her,
I sat down by my love thinking to woo her,
Whene'er she spake a word my tongue did quiver,
I dare not speak my mind while I was with her.

Love, here's a ring of gold, long time I've kept it;
Love, here's a ring of gold if you'll accept it,
And when you the posey read think on the giver,
Madam remember me undone forever.

[19] The best summary of the scandal associated with "Lovewell's Fight" and the role the ballad played in the aftermath appears in the *Bulletin of the Folk-Song Society of the Northeast*, #4, 3-8; #5, 17-19, #6, 3-4. A complete run of the *Bulletin* was printed in a single volume by the American Folklore Society (Philadelphia, 1960).

[20] G. Malcolm Laws, Jr., *Native American Balladry* (*NAB*), Philadelphia, 1964), 258.

[21] *GMS*, 22-23.

Thus this brave Wolfe took leave of his dear jewel,
And to his love he said oh don't prove cruel,
Although 'tis for a space I'm oblig'd to quit you,
Wherever I shall go I'll ne'er forget you.

Thus the brave and gallant Wolfe went to the ocean,
To free America from her invasion,
And landed at Quebec with all his party,
The city to attack all brave and hearty.

On the plains of Abraham before the city,
Brave Wolfe drew out his men in a line most pretty,
A distance from the town where the French did meet them,
With double number were resolv'd to beat them.

Being drawn up in this place for death prepared,
While in each other faces so boldly stared,
While Montcalm and brave Wolfe together talking,
And lovingly between their armies walking.

Then each one took his post at their retire,
And then this numerous host began their fire,
Then soon with crimson blood we were surrounded,
Which issued like a flood from dead and wounded.

Then sudden from his horse fell the brave hero,
And we lament the loss of him in sorrow;
As he lay weltering in his gore as he lay dying,
And many thousands more shrieking and crying.

The French begun to break, their troops were flying,
He seemed to awake as he lay dying,
And raised up his head while the drums did rattle,
And to his army said "how goes the battle?"

His Aid-de-camp replied "goes in our favour,
Quebec in all her pride nothing can save her,
She falls into our hands with all her treasure,"
"Oh then," replied brave Wolfe, "I die with pleasure."

Wolfe really did have a "true love," Katherine Lowther, at the time of his death during the seige of Quebec. He had been wounded in the battle that ensued after his men scaled the heights, and he did lie dying at his moment of victory. Knowing his condition, he is supposed to have asked for stimulants that he might go on leading his troops. The French commander, Louis Joseph de Montcalm was also slain in the fray. Perhaps the irony of having both brave leaders fall in this remarkable seige was reason enough to create the melodramatic scene in which the Frenchman and the Englishman walk arm and arm between the troops before separating to do fatal battle. Certainly, this scene, combining with the frustrated love affair and the motion picture ending make the song sure-fire in any place at any time. And if Hollywood has not seen fit to capitalize on it, the host of Catnachs have.

The Green Mountain Songster contains other fine examples of print-shop ballads that are known from traditional singers, like "The Bay of Biscay, O" and "The Maid in Bedlam."[22] The first is a rollicking come-ye-all which is also found under the titles "Ye Gentlemen of England" and "The Stormy Winds Do Blow." The other, like "Polly Oliver," is part of that endless stream of pieces in which lovers are parted and stubbornly reunite. Just as our era never tires of comic strips, movies, and TV shows which offer escape through this theme, so the print shops found an insatiable market for the harmless plot.

THE BAY OF BISCAY O.

Come all you jolly seamen with courage stout and bold,
Who value more your honour than misers do their gold;
When we receive our orders then we're oblig'd to go,
Cross the main to proud Spain let the wind blow high or low.

The twenty-fifth of January from Spithead we set sail:
The Rumzy our company blest with a pleasant gale,
There strait we sail'd together for the bay of Biscay O,
Then a long storm came on and the wind began to blow.

The wind and storm increasing, the Rumzy bore away,
And sailed for Gibraltar she could no longer stay,
And when she came to Gibraltar she told the people so,
That she thought we were lost in the bay of Biscay O.

[22] *GMS*, 21-22 and 9-10, respectively.

But as Providence would have it, it was not quite so bad,
The first we lost our fore mast therewith we lost our flag,
The next we lost our main mast and one of our guns also,
And five men were drowned then in the bay of Biscay O.

The losing of our main mast which prov'd a dismal stroke,
For on our larboard quarter there a great hole was broke,
The waves they did come rolling in which made our gun-room flow,
Thus she roll'd and she stroll'd in the bay of Biscay O.

It was both dark and dismal about twelve o'clock at night,
Our Captain on the forecastle was killed there outright,
The ring upon his fingers did burst in pieces too,
There he lay till next morning then him overboard did throw.

The wind and storm being over we raised jury masts,
And then for Gibraltar we did make all things fast,
But we could boil no victuals boys and that you well might know,
Obliged to eat our raw meat in the bay of Biscay O.

And when we come to Gibraltar we landed at the mole,
The people they came flocking down our shipwreck to behold,
They said it was a dismal sight as they ever did know,
We ne'er pine but drink wine so we wash'd away our wo.

THE MAID IN BEDLAM.

Through Morefields I walked one evening in the spring,
I heard a maid in Bedlam, so sweetly she did sing.
The chains she rattled on her hands, and then replied she,
'Tis I that loves my love, because my love loves me.

My love and I were parted, by friends that were unkind,
They have sent him away beyond the sea, which sore torments my mind,
But tho' I am ruin'd, for his sake contented can I be,
For 'tis I that loves my love, because my love loves me.

I wish I was a swallow—could mount the lofty air,
And though I lose my labor, and could not find him there,
Soon would I become a fish, I'd cross the raging sea,
For 'tis I that loves my love, because my love loves me.

Suppose my love be drowned all in the roaring main,
The waves away have carried him, to Turkey, France, or Spain,
To sleep within his frozen arms how happy should I be,
For 'tis I that loves my love, because my love loves me.

Oh that I were a turtle—could build upon his breast,
With blooming sprigs of myrtle, and there I'd make my nest,
To gaze upon his pretty eyes, how happy should I be,
For 'tis I that loves my love because my love loves me.

Of straw I'll make my garden, I'll make it very fine,
I'll stick the same with roses and lillies mix'd with thyme;
I'll present it unto my love, when he comes home from sea,
For 'tis I that loves my love, because my love loves me.

I'll wait it out with patience, I'll wear my heavy chain,
Who knows but in the space of time, my love may come again?
If ever that the day were, how happy should I be,
For 'tis I that loves my love, because my love loves me.

As this maid lay lamenting, her true-love came to land,
He heard she was in bedlam—he straight went out of hand;
Just as he enter'd in the gate, he heard her crying say,
'Tis I that loves my love, until my dying day.

O! do not you fright me, are you my love or no?
Oh yes, my dearest Nancy! what causes you to lament so?
For I am come to make you amends for all your unity,
For 'tis I that loves my love until the day I die.

He brought her to her senses, they married speedily,
And now they live in happiness, in joy and unity.
Come all you pretty maidens that have true loves at sea,
Come wait it out with patience, and take pattern by me.

Come all you jolly sailors, that sail upon the main,
I earnestly entreat of you to constantly remain;
Take pattern by my lilly, who proved so true to me,
If you do hope to prosper when you sail on the sea.

The Green Mountain Songster also contains "Jennie Jenkins,"[23] which was widely used as a dance song. The Sandgate soldier's

[23] *GMS*, 8-9.

version is pretty well garbled and thus appears to be directly from tradition. Possibly it was something he recalled from his youth, from those circle dances, Irish reels, and jigs, that were popular across the New England countryside of Colonial and early 19th century days.

JANE JENKINS.

Will you wear grey, Onere, Onere?
Will you wear grey, Jane Jenkins?
No, I won't wear grey for it's colour of the clay,
So buy me my tallawalawise, so buy me my tallawalawise.

Will you wear black, Onere, will you wear black, Onere?
I won't wear black, for the colour it is slack,
So buy me the tallawalawise, so buy me the tallawalawise,
So double rose Dillevally Sukey, Dicky,
So double rose Dillevally, Sukey, Dicky, white bands appear,
Where are the robes that you wear, Jane Jenkins.

Will you wear red, Onere, will you wear red, Onere?
I will not wear red for the colour I do dread,
So buy me my tallawalawise, so buy me my tallawalawise;
So double rose Dillevally, Sukey, Dicky, white bands appear.

Will you wear green, Onere, will you wear green, Onere?
I won't wear green for it's a colour that is mean;
So buy me my tallawalawise, so buy me my tallawalawise,
So double rose Dillivally, Sukey, Dickey, white bands appear.

Will you wear white, Onere, will you wear white, Onere?
O no I won't wear white 'tis a colour I dislike,
So buy me my tallawalawise, so buy me my tallawalawise,
So double rose Dillevally, Sukey, Dicky, white bands appear.

Will you wear yellow, Onere, will you wear yellow, Onere?
I will not wear yellow for it's a colour that is shallow,
So buy me my tallawalawise, so buy me my tallawalawise,
So double rose Dillevally, Sukey, Dicky, white bands appear.

Will you wear blue, Onere, will you wear blue, Onere?
O yes, I'll wear blue for the colour of it's true,
So you've bought me my tallawalawise, so you've bought
me my tallawalawise,
So double rose Dillevally, Sukey, Dicky, white bands appear.

Then there are a host of songs that must have been popular in the drawing rooms of the day. Sometimes these are hard to distinguish from the street ballads, as many of them were pirated or borrowed by the ballad-mongers. However, the ones I am thinking of are particularly precious or cute, "The Chamber Maid" being a good example.[24]

THE CHAMBER MAID.

Not far from town a country Squire,
An open hearted blade,
Had long confessed a strong desire
To kiss his chamber maid.

One summer's noon quite full of glee,
He led her to the shade,
And there beneath a mulberry tree,
He kiss'd his chamber maid.

The parson's wife from window high,
This amorous sport survey'd,
And softly wish'd, none can deny,
She'd been the chamber maid.

When all was o'er then Betsy cri'd,
Kind sir, I'm much afraid
That women there will tell your bride,
You've kiss'd your chamber maid.

The Squire conceiv'd a lucky thought
That she might not upbraid,
And instantly his lady brought
Where he had kiss'd her maid.

Then all beneath the mulberry tree,
Her ladyship was laid,
And there three times sweetly kiss'd was she,
Just like her chamber maid.

Next morning came the parson's wife,
For scandal was her trade,
I saw your Squire ma'am on my life,
Great with your chamber maid.

[24] *GMS*, 50-51.

When? cri'd the lady, where and how,
I'll soon discharge the jade;
Beneath the mulberry tree, I vow
I saw him kiss your maid.

This falsehood, cri'd her ladyship,
My spouse shall not degrade;
'Twas I that chanc'd to make a slip,
And not my chamber maid.

So both then parted in a pet,
Not trusting what each said,
And Betsey keeps her place as yet,
The pretty chamber maid.

Another, not dissimilar, and with a Revolutionary flavor to it, is called "The Damsel in Her Blooming Years," [25]

THE DAMSEL IN HER BLOOMING YEARS.

I'll tell you of a damsel all in her blooming years,
With grief and lamentation and many a melting tear,
'Tis of her best beloved as you may understand,
Who was oblig'd to travel into some foreign land.

Oh, stay at home Billy and do not go away,
For I am sorely grieved and very well I may,
For its sixteen weeks and better since I have loved thee;
Oh, stay at home love Billy, oh stay and marry me.

Oh, if I should stay at home love and another should take my place,
Oh it would be a shame, love, 'twould be a great disgrace,
For Washington he calls for men and I for one must go,
I dare not for my life love, I dare not answer no.

Well, since 'tis so love Billy, no better can I do,
I'll dress in men's attire and along with you will go,
And like a little foot page upon my love will wait,
I'll fear no manner of danger let it be e'er so great.

[25] *GMS*, 44.

Oh, it's a pity my Polly should be a servant man, [and fan,
I had rather see you dress'd love in your breast knot, mask
Besides love let me tell you your fingers are to fine
To stand behind my back love when I do sit and dine.

And since 'tis so my Polly that you have won my heart,
Then we will have a wedding before that we do part;
And now this couple married were in love and unity,
I wish them well together in North America.

Such songs, some narrative, some not, are examples of those incredibly dated pieces that were the popular songs of the day, the ditties which are sentimental ancestors to "Cheek to Cheek," "Misty," and "Stardust." They seldom survive for long, their triteness and vanity becoming more and more apparent as fashions shift. The ones favored by the Sandgate soldier are hard to read, even by title alone: "Fancy and Judgment," "Amours of Anacreon," "The Muse of Masonry," "The Maiden's Moan," "The Maiden's Address to her Fallen Lover."

Much more interesting is something like "Joel Baker."[26] This is a narrative obituary poem, like "Springfield Mountain," which evidentally was set to music and became, at least for a while, a song. However, it has faded from Vermont tradition, and I know of no other text.

JOEL BAKER.

Come all young lovers far and near,
A dismal story you shall hear,
A young man did in Alstead dwell,
Who lov'd a fair maid passing well.

To her he went with tears 'tis said,
And many solemn vows they made;
She false girl, fill'd his heart with wo.
Which sent him to the shades below.

And when so cruel she did prove,
And thus her true love did abuse,
By choosing of another one,
He cried I'm utterly undone.

[26] *GMS*, 39-40.

To her he went and thus he cried,
Dear Sally, will you be my bride?
For sure our vows must end the strife,
Or cut the brittle thread of life.

No answer from her could he gain,
To ease him from his bitter pain;
He said you've pierc'd my tender heart,
Alas, this world and I must part!

Now when her parents this did hear,
They said we fear his death draws near
With scornfulness the damsel spoke—
I soon will send to him a rope.

'Twas on July, the second day,
Oh when the sun had roll'd away;
Then by a musket's dismal sound,
His body by some friends was found.

His body did lay on the floor,
And from it ran the purple gore:
Three deadly groans he gave, 'tis true,
Then bid this sinful world adieu.

'Tis said this young man he was poor,
'Tis true, he had no great store;
I think I hear that fame does say,
What the other gains is by the way.

Now her new will I shall not name,
Although he says there's none to blame;
Oh, from my heart I wish them well,
For none but God alone can tell.

Scarce had a month then pass'd away,
When she with her new love did stay;
Much would they dread and greatly fear,
Then should his frightful ghost appear.

Now lovers all, I pray be true,
Don't break your vows, what ere you do;
The God above rules all below,
May punish you with nameless wo.

Some passed by his grave, 'tis said,
And there cast slurs upon the dead;
The time will come and soon will be,
They must lie there as well as he.

Now to conclude and make an end;
I sat me down—these lines I've pen'd—
God grant it may a warning be,
To all who do these verses see.

Brought from Europe, narrative obituary poetry flourished in America from the very beginnings of the Colonies down until the early 20th century. The custom was to compose or have composed a poem to be distributed and sometimes sung at the funeral. The poems told of the circumstances leading up to the death of the deceased, usually were set to the tune of "Old Hundred," and developed an easily recognizable style and meter. A few typified something that the listeners held dear. These continued to be sung, and as in the case of "Springfield Mountain," the most widely known obituary poem-song, became nationally disseminated ballads. Others were simply tossed into the grave with the coffin or lost and forgotten with the memory of the deceased. A few, like "Joel Baker," survived as songs for a short while, eventually to fade from tradition. There is no doubt a connection between this country custom and the broadside presses, which in urban areas had a stock of lines ready for whatever funeral might come along, somewhat in the fashion of the old Western Union singing telegrams. Such printers found as steady a commerce in death as does the mortician, and undoubtedly the relationships between the narrative obituary poem and the occasional ballads dealing with love crimes, the deaths of criminals and politicians, the train wrecks is closer than scholars have realized.

Phillips Barry actually made an effort to find out who Joel Baker might have been, but he had no luck, learning little from the histories of Alstead, New Hampshire (just across the river from Bellows Falls, Vermont) where the events of the song took place. However, it is not hard to reconstruct the scene for which the ballad must have been written. In the *Journal of American Folklore*, there is the following description preceding a copy of a narrative obituary ballad about one Isaac Orcutt.[27]

This ballad is communicated by Miss Julia D. Whiting, of Deerfield, Mass., who relates the circumstances of composition as follows: "About one hundred years ago, my grandmother, then a young woman of thirty, was living in Amherst, Mass. A young man by the name of Isaac Orcutt went to Westfield to work, and was there killed in an accident, and brought home to be buried. An old lady, whose name is unknown to me, composed these verses, and they were sung at his burial by six young women (of whom my grandmother was one), dressed in white, who stood around his grave. I dare say the old lady composed the tune as well as the words; at any rate, words and tune go well together."

Perhaps it was in a situation like this that the Sandgate soldier first heard the ballad. It is not impossible he knew Baker, not impossible that he wrote the original poem.

The Green Mountain Songster contains its share of political material. At the first announcement of the Stamp Act in 1765, the printers and local poets began to capitalize on the developing market for what we now consider "patriotic" pieces – even though at the time the Motherland must have seen them in somewhat different terms. Though this act was repealed in 1766, it wasn't long before duties on glassware, lead, paper, paints, and tea gave the print shops adequate opportunity for more statements such as the burden to "Song for the Sons of Liberty,"

For we must not, we will not be slaves, brave boys,
For we must not, we will not be slaves.

Subsequently, there was the Boston Massacre, the billeting of British troops in Boston, and the decade of events made famous by our schoolbooks. Printers capitalized on the tension. They re-wrote songs the British troops sang: a stanza like,

'Twas summer and softly the breezes were blowing,
And sweetly the nightingale sang from the tree;
At the foot of a rock where the river was flowing,
I sat myself down on the banks of the Dee.
Flow on, lovely Dee–flow on, thou sweet river,
Thy banks purest stream shall be dear to me ever

[27] *JAF*, 1900, 105-106.

For there I first gain'd the affection and favour
Of Jamie, the glory and pride of the Dee.

rapidly becoming,[28]

'Twas winter, and blue Tory noses were freezing,
As they marched o'er the land where they ought not to be;
The valiants complain'd at the fifers' curs'd wheezing,
And wish'd they'd remained on the banks of the Dee.
Lead on, thou paid captain! Tramp on, thou proud minions!
Thy ranks, basest men, shall be strung like ripe onions,
For here thou has found heads with warlike opinions,
On shoulders of nobles who ne'er saw the Dee.

Prominent figures, Francis Hopkinson, Joseph Warren, William Billings, and even a poet of the stature of Philip Freneau, were compelled to invective and parody. And when we recall that about three out of every ten colonists remained loyal to the Crown, we have also to recall that for every song such as "The Liberty Song"[29] of the Sandgate patriot there was a song such as the one Joseph Stansbury wrote for a Loyalist banquet in 1781.

THE LIBERTY SONG.

Awake, awake, Americans, put cheerful courage on,
If tyrants then shall you oppress, arise and say begone!
O let no Papist bear the sway, nor tyrant ever reign,
Treat such infringements of our rights with resolute disdain.

Yet we will loyal subjects be, to any loyal king,
And in defence of such a prince spend every precious thing:
But when our prince a tyrant grows, and Parliament grows worse,
New-England's blood will never bear the ignominious curse.

[28] The original song was written by John Tait, an Edinburgh judge; the parody by Oliver Arnold, a relative of the infamous Benedict. The pair of opening stanzas reproduced here are from Frank Moore, *Songs and Ballads of the American Revolution* (Moore), (New York, 1855), 79-82.

[29] *GMS*, 56. Political figures referred to in Stanza 3 are Sir Frederick North (1732-1792), the English statesman and prime minister; and Thomas Hutchinson (1711-1780) and Francis Barnard, both Royal Governors of Massachusetts and loyal subjects. In the "Loyalist Song" that follows, Clinton is Sir Henry Clinton (1738?-1795), British commander-in-chief in North America.

Then let Lord North and Huchinson and Barnard do their worst,
Their hated names through every age forever shall be curs'd;
But mortal tongue can ne'er express the praise that shall descend
Upon the head of every one who proves New-England's friend.

Tho' navies do around us lie, and troops invade the land,
Yet we'll defend our liberty as long as we can stand;
Though fighting be our last address, we'll bravely let them know,
That we will fight with all our might, before our rights shall go.

All for the sake of liberty our fathers first came here,
And hunger underwent, and cold and hardships most severe:
Then let no haughty tyrant think we are such a wretched brood
As to give up that liberty our fathers bought with blood.

We gladly will consent to peace, on reasonable terms,
Our liberty once well secur'd we will lay down our arms;
Yet never will resign those rights our fathers purchas'd so,
While any of their noble blood within our veins does flow.

Domestic enemies we have in almost every town,
Whose names to unborn ages shall always be handed down,
With infamy dishonour's yoke shall sink them in disgrace,
Amongst the sons of liberty, till time itself shall cease.

Unite, unite, Americans, with purse, with heart and hand,
Divided we shall surely fall, united we shall stand;
Then let our hearts be all as one, and all our veins be free,,
To fight and rather bleed and and die than loose our liberty.

Come, come, O brave Americans, let's drink a loyal bowl,
May the dear sound of liberty sink deep in every soul;
Here's a health to North America, and all her noble boys,
Their liberty and property, and all that she enjoys.

LOYALIST SONG.

Friends, push round the bottle and let us be drinking
While Washington up in his mountains is slinking.
Good faith, if he's wise he'll not leave them behind him,
For he knows he's safe nowheres where Britons can find him.
When he and Fayette talk of taking this city,
Their vaunting moves only our mirth and our pity.
But tho' near our lines they're too cautious to tarry,

What courage they show when a hen-roost to harry!
Who can wonder that Poultry and Oxen and Swine
Seek shelter in York from such Valour divine,

While Washington's jaws and the Frenchman's are aching
The spoil they have lost to be boiling and baking.
Let Clinton and Arnold bring both to subjection,
And send us more Geese here to seek our protection.
Their flesh and their feathers shall meet a kind greeting:
A fat Rebel Turkey is excellent eating:
A Lamb fat as butter, and white as a Chicken—
These sorts of tame Rebels are excellent picking.
Today a wild Rebel has smoked on the Table:
You've cut him and slic'd him as long as you're able.
He bounded like Congo, and bade you defiance;
And placed in his running his greatest reliance.
But Fate overtook him and brought him before ye,
To shew how Rebellion will wind up *her* story.
Then cheer up, my lads: if the Prospect grows rougher,
Remember from whence, and for whom 'tis, you suffer:
From whom Mild laws, and too happy Condition,
Have puffed up with pride and inflamed with Sedition:
For George, whose reluctance to punish Offenders
Has strengthened the hands of these upstart Pretenders.

There were Rebel shops and Tory shops, and a lot of opportunistic shops that saw a contract as a contract regardless of politics.

The Sandgate soldier sang a number of these political pieces down to the end of his days. It is interesting to note that the ones he preserves are generally better than the run-of-the-press and show real humor, real humanity. A particularly interesting text is "American Taxation," which traces at some length and with dated eloquence the origins of the War from an alliance between Lord North and Satan to a series of toasts to Colonial generals and allies. The poem has wit, naiveté, and real charm in its almost boyish outbursts: "Proud George you are engaged all in a dirty cause"; "I'll tell you George in metre if you'll attend awhile"; and "We truly were your betters hard by the Brandywine."[30]

[30] *GMS*, 15-19. The reference in Stanza 3 to "North, and Bute, his father" seems confused. North is of course Sir Frederick North. Bute

THE AMERICAN TAXATION.

Whilst I relate my story, Americans give ear,
Of Britain's fading glory you presently shall hear;
I'll give a true relation, attend to what I say,
Concerning the Taxation in North America.

The cruel Lords of Britain, who glory in their shame,
The project they had hit on they joyfully proclaim;
'Tis what they're striving after, to take our rights away,
And rob us of our Charter, in North America.

There are two mighty speakers who rule in Parliament,
Who always have been seekers some mischief to invent;
'Twas North, and Bute, his father, a horrid plan did lay,
To rob us of our charter, in North America.

They search'd the gloomy regions of the infernal pit,
To find among those legions one who excell'd in wit,
To ask of him assistance, to tell them how they may
Subdue without resistance this North America.

Old Satan, that arch traitor, a voyage resolv'd to make;
He reigns sole navigator upon the burning lake;
For the Brittanic ocean he launched fast away—
To land he had no notion, in North America.

He'll take his seat in Britain, it was his soul's intent,
Great George's throne to sit on and rule the Parliament;
His comrads were pursuing a diabolic way,
For to complete the ruin of North America.

---

should be John Stuart, the Third Earl of Bute (1713-1792), however, allusion is clearly made to a rumor of the time that North was the illegitimate son of Bute's father. Bute's father had nothing to do with "robbing" Americans of their charter. In Stanza 17, Hutchinson is again Thomas Hutchinson and Rogers is Robert Rogers of "Rogers' Rangers" fame. Rogers had become a violent Tory. In Stanza 28, the reference is to the well-known American generals of those names; in Stanza 30 to Sir Peter Parker (1721-1811), the British naval officer, who made an unsuccessful attack on Sullivan's Island in Charleston Harbor, S. C. in 1776; and in Stanza 31 to the famous British generals of those names. In Stanza 32, Warner is Seth Warner (1743-1784), the associate of Ethan Allen about whom we will hear more.

They tried the art of magic to bring their schemes about;
    At length the gloomy project was artfully found out;
The plan was long indulged in a clandestine way,
    At length it was divulged in North America.

These subtle arch combiners address'd the British court,
    All three were undersigners of this obscure report;
There is a pleasant landscape that lyeth far away,
    Beyond the wide Atlantic in North America.

There's a wealthy sort of people who sojourn in that land,
    Their churches all with steeples most delicately stand,
Their houses like the gilly they're painted red and gay,
    They flourish like the lilly in North America.

Their land with milk and honey continually doth flow,
    The want of food or money they seldom ever know,
They heap up gold and treasure, they have no debts to pay,
    They spend their time in pleasure in North America.

On turkey, fowls, and fishes, most frequently they dine,
    With gold and silver dishes their tables always shine;
They crown their feasts with butter, they eat & rise to play,
    In silks the ladies flutter in North America.

With gold and silver laces they do themselves adorn,
    The rubies deck their faces, refulgent as the morn,
Wine sparkles in their glasses, they spend each happy day,
    In merriment and dances in North America.

Let not our suit affront you when we address your throne,
    O king this wealthy country, and subjects, are your own.
And you, their lawful sovereign, they surely must obey,
    You have a right to govern this North America.

O king conceive the sequel from what we here prescribe,
    Is it not just and equal to tax this wealthy tribe?
The question being asked his Majesty did say,
    My subjects shall be taxed in North America.

Invested with my warrant my publicans shall go,
    The tenth of all their current they surely shall bestow:
If they indulge rebellion, or from my precepts stray,
    I'll send my war battalions to North America.

I'll rally all my forces by water and by land;
My light dragoons and horsemen shall go at my command,
I'll burn both town and city, the smoke shall cloud the day,
I'll shew no human pity in North America.

Go on my hardy soldiers you need not dream of ill,
There's Hutchinson & Rogers their functions will fulfil,
They tell such ample stories believe them sure we may,
That one half will turn tories in North America.

My gallant ships are ready to waft you o'er the flood,
Then in my cause be steady, which is supremely good;
Go ravage, steal and plunder, and your's shall be the prey,
They quickly will knock under in North America.

The laws I have enacted, I never will revoke,
Although they are neglected, my fury to provoke;
I will forbear to flatter, but rule with mighty sway,
I'll take away the charter from North America.

O George you are distracted! by sad experience find,
The laws you have enacted are of the blackest kind,
I'll make a short digression and tell you by the way,
We fear not your oppression in North America.

Our fathers were distressed while in their native land,
By tyrants were oppressed as we do understand;
For freedom and religion they were resolved to stray,
And try the desert regions of North America.

Heaven was their sole protector while on the raging tide,
Kind fortune their director, and providence their guide,
If I am not mistaken, about the first of May
This voyage was undertaken for North America.

If rightly I remember, this country to explore,
They landed in November on Plymouth's desert shore,
The savages were frightened, with fear they fled away,
In peace our fathers settled this North America.

We are their bold descendants, for liberty we'll fight,
The claim to independence we challenge as our right,
'Tis what kind heaven gave us, then who shall take away,
Kind Heaven too can save us in North America.

We never will knock under, O George, we do not fear
The rattling of your thunder, nor lightning of your spear;
Though rebbels you declare us we're strangers to dismay,
Therefore you cannot scare us in North America.

To what you have commanded we never will consent,
Although your troops are landed upon our Continent;
We'll take our swords and muskets & march in dread array,
And drive the British red coats from North America.

We have a bold commander who fears no sword or gun,
A second Alexander, whose name is Washington,
His men are all collected and ready for the fray,
To fight they are directed for North America.

We've Greene, we've Gates & Putnam to manage in the field,
A gallant train of footmen who'd rather die than yield,
A stately troop of horsemen train'd in the martial way,
For to augment our forces in North America.

Proud George you are engaged all in a dirty cause,
A cruel war have waged repugnant to all laws,
Go tell the savage nations, you're crueler than they,
To fight your own relations in North America.

I'll tell you George in metre if you'll attend awhile,
We forced your Sir Peter from Sullivan's fair isle;
At Monmouth town we gained the honors of the day,
A victory obtained in North America.

We truly were your betters hard by the Brandywine;
We led him fast in fetters whose name was John Burgoyne;
We made your Howe to tremble with terror and dismay,
True heroes we resemble in North America.

Confusion to the tories, that black infernal name,
In whom Great Britain glories, forever to their shame,
We'll send each foul revolter to smutty Africa,
Or noose them with a halter in North America.

Here's health to all our footmen that handle sword and gun,
To Warner, Gates & Putnam, & conqu'ring Washington,
Their names are wrote in letters which never shall decay,
While sun and moon shall glitter in North America.

Success unto our allies, in Holland, France and Spain,
Who arm'd their ships and gallies our freedom to maintain,
May they subdue the rancor of proud Brittania,
And drive them from their anchors in North America.

Success unto the Congress of the United States,
Who triumph in the conquests of Washington and Gates,
To all both land and seamen who glory in the day
When we shall all be freemen in North America.

Success to legislation that rules with gentle hand,
To trade and navigation by water and by land,
May all with one opinion our wholesome laws obey,
Throughout the vast dominion of North America.

The Sandgate soldier also liked "Old Granny Wales"; so well he decided to open his collection with it. This is a good song, in which Granny confronts Bute and Grenville on a London street with the accusation, "Are you the ringleaders of this here tea act?" Their masculine efforts to reason with her are brushed aside, and she tells them off in no uncertain terms.[31]

OLD GRANNY WALES.

As granny arose in the morning soon,
She put on her petticoat, apron and gown;
I've very bad news last night came to me,
They're wronging my children over the sea.

[31] *GMS*, 3-5. In Stanza 2, Lord Conner is probably Thomas Conolly (1738-1803), wealthy and prominent Irish politician, but I am by no means sure. He could be Roger Connor, father of the liberal Arthur O'Connor (1763-1852) and his brother Roger (1762-1834). In Stanza 4, Bute is John Stuart, and Granville is George Grenville (1712-1770), who is best known for the enactment of the Stamp Act of 1765. In Stanza 13, Warren is Joseph Warren (1741-1775), the American physician and patriot who sent Paul Revere on his famous ride and who was killed at Bunker Hill. In Stanza 15, Cornwallis is Charles Cornwallis (1738-1805) who surrendered at Yorktown in 1781; Graves is Samuel Graves (1713-1787), a naval officer; and Bixly is perhaps Sir Richard Bickerton (1727-1792). Granny Wales refers to Granuaile, a traditional name for Ireland.

Then granny mounted her gelding in rage,
    And strait up to Dublin it was her first stage;
As she was a riding up through Dublin street,
    'Twas there my lord Conner she chanced to meet.

He said noble granny come tell me in haste,
    What is the best news you have from the west?
I've very bad news which makes me complain,
    They're wronging my children that's over the main.

That news is too true, my lord Conner he said,
    They'll bring us to slavery I am afraid,
There is my lord Granville and infamous Bute,
    They've brought on this tea act that's now in dispute.

The weather being wet and her sorrows increas'd,
    She strait up to London it was her next stage,
As she was a riding up through London street,
    'Twas there my lord Granville and Bute she did meet.

She said noble gentlemen tell me in fact,
    Are you the ringleaders of this here tea act?
To enslave my sons that's in a foreign land,
    You are the two villains I do understand.

They say noble granny you're wrongly inform'd,
    To enslave America we never intend;
But this land is our king's we do solemnly say,
    And we will make laws for your sons to obey.

It's a lie! it's a lie! said old granny in haste,
    For it's very well known from the east to the west,
They ventur'd their lives all over the flood, [blood.
    And they purchas'd that land with the price of their

They say noble granny don't make such a vent,
We'll tame your sons courage, we'll make them repent,
Our great ships of war and our men in the fied,
They'll tame your sons courage & make them to yield.

You ne'er need to think for to frighten my sons;
At Lexington battle they made your men run,
They're men of experience in every degree,
And they'll turn your great ships with their helms alee.

I've thousands of sons that's American born,
To yield to you: slavery they highly it scorn,
They're men of experience in every respect,
And they scorn to be held down now by your tea act.

Now says noble granny I'll take leave to tell,
The battle we fought on yon Bunker's hill,
Where nine hundred Britons lay dead on the ground,
And five hundred more since have died of their wounds.

They say noble granny don't boast of your sons,
Although it was bloody the battle we won;
And then you had Warren, but now he is dead,
And you have no Warren your armies to head.

I well know say, granny our Warren is dead,
But we have a Washington our armies to head;
He'll handle your troops as polite as you please,
And pay them trouble for crossing the seas.

We allow noble granny your sons they are brave,
But now do you think of the armies we have;
We'll send over Cornwallis, our Bixly and Graves,
And your sons shall submit or we'll make them all slaves.

Well, well, says old granny go on with your cause,
My sons they will never submit to your laws,
They ventur'd their lives all over the flood,
And they purchas'd that land with the price of their blood.

I've millions of sons that's American born,
To hold to your slavery they highly it scorn,
They're men of experience in every degree,
And they'll turn your great ships with their helms alee.

Now says noble granny I'll this to you state,
You'll repent of your crimes when it is too late,
And when we have whip'd you and sent your troops home,
My sons shall be free and make laws of their own.

Oh rubber! oh rubber! cries old granny Wales,
The fox in the trap is caught by the tail;
We've men of experience that never will fail,
Here's success to the sons of old granny Wales.

This is the song I mentioned earlier in connection with Potter County and its possible relationship to *The Songster*. The fragment John C. French reported as "sung by Old People" under the title "Revolutionary Song" is one of the few times this piece has been collected from oral tradition.[32]

> Have you any good news
> from the East or the West?
> Oh! very bad news last
> night came to me,
> The wronging my children
> over the sea.
>
> There's a Fox in the trap
> and he's caught by the tail.
> Lord North and Cornwallis and Bute
> made this tea act that
> caused the dispute.

These few lines give you a glimpse of how little may remain of a print shop song after 150 years or so have passed.

Before leaving *The Green Mountain Songster*, it is only fair to point out that the Sandgate soldier had other facets to his repertory. First, there are a good many songs in the booklet that date from years after the Revolution. The Sandgate patriot was a practicing singer, and he added such pieces as "The Lame Sailor," "The Capture of the Java," "Old England Forty Years Ago," "Eliot and Monturet," "Perry's Victory," and "The Capture of the Macedonian" – all songs which celebrate events in that 1812 epilogue to the War of Independence. In addition, he must have known a number of off-color songs as soldiers always do. These he did not choose to publish, the closest we get to such matters being the not too racy, "Adam and Eve."[33]

[32] Shoemaker, 298. Reported by John C. French as "sung by Old People in Potter County."

[33] *GMS*, 68-69.

ADAM AND EVE.

Adam the first was form'd of dust as scripture doth record,
And did receive a wife call'd Eve of his creator Lord;
From Adam's side the crooked bride the Lord was pleas'd to form,
Ordain'd that they in bed might lay and keep each other warm.

This new made pair full happy were and happy might remain'd,
If his helpmate had never ate the fruit that was restrain'd;
Though Adam's wife destroy'd his life in manner that was awful,
Yet marriage now we all allow to be both just and lawful.

But woman must be courted first because it is the fashion,
And they oft times commit great crimes caus'd by a lustful passion,
And now a days there are two ways which of the two is right,
To lie between the sheets neat and clean or set up all the night.

Nature's request is great for rest our bodies seek repose,
Night is the time and 'tis no crime to bundle in our clothes,
But some suppose bundling in clothes does heaven sorely vex,
Then let me know which way to go to court the fairer sex.

Whether they must be hug'd and buss'd while setting by the fire,
Or whether they in bed may lay which doth the Lord require?
Let coat and shift be thrown adrift and breeches take their flight,
An honest man and woman can be quiet all the night.

But if there be dishonesty implanted in their mind,
Breeches nor smocks nor scarce pad locks the rage of lust can bind;
Kate and Sue both find it true who bundling do use.
Ruth is beguil'd and got with child who bundling did refuse.

Whore will be whore and on the floor it has been often said,
To sit o'er smoke and ashes poke won't keep a girl a maid.

There are 49 ballads and lyrics in *The Green Mountain Songster*, and it would be tedious to discuss each of them here. However, by now you have a good idea of what at least one Revolutionary singer, albeit a pretty literary singer, considered important in 1823. Omitting material that can't date back to the time of the Revolution and projecting the residue into the singing tradition of the time, I think we get a rather good view of what a soldier would have wanted to hear and thus wanted to sing around 1780 in Vermont. It is interesting to note how few of these songs are about the war. As we saw with Tarbox's tales at Valley Forge, the Sandgate soldier simply went to battle taking with him the lore he had known at home. In fact, it is not far-fetched to suspect that a number of the war songs may have entered his repertoire later, long after his soldier days were done.

The thesis that the repertoire of the Revolutionary folksinger was close to print is more than implicit in my decision to use *The Green Mountain Songster* as a glass through which we can look backward. But I feel this is realistic. The soldiers who fought for and against the Colonial cause were not persons isolated from the mainstream of the ever-growing city and town life of Britain and America. While many of them were illiterate or at best semi-literate, many of them were not, and all of them lived in or near a world where literacy was present and increasing. I am content to believe that what *The Green Mountain Songster* shows is, allowing for the time element, a fair view of what the soldiers sang.

4 "Yankee Doodle Dandy"

SO FAR WE HAVE BEEN LOOKING at the repertoire of folk tale-tellers and singers. It is time to turn to a specific item of lore in order to see how complex the histories of such things are, how much of the background of a war folksong is unrelated to the conflict identified with it. Take something like "Yankee Doodle." Everyone knows that "Yankee Doodle" is a Revolutionary folksong. Most people, if they think about it at all, figure "Yankee Doodle" was composed lock-stock-and-barrel at a specific moment, sung by first the British and then the Americans, eventually establishing itself as a folksong. Unfortunately, things aren't that pat. Certainly the soldiers of the Revolution sang "Yankee Doodle." It nearly became our national anthem. In 1909 Oscar G. T. Sonneck was commissioned to do a study of it, "The Star-Spangled Banner" and "Hail, Columbia."[1] His efforts were thorough, and what he had to say about "Yankee Doodle" has remained pretty much the last word on that song until today. The trouble with Sonneck's work is, however, that Sonneck was not a folklorist, and he fell into traps that a folklorist would have

[1] Oscar G. T. Sonneck, *Report on the Star Spangled Banner, Hail Columbia and Yankee Doodle* for the Library of Congress (Washington, D. C., 1909).

easily avoided. Basically, Sonneck approached the history of "Yankee Doodle" as though it had a single history, when clearly, like most folk items, it does not. "Yankee Doodle" has four interrelated histories: the history of its melody, really of the family of tunes to which its melody belongs; of the related nursery rime; of the derogatory term "yankee"; and of the popular song itself, a song which incidentally is not a ballad. If one doesn't keep these distinctions in mind (and as far as I can tell no one working on "Yankee Doodle" to date has done so), he has trouble arriving at conclusions concerning "Yankee Doodle." If he does keep those distinctions straight, the history of the whole matter is relatively clear.

Let me start with the tune family. Every folklorist knows that song tunes and song texts live independent lives. Some wag has described them as Hollywood stars, who marry for awhile, then separate, and marry others, always keeping their identity in the process. And like Hollywood stars, a marriage here and there seems to be made in heaven and to endure, so that it is not unusual to find a tune and a text that stay together for life. But the point remains, one does not trace the origin of the text of a song by means of the tune or vice-versa; usually such investigations prove deceptive.

Now this is one of the problems with persons working on "Yankee Doodle." The tune that we associate with the Revolutionary patriotic song, with the text that goes,[2]

Father and I went down to camp,
Along with Captain Gooding,
And there we see the men and boys,
As thick as hasty pudding.

Chorus: Yankee Doodle, keep it up,
Yankee Doodle, dandy,
Mind the music and the step,
And with the girls be handy.

[2] This is the text of a broadside owned by the American Antiquarian Society of Worcester, Massachusetts. The printer is N. Coverly, Jr., Milk Street, Boston.

And there we see a thousand men,
As rich as 'Squire David;
And what they wasted every day,
I wish it could be saved.

The 'lasses they eat every day,
Would keep a house a winter;
They have so much that, I'll be bound,
They eat it when they're a mind to.

And there we see a swamping gun,
Large as a log of maple,
Upon a deuced little cart,
A load for father's cattle.

And every time they shoot it off,
It takes a horn of powder,
And makes a noise like father's gun,
Only a nation louder.

I went as nigh to one myself,
As Siah's underpinning;
And father went as nigh again,
I thought the deuce was in him.

Cousin Simon grew so bold,
I thought he would have cock'd it;
It scar'd me so, I shrink'd it off,
And hung by father's pocket.

And Captain Davis had a gun,
He kind of clapped his hand on't,
And stuck a crooked stabbing iron
Upon the little end on't.

And there I see a pumpkin shell
As big as mother's basin;
And every time they touch'd it off,
They scampered like the nation.

I see a little barrel too,
The heads were made of lether,
They knock'd upon't with little clubs,
And call'd the folks together.

And there was Captain Washington,
And gentlefolks about him,
They say he's grown so tarnal proud,
He will not ride without 'em.

He got him on his meeting clothes,
Upon a slapping stallion,
He set the world along in rows,
In hundreds and in millions.

The flaming ribbons in his hat,
They look'd so tearing fine ah,
I wanted pockily to get,
To give to my Jemimah.

I see another snarl of men
A digging graves, they told me,
So tarnal long, so tarnal deep,
They 'tended they should hold me.

It scar'd me so, I hook'd it off,
Nor stopp'd, as I remember,
Nor turned about, till I got home,
Lock'd up in mother's chamber.

is extremely old, much older than the word "yankee," and much older than any of the rimes or lyrics now associated with it. Variants of the "Yankee Doodle" melody, that is melodies that might be considered part of the same family of tunes, have been traced back to medieval Italian church music, to vintage and reaping songs in France and the Low Countries, to dance songs in Hungary. The tune itself can be called a folk tune. It was a popular country jig in Britain, and, as such, was well-known to composers and musical hacks in the 17th and 18th century England and Ireland. Sonneck[3] traces all the appearances of its variants that he could find, and the discoveries are copious and tedious. Briefly, the "Yankee Doodle" tune was widely known, widely borrowed, and a very good one, which served as well for a night in the theatre as it did for a Colonial dance.

[3] See Sonneck, 95 f.

Somewhere in its travels it associated itself with a series of folk rimes. In Holland the lyric,

> Yanker, dudel, doodle, down,
> Diddle, dudel, lanther;
> Yanker, viver, voover, vown
> Botermilk and tanther.

which refers to Jan, the doodle, and his wages of milk plus a tenth of the harvested grain was sung to it by reapers. The melody and this lyric must have been brought to Nieuw Amsterdam. In England, a persistent legend exists that unhappy Cavaliers jeered Oliver Cromwell by setting the following doggerel to it and singing it as he rode into Oxford on a small horse,

> Nankie doodle came to town
> Upon a Kentish pony;
> He stuck a feather in his hat
> And called it macaroni.

This may well have happened, although the lines above are not likely to have been the ones used, for the word "macaroni" as it refers to foppery doesn't seem to have been in existence in Cromwell's day. Perhaps the rime most consistently associated with the melody is,

> Lucy Locket lost her pocket,
> Kitty Fisher found it–
> Nothing in it, nothing on it,
> But the binding round it.

Lucy Lockit was the name given Polly Peachum's main rival for MacHeath's affections in *The Beggar's Opera,* and Kitty Fisher was a lady painted several times by Joshua Reynolds between 1758 and 1765. Kitty Fisher was married to a Kentish squire named Norris, and she died in March of 1767. Of course, these ladies' names do not really date the rime. The pattern of the verse was probably much older, and the names come and go like Charlie Chaplin, Don Ameche, and Elvis Presley in grammar school jump-rope games. In fact, in New England, Kitty Fisher is usually Lydia Fisher, whom I can't identify, and the melody was generally known as "Lydia Fisher's Jig."

It was during the associations of this melody to these and similar rimes that the word "macaroni" entered the scene. In the 15 years just before the American Revolution, there was a fad in London that centered on the Italian food. It was not dissimilar to the sloppy dress, hippie fad that has lately swept the Western world. Macaroni clubs were formed. The men wore immense top knots of hair and small cocked hats. Clothes were tight-fitting, and walking sticks with long tassels were carried everywhere. Foppish manners were cultivated, and people embracing the fad served macaroni at all meals, developed macaroni schools of art, macaroni music. By extension, the word could be used to describe almost anything that was "in" with the group. In the supposedly Cromwellian rime, the Lord Protector sticks a feather in a knot, a macaroni, on his hat, and putting on foppish ways, enters town on a silly Kentish pony. Such references tend to date this particular variant of the rime no earlier than the 1760s, and it is certain some other derogatory verse was sung to the old tune that day in Oxford more than 100 years before.

Furthermore, it seems certain the word "yankee" entered the British rimes from the Dutch phrase "yanker, dudel, doodle, down," which must have been heard by Britishers both on the Continent and in the northeastern American colonies. The English word "yankee" is usually traced back to Dutch anyhow. Originally, it seems to have derived from a back-formation of the name Jan Kees, a variation of Jan Kaas (John Cheese), that was used scornfully to describe Hollanders in Flanders and Germany. It seems likely that the Dutch in New York began to use the word for New Englanders and that eventually all New Yorkers started using it to describe their troublesome neighbors to the east. An officer, writing from Quebec in 1775-1776, comments,[4]

> The New Yorkers look upon themselves as being far superior to what they call *Yankies*, meaning the people of Connecticut, Massachusetts, Rhode Island and New Hampshire, who effect a disgusting preeminence and take the lead in every thing.

[4] From a "Journal of the most remarkable occurrences in Quebec, 1775-1776, by an officer of the garrison," as reprinted by the New York Historical Society in 1880. See p. 222.

"The Macaroni Card Players"

This use was undoubtedly shored up by the Scottish dialect verb "to yankie" which means to cheat someone or drive an unfair bargain. At any rate, by the middle of the 18th century, the word "yankee" was fully established in English usage, referring not only to New Englanders as a proper noun, but frequently carrying with it the connotation of acuteness and trickery.

Consequently, it seems sound to assume that the chorus, the only part of the song "Yankee Doodle" most people know,

Yanee Doodle came to town
A-riding on a pony,
He stuck a feather in his hat
And called it macaroni.

Yankee Doodle keep it up,
Yankee Doodle Dandy,
Mind the music and the step
And with the girls be handy.

is essentially a rime that dates, in this particular form, from the middle of the 18th century, from perhaps but ten years before the Revolution, that it opens with a variation of the old Dutch reaping rime, includes references to the verse (whatever it was) which was used to jeer Cromwell's entrance to Oxford, includes references to the macaroni fad of the 1760s and '70s, and reflects the use of the melody as a dance tune in the last two lines. It seems also sound to assume that this chorus existed quite independently, and entered the full song "Yankee Doodle," partly because it was so popular and partly because it was a better chorus than the one that was originally present. In short, a folk tune family and a series of folk rimes were fully established not only in tradition, but in polite circles, by the time anyone came to write a set of lyrics that might be considered the archetype of the song "Yankee Doodle."

There need no longer be much dispute over this archetype. Pretty well authenticated legend has it that a British surgeon, Richard Shuckburgh, sat at the well-curb in the yard of the Van Rensselaer mansion, Fort Crailo (Crailo House) at Greenbush on the banks of the Hudson near Albany, in what must have been the summer of 1755, watched ragged Colonial re-enforcements preparing to support the British against the French at Lake George, and was inspired to write the stanzas that have since become the main text of the full song. Sonneck quotes a grand-daughter of General Robert Van Rensselaer concerning the family legend,[5] which almost surely is dated three years late.

> The story of "Yankee Doodle" is an authentic tradition in my family. My grandfather, Brig. Gen. Robert Van Rensselaer, born in the Green Bush Manor House, was a boy of seventeen at the time when Doctor Shackbergh, the *writer of the verses,* and General Abercrombie were guests of his father, Col. Johannes Van Rensselaer, in *June 1758.*
>
> We have a picture of the old well, with the high stone curb and well-sweep, which has always been associated with the lines written while the British surgeon sat upon the curb . . .

He also cites a legend surviving among the Douw family in the late 19th century which presents a mild contradiction to the Van Rensselaer story.

> . . . It was on the farm of the Douw family that the English army, and the sixteen Colonial regiments, were encamped in 1755, under General Abercrombie, previous to the attack on Fort Ticonderoga in the French and Indian war. And it was at this historical spot where "Yankee Doodle" was composed by Dr. Shackleferd, and sung in derision of the four Connecticut regiments, under the command of Col. Thomas Fitch, of Connecticut . . .

The differences are of little account. Shuckburgh's name was often spelled Shackburg or Schuckborough, so Shackleferd is not much of a distortion after 100-odd years. Furthermore, it matters little whether the song was acutally composed at Douw Farm or Crailo House. If it were sung early in the game at both places, both places might well be claimed by the interested families as the origin spot. Nothing is more common in folklore. Then, too, Fitch and Shuckburgh are related by tradition: there being a sentimental Connecticut legend that tells how one Colonel Thomas Fitch of Norwalk led his shabbily dressed troops to Albany during the French-Indian Wars inspiring a British Army surgeon to compose "Yankee Doodle." Supposedly

[5] See Sonneck, 154 for this quotation and the one that follows.

Elizabeth Fitch on seeing the ragged and ill-assorted outfits of her husband's "troops" exclaimed, "You must have better uniforms than that!" and ran into the chicken yard where she gathered a bunch of feathers. She made each soldier put a feather in his hat, and when Shuckburgh saw them arriving in Albany, he burst out, "God damn me, they're macaronis!"

The account in *Farmer and Moore's Literary Journal* of 1824 is quite similar, although no mention is made of Fitch.[6]

> . . . The British army lay encamped in the summer of 1755, on the eastern bank of the Hudson, a little south of the city of Albany. . . . In the early part of June the eastern troops (Colonial) began to pour in, company after company, and such a motley assemblage of men never before thronged together on such an occasion. It would . . . have relaxed the gravity of an anchorite to have seen the descendants of the Puritans making through the streets of our ancient city to take their station on the left of the British army, some with long coats, some with short coats, and some with no coats at all. . . . Their march, their accoutrements, and the whole arrangement of their troops furnished material of amusement to the wits of the British army. Among the club of wits that belonged to the British army there was a physician attached to the staff, by the name of *Doctor Shackburg*, who combined with the science of the surgeon the skill and talents of a musician. To please Brother Jonathan he composed a tune, and, with much gravity, recommended it to the officers as one of the most celebrated airs of martial musick. The joke took, to no small amusement of the British Corps. Brother Jonathan exclaimed that it was a "nation fine," and in a few days, nothing was heard in the Provincial camp but "Yankee Doodle!"

Of course, sentimental histories are scarcely a trustworthy source for detail, but one doesn't want to discard them either. Most often they have a core of accuracy to them, legend being a formulaic elaboration of things that did happen.

Suffice it to be believed, then, that Richard Shuckburgh composed the song about Connecticut troops, probably those of Colonel Thomas Fitch, in the days of the French-Indian Wars, in 1755.[7] This

[6] As quoted by Benjamin A. Botkin in *A Treasury of New England Folklore* (New York, 1947), 516. Botkin also quotes a variant of the chicken feather anecdote on p. 516.

Shuckburgh was born in or about 1710. A British Army surgeon, he is known to have been in the New World involved in surveying along the Mohawk and Delaware Rivers by 1734-1735. In 1736 there is a record of his receiving a warrant for medicine to be used for independent English regulars at the garrison at Oswego. The records on him are not particularly good, but it is also certain he resided in New York City on the Broad Way until 1769, living with his wife and a daughter, Betsey. After Betsey's marriage, he moved to land along the Mohawk and became Secretary for Indian Affairs.

During much of this period he was closely associated with Sir William Johnson, who came from Ireland in 1738 to look after holdings on the Mohawk belonging to his uncle Peter Warren. Johnson, who learned the Mohawk language and became genuinely friendly with the Indians, went on to develop huge personal holdings in the area, including Fort Johnson, and the sort of neo-baronial manor he called Johnson Hall. As chief representative for the Crown in the French-Indian Wars of the 1750s, as a major general in the militia, and later as a baronet, Johnson became one of the most powerful figures in New World affairs. He kept careful records, for which he is much appreciated by historians, and later sided with the Loyalists in pre-Revolutionary days, using his influence with the Mohawks as a powerful lever, for which he is much disparaged by American schoolteachers. James Flexner reconstructs life at Johnson's manor in his book *Mohawk Baronet*,[8]

Though one of Johnson's tenants kept "an excellent inn at Johnstown"—he went bankrupt—Sir William invited the visitors who came to his capital "from all parts of America, from Europe, and from the West Indies . . . to repair to the Hall," where, so wrote Sir William's friend, Judge Jones, they "all were equally and hospitably entertained. . . . The gentleman and ladies breakfasted in their respective rooms, and, at their option, had either tea, coffee, or chocolate, or if an old

[7] In spite of Sonneck's doubts about Shuckburgh, Lewis A. Maverick in a fine article in *The American Neptune*, April 1962, 106-135 makes it pretty clear that Shuckburgh should be given credit for composing the group of stanzas that created the song, as opposed to the rime, "Yankee Doodle."

[8] James T. Flexner, *Mohawk Baronet* (New York, 1959), 304-306.

rugged veteran wanted a beef steak, a mug of ale, a glass of brandy, or some grog, he called for it, and it always was at his service. The freer people made the more happy was Sir William. After breakfast, while Sir William was about his business, his guests entertained themselves as they pleased. Some rode out, some went out with guns, some with fishing tackle, some sauntered about the town, some played cards, some backgammon, some billiards, some pennies, some even at nine pins.

Thus was each day spent until the hour of four, when the bell punctually rang for dinner [the dinner bell weighed 100 pounds] and all assembled. He had besides his own family, seldom less than ten, sometimes thirty. All were welcome. All sat down together. All was good cheer, mirth, and festivity. Sometimes seven or eight or ten of the Indian sachems joined the festive board. His dinners were plentiful. They consisted, however, of the produce of his estate, or what was procured from the woods and rivers, such as venison, bear, and fish of every kind, with wild turkeys, partridges, grouse, and quails in abundance. No jellies, creams, ragouts, or sillabubs graced his table. His liquors were Madeira, ale, strong beer, cider, and punch. Each guest chose what he liked and drank as he pleased. [He now ordered limes by the thousand.] The company, or at least part of them, seldom broke up before three in the morning. Everyone, however, Sir William included, retired when he pleased. There was no restraint."

As the wilderness baronet presided over Gargantuan consumption of food, punch, and wine, John Kain, a blind Irish harper he had imported, sang ancient eddas. Kain, finally drifted away to Philadelphia, where he committed a murder. He was replaced as castle musician by a tiny and chirpy violinist called Billy, who grimaced as he played duets and a bewigged Indian able to scrape European tunes "tolerably" out of a fiddle. Among the applauders was a man famous—or notorious—in musical literature. Richard Shuckbaugh, a physician who preferred drinking to doctoring, long Johnson's friend and after 1765 official Indian Secretary, is said to have convulsed a festivity at Albany during the French and Indian War by setting to a tune either original or traditional—how the musicologists argue!—a jingle—ah fatal act!—mocking the New England militia and called *Yankee Doodle.*

Flanking the rear of Johnson Hall were two freestanding stone blockhouses built during Amherst's War and large enough to shelter the whole community: They were connected to the Hall by tunnels. One was used as Negro quarters; the other, which was over the wine cellar, was probably Johnson's private study. The bowmaster (overseer) had a stone house of one room. There was a blacksmith's shop, a red coach house, stables, a coop for the peacock and his hen, a cage for the monkeys, kennels, a large framed barn, more slave quarters, "a good saw and gristmill," and "many little buildings for the accommodation of the Indians." Nearby were a large, thriving orchard, flower gardens where "a West Indian bird called a flamingo" drank from the fountain, and the 500 acres Hall farm "chiefly enclosed with board fence and hedges."

The farm, so Valley gossip remembers, was worked by some fifteen slaves who were dressed like Indians except that their blankets were stitched into coats. The many household slaves obeyed a very active German butler called Frank. Two dwarfish looking waiters, both named Bartholomew, were squawked at by the parrot in the entrance hall. An Indian boy in livery handed around tobacco. So effective were what Croghan called "the fertile loins of your estate" that when the children needed shoes, the order overflowed Johnstown and had to be farmed out among several Schenectady shoemakers.

In September of 1755, the 8th or 9th to be accurate, this neo-medieval figure, by then a major general in the militia, was involved in battling the French on Lake George. Shuckburgh, who had been in London during the summer, returned just after this fight and seems to have gone to Albany and to Johnson's camp to deliver messages to the General, who was recuperating from wounds. By late September, Shuckburgh was certainly in Albany, where the colonial governors were sending fresh militia as re-enforcements against the French. These re-enforcements were a particularly ragged bunch. Inadequately fed and clothed, they slept in makeshift huts, used sticks and cornstalks for guns in their drills, and were poorly commanded. Shuckburgh, who was described in his obituary in the *New York Gazette* of August 26, 1773 as "a man of infinite jest and humour," saw these men. The result was the song "Yankee Doodle."[9] Lewis A. Maverick has speculated these were the original words.

[9] Maverick, 125-126 writes "I submit that the following nine stanzas, a unified group, are probably the portion of the song that was written by Shuckburgh about October first, 1755 . . . at Greenbush, on the bank of the Hudson." I believe him in this. He further argues (115-117) that the identifying or chorus stanzas of "Yankee Doodle" were composed in London in 1744-1755. I don't accept his thesis on this point. I feel, as indicated above,

Father and I went down to camp
Along with Captain Gooding
And there we saw the men and boys
As thick as hasty pudding.

Refrain: Corn stalks twist their hair,
Carts wheel around them,
Great wagons carry them off,
And mortar pestles pound them.

And there was Captain Washington
Upon a strapping stallion,
A-givin' orders to his men.
I guess there was a million!

And Oh! The feather in his hat!
It look'd so tarnal fine, sah.
I wanted pescally to get
To give to my Jemima.

And there we marched around and round.
Some played on cornstalk fiddles.
And some had ribbons red as blood
All bound about their middles.

And there they had a swampin' gun,
Big as a log of maple,
Upon a deuced little cart,
A load for Father's cattle.

And ev'ry time they fired it off
It took a horn of powder.
It made a noise like Father's gun,
Only a nation louder.

And troopers they would gallup up
And fire in our faces.
It almost skeer'd me half to death
To see them run such races.

---

that the rime which eventually served as a chorus to the song (in addition to surviving independently as a rime) was in oral circulation in both England and America long before the 1740s. The fact that names such as Lucy Locket and words such as "macaroni" appear in that rime do not date anything but the particular variants under discussion.

I just can't tell you half I seen,
They kept up such a smother.
So I took off my hat, and made my bow,
And scamper'd home to Mother.

Except for the fact that no one knows who Captain Gooding was and that Captain Washington, presumably George, was not in the north in 1755, these lines are probably close to those Shuckburgh composed. At least, this is as good a guess as any.

It is from this, or some similar, beginning that oral tradition takes over, and to my way of thinking it is to this set of words that the widely known "Yankee Doodle" rime attached itself. Of course, if I am correct, Shuckburgh wrote the lyrics that eventually became the song, but did not write the chorus, perhaps was not even the one to add the chorus that eventually came to identify his song. At any rate, the song became immediately popular in camp and ultimately all across the northern colonies. New stanzas, as well as the new chorus, were added, parodies developed, and a genuine folk song was being born. Before long the British troops used it to belittle the American troops around Boston, and subsequently the Americans took the verses over as their own patriotic anthem. Sonneck documents this evolution with a series of interesting quotations.[10]

In the New York Journal, October 13, 1768, we read in the "Journal of Transactions in Boston, Sept. 28, 1768:"

Sept. 29. The Fleet was brought to Anchor near Castle William, that Evening there was throwing of Sky Rockets, and those passing in Boats observed great Rejoicings and that the Yanbey Doodle Song was the Capital Piece in their Band of Music."

Writing of the events at Boston in 1769, the late Mr. Fiske in his work on the "American Revolution" (vol. 1, p. 65) says:

On Sundays the soldiers would race horses on the Common, or play Yankee Doodle just outside the church-doors during the services.

Unforunately Mr. Fiske did not refer to his authority for this almost incredible bit of information; nor did Mr. Elson, when he wrote in his book on our national music (p. 145):

[10] Sonneck, 108-109.

> A little later [than 1769], when the camps were in the town of Boston, the British custom was to drum culprits out of camp to the tune of "Yankee Doodle," a decidedly jovial *Cantio in exitu.*

The next reference carries us to the commencement of hostilities. When the news of the affair at Lexington (Apr. 19, 1775) reached Lord Percy in Boston, says the Reverend Gordon in his History in a letter dated "Roxbury, April 26, 1775," he ordered out a reeinforcement to support his troops.

> The brigade marched out playing, by way of contempt, *Yankee Doodle* . . .

James Thacher has almost literally the same in his Military Journal under date of April 21, 1775. A further contemporary reference is found in the "Tarvels (1st ed., vol. 2, p. 50) of Thomas Anburey, the British officer, who, under date of "Cambridge, in New England, Nov. 27, 1777," wrote as follows:

> . . . the name [of Yankee] has been more prevalent since the commencement of hostilities. The soldiers at Boston used it as a term of reproach, but after the affair at Bunker's Hill, the Americans gloried in it. *Yankee Doodle* is now their paean, a favorite of favorites, played in their army, esteemed as warlike as the Grenadier's March–it is the lover's spell, the nurse's lullaby. After our rapid successes, we held the Yankees in great contempt, but it was not a little mortifying to hear them play this tune, when their army marched down to our surrender.

Anburey, of course, alludes to General Burgoyne's surrender at Saratoga, October 17, 1777. Again the military bands of the Continental army are said to have used "Yankee Doodle" as their *paean* at the climax of the war when Lord Cornwallis surrendered at Yorktown, October 19, 1781, but Robin, Knox, Thacher, Anburey, Chastellux, Gordon, and Johnston do not confirm this popular legend. I distinctly recall having seen it told by a French memoir writer of the time, but unfortunately am unable to retrace my source.

With a background like this, it is of course easy for scholars to make just about any claim for dating and authorship they wish, especially if they fail to distinguish between the melody, the rime, and the Shuckburgh song. At one point, Sonneck actually lists 16 theories of origin for "Yankee Doodle,"[11] a number of which I have already referred to.

1. The song of "Yankee Doodle" was composed by a British officer of the Revolution.

2. The air had its origin in a military march "Schwälmer Tanz," introduced into this country by the Hessians during the war for Independence.

3. The first part of the tune is identical with the *Danza Esparta* and the tune had its origin in the Pyrenees.

4. The air is of Hungarian origin.

5. The tune was introduced by German harvest laborers into Holland.

6. The air was composed by the fife-major of the Grenadier Guards about 1750 as a march.

7*a*. The tune was founded on an English tune common among the peasantry of England previous to the time of Charles I.

7*b*. It was set during the time of Cromwell to various ditties in ridicule of the protector. One of these began with the words "The Roundheads and the Cavaliers;" another

Nankee Doodle came to town
Upon a Kentish pony [or Upon a little pony]
He stuck a feather in his hat
And called him Macaroni.

were known as early as Cromwell's time, and indeed applied to him.

8. In the reign of Charles II the tune was sung to the words, perpetuated as a nursery rhyme:

Lucy Locket lost her pocket
Kitty Fisher found it.
Nothing in it, nothing in it
But the binding round it.
[or, Not a bit of money in it
Only binding round it]

9. The air is the same as of the New England jig "Lydia Fisher," which was a favorite in New England long before the American Revolution.

10. The earliest printed version of the air "Yankee Doodle" appears in 6/8 time in "Walsh's collections of dances for the year 1750" under the title of "Fisher's Jig."

[11] Sonneck, 107.

11. The air is identical with "Kitty Fisher's Jig" as printed in one of Thomson's country dance books in triple time.

12. "Yankee Doodle" is identical with an "*Air from Ulysses*," opera by J. C. Smith.

13. The air "Did little Dickey ever trick ye" in an opera by Arne, composed about 1750, is the same as "Yankee Doodle."

14. Doctor Shackburg, wit and surgeon in the British army encamped in 1755 near Albany, composed a tune and recommended it to the provincial officers as one of the most celebrated airs of martial music and that this joke on the motley assemblage of provincials took immediately.

15. Doctor Shuckburgh wrote the Yankee Doodle verses to an old-fashioned jig.

16. The air is of Irish origin and is identical with "All the way to Galway."

The trained folklorist knows that all these theories are correct, in a sense, depending on which portion of the tradition one cares to focus upon and depending whether or not one allows authorship to a person who merely sets the old melody to new words. After all, when someone like Edward Everett Hale attributes authorship of the song to Edward Bangs in 1775, I am willing to believe him to the extent that Bangs wrote a version of it at that time. One can claim "Yankee Doodle" to be a hundred things, each true, for the melody, the rime, and the Shuckburgh song have wandered like silver dollars from hand to hand, and like all folk materials belonged to no one and everyone along the way.

We have, of course, a particular interest in the variations that developed during the Revolution, when the chorus and the melody seem to have been used by both sides for every conceivable purpose. The Tories had short rimes,[12]

Yankee Doodle came to town
　　For to buy a firelock:
We will tar and feather him
　　And so we will John Hancock.

[12] As quoted from earlier sources by the Opies in *The Oxford Dictionary of Nursery Rhymes*, 441-442. The patriots derided were all men active in the cause about 1775-1776.

Madam Hancock dreamt a dream;
She dreamt she wanted something;
She dreamt she wanted a Yankee King,
To crown him with a pumpkin.

as well as more elaborate songs.[13]

Arnold is as brave a man
As ever dealt in horses,
And now commands a numerous clan
Of New-England Jack-asses.
Yankey Doodle, &c.

With sword and spear he vows and swears
That Quebec shall be taken;
But if he'd be advised by me,
He'd fly to save his bacon.

But th'other day he did assay
To do some excution;
But he thought fit to run away,
For want of resolution.

The next came in was Colonel Green,
A blacksmith by his trade, Sir;
As great a black as e'er was seen,
Tho' he's a Colonel made, Sir.

The Congress, who're a noted set
Of very honest fellows,
And being upon business met,
Told Green to sell his bellows.

He took the hint–away he went,
And all his hammers sold, Sir;
And for to fight was his intent,
Like to a hero bold, Sir.

In order for to prove the same,
(Believe me, it is true, Sir,)
When others into action came,
He to a cellar flew, Sir.

[13] See Opies, 440-441.

Next Bigalow, of Vulcan race,
Hearing of Green's success, Sir;
Resolved was to get a place,
So went to the Congress, Sir.

A sword made of an iron hoop,
(An emblem of his trade, Sir,)
To Philadelphia he took up,
To show his rusty blade, Sir.

They gave him a commission straight,
And bid him not abuse it;
Told him his rusty sword to whet,
And sent him here to use it.

Then butcher Jophen he step'd in,
And wished he might not thrive, Sir,
If he would spare one single skin,
He'd flea us all alive, Sir.

Well said, says tanner Ogden strait,
If you'll by that abide, Sir,
The villains all share share one fate;
I'll surely tan their hide, Sir.

Then Gullege swore, by all his shoes,
Alive he would not leave us;
That nothing should our fault excuse,
And Captain Thayer should shave us.

'Tis thus, my friends, we are beset,
By all those d——n'd invaders;
No greater villains ever met,
Than are those Yankey leaders.
Yankey Doodle, &c.

This latter piece was discovered in England in *The Bath Chronicle* of November 21, 1776, as brought back by a gentleman "just arrived from Newfoundland" who claimed the verses were written at Quebec, "soon after the late seige thereof."

The patriots made their uses of the material, and besides the famous text printed at the start of this chapter, there were songs such as the rather fanciful "The Plymouth Colony" which concludes *The Green Mountain Songster.*[14]

THE PLYMOUTH COLONY.

If yankees you would have a song a duced nation fine one,
Then in the chorus all along I guess you'd like to join one;
Then yankee doodle roar away keep up the chorus handy,
For some can sing and all can say yankee doodle dandy.

Our grandsires lived a great way off and if you think to doubt it,
And if I'd only time enough I'd tell you all about it,
I'd tell you all how hard they were for tithes and taxes haunted,
And how they did not think twas fair and how they got affronted.

Not knowing what might them befal they nothing were afaid in,
So took their wives and children all and off they push'd to London,
And there they got a monstrous ship as big as any gun boat,
And all to fit her for a trip I guess 'twas nice done to't.

Then every man he seiz'd a rope and pull'd with all his soul sir,
And haul'd the tow cloth all way up and ti'd it to the pole sir;
Then yankee doodle now they go all in their ships so handy,
And sing All Saints Old Hundred too and yankee doodle dandy.

And when they'd got away from shore and fore the wind did strike it,
And heard the ocean's billows roar I guess they did not like it;
But yankee doodle never mind keep up the chorus handy,
They'd left the oppressors far behind so yankee doodle dandy.

The billows they rose up so high enough the ship to fll sir,
And toss'd the vessel at the sky as high Cushit hill sir,
And there they saw a great big fish that thresh'd about his tail sir,
And look'd so deuced saucyish I guess it was a whale sir.

And when they were all landed so our granddaddys & granddames,
And Sal and Sue and Bill and Joe all had a feast on sand clams,
Then yankee doodle all you know struck up their chorus handy,
And Sal and Sue and Bill and Joe sung yankee doodle dandy.

To keep the bears and painters out and not less savage wild men,
Of white pine logs each built a hut as big as father's hog pen,
They planted fields enclos'd with stakes and worked dogs or asses,
Made pumpkin pies and Indian cakes and eat them up with lasses.

[14] *The Green Mountain Songster*, 60.

Then yankee doodle all you know struck up their chorus handy,
And Sal and Sue and Bill and Joe sung yankee doodle dandy,
And every day for many weeks beginning each on Monday,
They watch'd and work'd and fought like Greeks and went to church
on Sunday.

Then yankee doodle one and all struck up their chorus handy,
And sung All Saints, Old Hundred too and yankee doodle dandy;
Then yankee doodle all once more strike up your chorus handy,
As loud as you can sing and roar, yankee doodle dandy.

Today, the rime, its variations, and the chorus are still widely known in folk tradition, but the full song and its re-writings are much more difficult to come by. The texts that have been taken from folk informants seldom derive directly from the Shuckburgh original, but rather are print shop parodies like the one quoted by John Lomax out of the *Providence Journal* and beginning,[15]

Let gouty monarchs share their shams
'Neath silken-wove pavilions;
But give us Narragansett clams—
The banquet for the millions.
Yankee Doodle, etc.

Along the Narragansett shore,
Polite in their salams, sir,
Sat copper-colored kings of yore
And feasted on their clams, sir.
Yankee Doodle, etc.

or the Civil War fragment Lomax gives "from the South" beginning,

Yankee Doodle had a mind
To whip the Southern traitors,
Just because they did not choose to live
On codfish and potatoes.
Yankee Doodle, fa, so, la,
Yankee Doodle dandy,
And so to keep his courage up
He took a drink of brandy.

[15] See John and Alan Lomax, *American Ballads and Folk Songs* (New York, 1934), 524-526.

Yankee Doodle drew his sword
And practiced all his passes;
Come, boys, we'll take another drink
When we get to Manassas.
Yankee Doodle, fa, so la,
Yankee Doodle dandy
Never got to Manassas plain
And never drank his brandy.

Such variations stem from the popularity of the melody and chorus in the songsters of the early 19th century and from music hall and stage uses, such as the one Royall Tyler made of it in developing his character Jonathan of *The Contrast* ——— our first stage yankee![16]

Jenny: What is it called?

Jonathan: I am sure you have heard folks talk about it, it is called Yankee Doodle.

Jenny: Oh! it is the tune I am fond of, and, if I know any thing of my mistress, she would be glad to dance to it. Pray, sing?

Jonathan [Sings]:

Father and I went up to camp,
Along with Captain Goodwin;
And there we saw the men and boys,
As thick as hasty-pudding.
Yankee Doodle do, etc.

And then we saw a swamping gun
Big as a log of maple,
On a little deuced cart,
A load for father's cattle.
Yankee Doodle do, etc.

And every time they fired it off
It took a horn of powder,
It made a noise like father's gun,
Only a nation louder.
Yankee Doodle do, etc.

There was a man in our town
His name was–

No, no, that won't do. . . . [after some dialogue]

Jonathan: No, no, I can sing no more, some other time, when you

[16] See Act III, Scene 1 of *The Contrast.*

and I are better acquainted, I'll sing the whole of it—no, no—that's a fib—I can't sing but a hundred and ninety-nine verses: Our Tabitha at home can sing it all—[Sings]

Marblehead's a rocky place,
And Cape-Cod is sandy;
Charlestown is burned down,
Boston is the dandy.
Yankee doodle, doodle do, etc.

I vow my own town song has put me into such topping spirits, that I believe I'll begin to do a little, as Jessamy says we must when we go a courting— . . .

Finally, my sense of completeness demands that I tell you what happened to Dr. Shuckburgh whose satire is so pivotal in all this. Johnson made him temporary Secretary of Indian Affairs after the death of Peter Wraxall in July 1759. However, much to the chagrin of both, London sent William Marsh to assume the post on a permanent basis in May 1760. Shuckburgh, who had sold his commission in the English Army on the "certainty" of his permanent appointment as secretary, was out of a job. Through Johnson, he was able to get a new commission in the Army from General Amherst, selling land to pay for it. By 1766, he was unhappily in Detroit, the Far West of those days, on detached service from the Army, perhaps working for Johnson. Johnson, who was still trying to get Shuckburgh the old position of Secretary of Indian Affairs, finally succeeded that year. Marsh, it seems, had not worked out well. Shuckburgh died in 1773; Johnson, a year later. *The Johnson Papers*, VIII, 866-867 contain a letter from Daniel Claus of Schenectady dated August 20, 1773.

I suppose you will also by this Post be inform'd of poor Dr. Shuckburgh's Death, who died suddenly last Monday morning about 7 o'clock of an apoplectic fit, and was buried on Tuesday evening. Col. Johnson was at the Burial. The Governor and I happen'd to be in Schenectady that afternoon, but much hurried to pay his Visit to Sir John and Lady and return. I went to Mrs. Shuckburgh to condole with her and make an Appology for not attending the Burial, in which she chearfully acquiesced.

So ended the life of the man who, the folklorist knows, did and did not write "Yankee Doodle."

5 Legends in Song

WE ARE NOW DONE TRYING to reconstruct and analyze the folklore which was carried by participants to the American Revolution, so let's turn to the other side of the coin: to the legends that recount highlights of the war and to the effect of the war situation on tradition in general. The next two chapters deal with these matters: this one with ballads that tell of Revolutionary events; the next one with the influence of William Billings on religious folksong in the South.

There is, and always will be, tremendous romantic fascination in the idea that the "great unwashed" create songs and other lore spontaneously from the events in which they participate and that they preserve these then historical accounts to teach their generations what the forefathers accomplished. The idea is charming. Unfortunately, it doesn't offer a particularly accurate way of approaching historical folksong. Whether we like it or not, most historical folksong develops at a pretty sophisticated level, is heard by the folk because it is widely distributed by whatever mass media methods are available, and is preserved because of the pretty tune or because it reveals something about humanity that seems important. North Carolinians singing,

We're marching down to Old Quebec
And the drums are loudly beating;
The American boys have gained the day,
The British are retreating.

as they dance at a country frolic are not really recalling history (in fact, few of them could tell you where Quebec is or what war is involved). They are just singing words that mean about as much to them as "all that meat and no potatoes" means to a white teenager who doesn't know or care about Negro slang. And, clinching my point, we may find them changing the words to such historical confusion as,

We're marching down to Old Quebec
And the drums are loudly beating;
The Rebels brave have won the day,
The Yankees are retreating.[1]

Unfortunate as it may be for persons who wish to use folklore for national purposes, the folk idea of history is parochial, and if a ballad about a battle lives it will live either because of the reasons given above or because the history has local significance.

G. Malcolm Laws, Jr. lists but forty American war ballads in his bibliographical study, *Native American Balladry*[2]——and only five of these (plus two, recorded elsewhere and derived from British tradition) deal with our Revolution. Only forty war ballads, three-fourths of which are rarely collected, have entered American oral tradition from the literally thousands pumped out by patriotic entrepreneurs during the struggles that usurp so many pages in the formal histories. A paltry bag!

I stress the point because at "centennial time" everyone hops aboard the bandwagon. From 1960-1965 the bookstores were clogged with anthologies entitled *Ballads of the Civil War*, *A Treas-*

[1] For these two rimes, see *The Frank C. Brown Collection of North Carolina Folklore*, 7 volumes (Durham, N. C., 1952-1964), I, 118.

[2] G. Malcolm Laws, Jr., *Native American Balladry* (Laws, *NAB*) (Philadelphia, 1964). In this bibliographical study, Laws has labelled each ballad with a letter denoting subject and a number. References to Laws' labels refer to this book or the companion volume cited above: Laws, *ABBB*.

ury of Civil War Songs, Folksongs Blue and Gray. Now that it is two hundred years since the flag was "unfurled to the April breeze," there will be a plethora of Revolutionary songbooks. These will be handsome, heavily illustrated packages with ballads (the verses clearly printed, the music set for piano or guitar) that relate in subject matter to the struggle for independence. They can be pasted together in a few hectic days, and they will be done by modern hacks somewhat in the spirit of Jamie Catnach.

There is nothing wrong with these books. They will bring joy to a lot of people and they will serve in their fashion to circulate currency, but most of them will fly under flags as false as those of Blackbeard and Captain Kidd. They will not be books of folksongs, and should not be thought of as such. Most of them will be made up of the popular songs of Revolutionary days, songs that were hawked and sung in the Colonial cities much as "Praise the Lord and Pass the Ammunition" and "The White Cliffs of Dover" were hawked and sung during World War II. The people who wrote them were quite literate, and sometimes even talented; the people who heard them and sang them were Mother Machree and the girl-next-door. Very few will enter the repertoire of even one traditional singer, and even fewer will begin to circulate and vary among the folk groups in that way necessary for them to become folksongs. Just recall how few of the commerical songs of the time the Sandgate soldier saw fit to include in *The Green Mountain Songster* and how few of the ones he did include have been sung by enough folksingers to become folksongs. There is an analogy to be drawn between songs and frog's eggs: tradition is a river into which many eggs are laid, few become tadpoles, even fewer full-grown frogs.

We make then a definite distinction between the hundreds of songs that we might call "songs of the American Revolution" and the handful that we can call "folksongs of the American Revolution" or the seven that Laws would allow us to call "ballads of the Revolution." Undramatic as it may be that the American folk are not more interested in recalling the events of our struggle for freedom, facts are facts, and I intend to abide by them.

Laws names the seven Revolutionary ballads that he feels have entered American oral tradition in his two standard bibliographies,

Native American Balladry and *American Balladry from British Broadsides.* They are "Major André's Capture"; "Paul Jones, the Privateer"; "Paul Jones's Victory"; "Revolutionary Tea"; "The Dying British Sergeant"; "Donald Monroe"; and "The Sons of Liberty."[3] The first five are listed in *Native American Balladry* and seem to have their widest distribution through the Maritimes, the northeastern states, and along the Appalachians, close to the very regions in which the bulk of the Revolution was fought, though "The Dying British Sergeant" is so rare it is put in a kind of reject heap under the heading "Ballads of Doubtful Currency in Tradition." The final two, given as derivatives of British broadsides, seem to be distributed in roughly the same way. "Donald Monroe," stripped of its war setting, is relatively common, especially in Canada. "The Sons of Liberty" is not much more widely known than "The Dying British Sergeant."

None of the seven are what one would label popular among the folk. The first four glorify specific historical events; the last three are somewhat more personal. None are notably different from hundreds of other songs that were pumped out by the print shops on both sides of the ocean. Why these have survived, feeble as that survival may be, while so many others have not is a mystery. No one has ever figured out why some songs live and others don't, anyhow—and I don't expect anyone ever will. Certainly, chance has a good bit to do with it. If a prominent and energetic singer takes a fancy to it, a song is going to be heard. The old motto of the music rackets, "you like what you hear," applies. If a song appears in a songster, especially a widely distributed songster, that can help too. It is also important that a collector happen to collect from an informant who happens to sing it. When a song is not widely known, there is always the chance no collector will stumble upon it. Finally, the tune means a lot. Any song with a tune that appeals to the folk ear will outlive a song that is dull or insipid. But these ideas don't account for everything. Perhaps there is something reminiscent of the emotional appeal of "Mary Hamilton" in the capture and death of young Major André; Paul Jones was a genu-

[3] These songs are Laws A2, A3, A4, A24, dA29, J12, and J13 respectively.

inely fascinating figure whose exploits were glorified even in Britain; and "Revolutionary Tea" makes a pretty good human interest story when removed from its parable context, as do "Donald Monroe," "The Sons of Liberty," and "The Dying British Sergeant." At any rate, all of them deserve a closer look.

As I plan to discuss "Major André's Capture" in a later chapter on spies, I'll begin with Paul Jones. John Paul (he later added the name Jones) was born son of the gardener to a landowner, William Craik, in Kirkbean, Scotland on July 6, 1747.[4] As a youth he went to sea from Whitehaven, a port he was to raid as Captain of the *Ranger*, and worked his way up from apprentice seaman to master of a merchant ship. He was on his way to amassing a comfortable fortune, when a mutinous brawl over wages resulted in his killing one of his own seamen in Tobago. He found it expedient to flee, to change his name, and eventually to take up residence in Virginia. The Revolution broke out right after this, and John Paul Jones decided to work for the Colonial cause. Commissioned as a First Lieutenant, he is reputed to have raised the first flag of the American Navy (actually a Union Jack with stripes to symbolize loyalty but resistance) aboard Ezek Hopkins' ship the *Alfred* in the Delaware River in December of 1775. In 1777 at Badger's Island, Maine, the 18-gun *Ranger*, one of the two famous ships he was to command, was launched. In her *Minstrelsy of Maine*, Fannie Eckstorm writes,[5]

In entering Maine by the Memorial Bridge between Portsmouth and Kittery the first Maine soil touched is Badger's Island, where was built, and on May 10, 1777, was launched, the Continental sloop-of-war *Ranger*, the first war vessel that ever flew the Stars and Stripes. John Paul Jones commanded her and was a familiar figure about Portsmouth and the Maine shore while she was building and fitting out. Not visible from the highway, yet not far from it, is a bronze tablet erected by the Sons of the American Revolution of Portsmouth commemorating the historic spot.

[4] The definitive biography of Jones, about whom there is much misinformation abroad, is Samuel E. Morison's, *John Paul Jones* (Boston and Toronto, 1959).

[5] Fannie H. Eckstorm and Mary W. Smyth, *Minstrelsy of Maine* (Boston and New York, 1927), 208.

On June 14, 1777 Congress officially appointed Jones captain of this vessel, and on November 1 she sailed from Portsmouth, New Hampshire carrying news of Burgoyne's surrender to Benjamin Franklin, among others, in Paris. Jones anchored her near Nantes one month after embarking and by mid-January was given the green light to raid and harass the British in whatever fashion he saw fit. On February 14, the *Ranger* exchanged salutes with a French Squadron and became the first vessel flying the Stars and Stripes to receive this accolade from a foreign power. By late April she was raiding off the Irish and English coasts, attacking Whitehaven in Cumberland directly. He knew this area as well as his rivals and was able to capture the 20-gun *Drake* in a brief skirmish, this being the first British ship to be taken by an American man-o-war.

There is a fine anecdote about these days, and I'll repeat it here as Horace P. Beck told it to me, although there is a version complete with names, Scottish dialect, and nautical details on pages 218-219 in Morison's biography of Jones. It seems that Edinburgh was threatened by Jones, and one of the local Presbyterian ministers went on record as instructing the good Lord He would have to save the town from this overpowering marauder. The minister announced he would take his chair down to the banks of the Firth to sit there, come hell or high water, until the Lord turned back Jones. He did this, and as the tide came in Jones capitalized on a favorable breeze to sail up toward Edinburgh. He approached the city about the time the rising tide approached the minster's chin. But behold! Just as Edinburgh was to be attacked and the minister to drown, a huge gale arose blowing in Jones' face, forcing him back down the Firth and saving not only the day, but the preacher, who splashed ashore secure in this manifestation of Providence.

"Paul Jones, the Privateer" or "The Yankee Man-o-War" commemorates an engagement in this campaign, almost certainly one that took place in the Irish Channel in the spring or early summer of 1778, obviously before the *Ranger* returned to New Hampshire in October. Miss Eckstorm says the following about her text,[6]

The places named, when recognizable, are on the southern shore

[6] Eckstorm and Smyth, 212-213.

of Ireland. Apparently, coming up from France, Paul Jones made the light on the Old Head of Kinsale to the west, and then, turning eastward, kept along the Irish coast until he saw a British ship and her consorts bearing down. At the Saltee Islands and Tuskar Rock, on the very southeastern point of Ireland, he had to display consummate seamanship to throw off the British ships as he turned northward into the Irish Sea. Sailing northward through the Irish Sea he came out by the North Channel. A hundred and fifty years of singing have mixed up the verses and the places are sometimes obscured, as in one version we have where he raised the light on 'old King's Ale,' and later on

The mists hung heavy o'er the sea from father's to King's Ore.

The song is a very good one, and under the title "The Stately Southerner" is a well-known American fo'c'stle piece. The title, which may seem strange to modern ears, makes good sense in the slang of the time, when Virginians, and Jones made that his American home, were called "Southerners" by deprecating New Englanders much in the way modern Southerners refer to Northerners as "Yankees."

The text below is supposedly from the recitation of a sailor, and the more enthusiastic of the scholars like to think of it as having been composed by a member of the *Ranger's* crew and handed down from gob to gob since Paul Jones strode the decks.[7]

'Tis of a gallant Yankee ship that flew the stripes and stars,
And the whistling wind from the west-nor'-west blew through the pitch-pine spars,—
With her starboard tacks abroad, my boys, she hung upon the gale,
On an autumn night we raised the light on the old head of Kinsale.

It was a clear and cloudless night, and the wind blew steady and strong,
As gayly over the sparkling deep our good ship bowled along;
With the foaming seas beneath her bow the fiery waves she spread,
And bending low her bosom of snow, she buried her lee cat-head.

There was no talk of short'ning sail by him who walked the poop,
And under the press of her pond'ring jib, the boom bent like a hoop!

[7] Reproduced from Stephen B. Luce, *Naval Songs* (New York, 1902), 56 in Robert W. Neeser, *American Naval Songs and Ballads* (New Haven, 1938), 25-26.

And the groaning water-ways told the strain that held her stout main-tack,
But he only laughed as he glanced abaft at a white and silv'ry track.

The mid-tide meets in the channel waves that flow from shore to shore,
And the mist hung heavy upon the land from Featherstone to Dunsmore,
And that sterling light in Tusker Rock where the old bell tolls each hour,
And the beacon light that shone so bright was quench'd on Waterford Tower.

The nightly robes our good ship wore were her own top-sails three,
Her spanker and her standing jib—the courses being free;
"Now, lay aloft! my heroes bold, let not a moment pass!"
And royals and top-gallant sails were quickly on each mast.

What looms upon our starboard bow? What hangs upon the breeze?
'Tis time our good ship hauled her wind abreast the old Saltee's.
For by her ponderous press of sail and by her consorts four
We saw our morning visitor was a British man-of-war.

Up spake our noble Captain then, as a shot ahead of us past—
"Haul snug your flowing courses! lay your top-sail to the mast!"
Those Englishmen gave three loud hurrahs from the deck of their covered ark,
And we answered back by a solid broadside from the decks of our patriot bark.

"Out booms! out booms!" our skipper cried, "out booms and give her sheet,"
And the swiftest keel that was ever launched shot ahead of the British fleet,
And amidst a thundering shower of shot with stun'-sails hoisting away,
Down the North Channel Paul Jones did steer just at the break of day.

Paul Jones' most famous ship was, however, an old, re-fitted merchantman, the *Bonhomme Richard,* named after Benjamin Franklin's "Poor Richard" of the *Almanack.* On the night of Sep-

The "Bonhomme Richard"
Scale model owned by the Naval Academy Museum

tember 22 and into the morning of September 23, 1779, the *Bonhomme Richard* and the *Pallas* won a victory over the British ships *Serapis* and the *Countess of Scarborough* in what has been long considered one of the classic naval battles of history. Nathaniel Fanning, who served under Jones in the battle, has left a vivid account of the *Bonhomme Richard-Serapis* struggle in which Jones, outgunned, managed to run his "merchantman" alongside his newly built rival. So close did the ships lie, their yardarms interlocked and their decks formed a sort of mutual battlefield. Near the conclusion of his account, Fanning tells how the American frigate, *Alliance*, coming to help, gets confused in the darkness and pours shot into both ships. Eventually, by means of a lantern signal, the Americans are able "to undeceive the *Alliance*" and the firing from that quarter ceases. Fanning continues,[8]

> At thirty-five minutes past twelve at night, a single hand grenado was thrown by one of our men out of the maintop of the enemy, designing it to go among the English who were huddled together between her gun decks. On its way it struck on one side of the combings of her upper hatchway and, rebounding from that, took a direction and fell between their decks, where it communicated to a quantity of loose powder scattered about the enemy's cannon: and the hand grenado, bursting at the same time, made a dreadful explosion and blew up about twenty of the enemy. This closed the scene, and the enemy now in their turn (notwithstanding the gasconading of Captain Pearson) bawled out, "Quarters, quarters, quarters, for God's sake!" It was, however, some time before the enemy's colors were struck. The Captain of the *Serapis* gave repeated orders for one of his crew to ascend the quarter deck and haul down the English flag, but no one would stir to do it. They told the Captain they were afraid of our riflemen, believing that all our men who were seen with muskets were of that description. The Captain of the *Serapis* himself therefore ascended the quarter-deck and hauled down the very flag which he had nailed to the flagstaff a little before the commencement of the battle, and which flag he had at that time, in the presence of his

[8] See the *Memoirs of Nathaniel Fanning, an officer of the Revolutionary Navy, 1778-1783* as edited and annotated by John S. Barnes (New York, 1912), 32 f.

principal officers, sworn he never would strike to that infamous pirate J. P. Jones.

The enemy's flag being struck, Captain Jones ordered Richard Dale, his First Lieutenant, to select out of our crew a number of men and take possession of the prize, which was immediately put in execution. Several of our men (I believe three) were killed by the English on board of the *Serapis* after she had struck to us, for which they afterwards apologized by saying that the men who were guilty of this breach of honor did not know at the time that their own ship had struck her colors. Thus ended this ever-memorable battle, after a continuance of a few minutes more than four hours. The officers, headed by the Captain of the *Serapis,* now came on board of our ship; the latter (Captain Pearson) inquired for Captain Jones, to whom he was introduced by Mr. Mase, our purser.

They met, and the former accosted the latter, in presenting his sword, in this manner: "It is with the greatest reluctance that I am now obliged to resign you this, for it is painful to me, more particularly at this time, when compelled to deliver up my sword to a man who may be said to fight with a halter around his neck!"

Jones, after receiving his sword, made this reply: "Sir, you have fought like a hero, and I make no doubt but your sovereign will reward you in a most ample manner for it."

Captain Pearson then asked Jones what countrymen his crew principally consisted of. The latter said, "Americans." "Very well," said the former, "it has been 'diamond cut diamond' with us."

Later, when Pearson was knighted as a reward for his gallantry in the affair, Jones is reported to have commented, "Let me fight him again . . . and I'll make a lord of him."

Jones did not receive immediate credit for his part in the fray, but as time went on poets, even distinguished ones like Philip Freneau, began to glorify his escapades. Freneau submitted a glowing description of the *Serapis* encounter to *The Freeman's Journal* in the summer of 1781. The final two stanzas are typical, showing how happy it is we have other pieces by which to judge his literary stature.[9]

[9] These are the final two stanzas of the poem entitled "On the Memorable Victory" which appeared in the issue of August 8, 1781.

Go on, great man, to scourge the foe,
And bid these haughty Britons know
    They to our *Thirteen Stars* shall bend;
Those *Stars* that, veil'd in dark attire,
Long glimmer'd with a feeble fire,
    But radiant now ascend.

Bend to the Stars that flaming rise
In western, not in eastern skies,
    Fair Freedom's reign restored—
So, when the Magi, come from far,
Beheld the God-attending Star,
    They trembled and ador'd.

However, it was through such tributes, especially those on the broadsides and in the chapbooks, that full notoriety came to Jones, who at first was more *fameux* in Europe than he was at home.[10] All his publicity was not complimentary, and lines like,

It vexes my patience, I'm sure, night and day
To think how that traitor Paul Jones got away.

or,

He took the *Serapis*, tho' the battle it was hot;
But a rogue and vagabond,
        Is he not?

were common. Yet Jones had a magic about him, and most the publications gild his escapades with derring-do. Morison prints a ditty called *Hier Komt Paul Jones Aan* which tells what a "nice fellow" he is and which is still being sung as a children's rime in the Netherlands, and someone in Yorkshire produced a broadsheet right after the battle calling Jones "a noble commander." This is "Paul Jones's Victory," a piece that had wide distribution on both sides of the Atlantic and eventually entered oral tradition. The variants show all sorts of foolish changes in fact—one even naming the British ship the *Richards*, but the details of the battle remain reasonably clear.

[10] For a list of some of these, see W. Roy MacKenzie, *Ballads and Sea Songs from Nova Scotia* (Hatboro, Pa., 1963), 205. This is a reprint of the 1928 edition published at Cambridge, Massachusetts. See also Morison, 246-251, 254-258.

The text below, direct from an American broadside, is particularly complete.[11]

PAUL JONES'S VICTORY.

(September 23, 1779)

An American frigate, a frigate of fame,
With guns mounting forty, the *Richard* by name,
Sail'd to cruise in the channels of old England,
With valiant commander, Paul Jones was the man.
Hurrah! Hurrah! Our country for ever, Hurrah!

We had not cruised long, before he espies
A large forty-four, and a twenty likewise;
Well-manned with bold seamen, well laid in with stores,
In consort to drive us from old England's shores.
Hurrah! Hurrah! Our country for ever, Hurrah!

About twelve at noon Pearson came alongside,
With a loud speaking trumpet, "Whence came you?" he cried,
"Return me an answer, I hail'd you before,
Or if you do not, a broadside I'll pour."
Hurrah! Hurrah! Our country for ever, Hurrah!

Paul Jones then said to his men, every one,
"Let every true seaman stand firm to his gun!
We'll receive a broadside from this bold Englishman,
And like true Yankee sailors return it again."
Hurrah! Hurrah! Our country for ever, Hurrah!

The contest was bloody, both decks ran with gore,
And the sea seemed to blaze, while the cannon did roar;
"Fight on, my brave boys," then Paul Jones he cried,
"And soon we will humble this bold Englishman's pride."
Hurrah! Hurrah! Our country for ever, Hurrah!

"Stand firm to your quarters–your duty don't shun,
The first one that shrinks, through the body I'll run;
Though their force is superior, yet they shall know,
What true, brave American seamen can do."
Hurrah! Hurrah! Our country for ever, Hurrah!

[11] As reproduced with slight variation from a broadside in the possession of the American Antiquarian Society in Neeser, 26-29.

The battle rolled on, till bold Pearson cried:
"Have you yet struck your colors? then come alongside!"
But so far from thinking that the battle was won,
Brave Paul Jones replied, "I've not yet begun!"
Hurrah! Hurrah! Our country for ever, Hurrah!

We fought them eight glasses, eight glasses so hot,
Till seventy bold seamen lay dead on the spot.
And ninety brave seamen lay stretched in their gore,
While the pieces of cannon most fiercely did roar.
Hurrah! Hurrah! Our country for ever, Hurrah!

Our gunner, in great fright to Captain Jones came,
"We gain water quite fast and our side's in a flame;"
Then Paul Jones said in the height of his pride,
"If we cannot do better, boys, sink along-side!"
Hurrah! Hurrah! Our country for ever, Hurrah!

The *Alliance* bore down, and the *Richard* did rake,
Which caused the bold hearts of our seamen to ache;
Our shot flew so hot that they could not stand us long,
And the undaunted Union of Britain came down.
Hurrah! Hurrah! Our country for ever, Hurrah!

To us they did strike and their colors hauled down;
The fame of Paul Jones to the world shall be known;
His name shall rank with the gallant and brave,
Who fought like a hero our freedom to save.
Hurrah! Hurrah! Our country for ever, Hurrah!

Now all valiant seamen where'er you may be,
Who hear of this combat that's fought on the sea,
May you all do like them, when called for the same,
And your names be enrolled on the pages of fame.
Hurrah! Hurrah! Our country for ever, Hurrah!

Your country will boast of her sons that are brave,
And to you she will look from all dangers to save;
She'll call you dear sons, in her annals you'll shine,
And the brows of the brave with green laurels entwine.
Hurrah! Hurrah! Our country for ever, Hurrah!

So now, my brave boys, have we taken a prize—
A large 44, and a 20 like-wise!
Then God bless the mother whose doom is to weep
The loss of her sons in the ocean so deep.
Hurrah! Hurrah! Our country for ever, Hurrah!

When collected from oral tradition, the song is almost always a great deal shorter, but, as so often is the case, without loss of much significant matter.[12]

PAUL JONES.

1 A forty-gun frigate from Baltimore came,
Her guns mounted forty, and *Richard* by name,
Went cruising the channel of old England,
With a noble commander, Paul Jones was the man.

2 We had not sailed long before we did spy
A large forty-four and a twenty close by,
All these warlike vessels full laden with store;
Our captain pursued them on the bold York shore.

3 At the hour of twelve Pierce came alongside
With a large speaking trumpet: 'Whence came you?' he cried.
'Quick give man an answer, I've hailed you before,
Or at this moment a broadside I'll pour.'

4 We fought them five glasses, five glasses so hot,
Till sixty bright seamen lay dead on the spot,
Full seventy wounded lay bleeding in gore.
How fierce our loud cannons on the *Richard* did roar.

5 Our gunner got frightened, to Paul Jones he came.
'Our ship she is sinking, likewise in flame.'
Paul Jones he smiled in the height of his pride,
Saying, 'This day I'll conquer or sink alongside.'

6 Here's health to those widows who shortly must weep,
For the loss of their husbands who sunk in the deep.
Here's a health to those young girls who shortly must mourn
For the loss of their sweethearts that's overboard thrown.

[12] Brown, II, 524. Contributed by P. D. Midgett, Jr. from Wanchese, N. C.

7 Here's a health to Paul Jones with sword in hand–
He was foremost in action, in giving command.
Here's a health to Paul Jones and all his crew–
If we hadn't a French Captain, boys, what could we do!

The two texts taken together show quite clearly what the first city printer and then oral tradition deem important when describing an historical event.

After the Revolution, Paul Jones spent most of his time in Europe. He was an American agent in Paris for awhile, and later became a Rear-Admiral in the Russian Navy. He died in 1792, but it wasn't until 1905 that his body, rediscovered, was disenterred and brought back to the United States Naval Academy at Annapolis to rest *in bello* as well as *in pace*.

Most people learned about the Boston Tea Party in grade school; few however recall why it occurred. The Townshend Acts of 1767 followed a series of unpopular attempts by the English government to improve mercantile control of her colonies. These Acts, which were supposed to provide the revenue necessary to pay Colonial administrators, placed duties on paper, glass, lead, painters' colors, and tea; provided for writs of assistance for enforcement; and stated that violators were to be tried, without jury, in the admiralty courts. Needless to say, they caused quite a furor, especially in Boston where Colonial irritation was rawest. Among other things, they were in back of the street brawl between British troops and local citizens in which four or five Bostonians were slain and to which history has given the magnificent title, "The Boston Massacre." Before long the British repealed the Townshend Acts, excepting the one on tea. However, the Act of 1773, which was designed to aid the East India Company to sell its surplus tea soon followed. Parliament relieved the Company of the duty on tea in England and granted it a monopoly of the transport of tea to America where it could be sold by Company agents subject to a small import duty. As this ruling discriminated against local merchants, it was true salt into the wounds. Every British tea ship that entered a Colonial port offered an excellent test of authority and a chance for the rebellious to perform.

On the night of December 16, 1773, about fifty Bostonians operating under the organization of the "Man of the Town Meeting," Sam Adams, disguised themselves as Indians and boarded British ships anchored in the harbor. They burst open about 350 chests of tea and steeped the contents in harbor water in what became known as the Boston Tea Party. On December 18, 1773, John Andrews wrote as follows,[13]

> . . . They mustered, I'm told, upon Fort Hill, to the number of about two hundred, and proceeded, two by two, to Griffin's wharf, where Hall, Bruce, and Coffin lay, each with 114 chests of the *ill fated* article on board; the two former with *only* that article, but ye. latter arriv'd at ye. wharf only ye. day before, was freighted with a large quantity of other goods, which they took the *greatest* care not to injure in the least, and before *nine* o'clock in ye. evening, every chest from on board the three vessels was knock'd to pieces and flung over ye. sides. They say the actors were *Indians* from *Narragansett.* Whether they were or not, to a transient observer they appear'd as *such,* being cloath'd in Blankets with the heads muffled, and copper color'd countenances, being each arm'd with a hatchet or axe, and pair pistols, nor was their *dialect* different from what I conceive these geniusses to *speak,* as their jargon was unintelligible to all but themselves. Not the least insult was offer'd to any person, save one Captain Conner, a letter of horses in this place, not many years since remov'd from *dear Ireland,* who had ript up the lining of his coat and waistcoat under the arms, and watching his opportunity had nearly fill'd 'em with tea, but being detected, was handled pretty roughly. They not only stripp'd him of his cloaths, but gave him a coat of mud, with a severe brusing into the bargain: and nothing but their utter aversion to make *any* disturbance prevented his being tar'd and feather'd.
>
> Should not have troubled you with this, by Post, hadn't I thought you would be glad of a more particular account of so *important a transaction,* than you could have obtain'd by common report: and if it affords my brother but a *temporary* amusement, I shall be more than repaid for the trouble of writing.

This event is sometimes cited as the spark that set off the Revolution. Certainly, it was one of the first manifestations of the Colo-

[13] From the *Letters of John Andrews, Esq. of Boston, 1772-1776* as edited from the original manuscript by Winthrop Sargent in *Proceedings of the Massachusetts Historical Society* (Cambridge, 1866), 12-13.

nists' growing desire to protest physically. Poets and hacks found the Tea Party irresistible, and they capitalized on its drama for years—long after the conflict was over, even to the time of Jackson.[14]

Deep into the sea descended
Cursed weed of China's coast,
Thus at once our fears were ended
Rights shall n'er be lost.

Such political songs do not, of course, survive well among the folk. Once Americans moved West and the Revolution faded into the past, interest in Sam Adams' cause waned. The farmer in Indiana, the miner in Utah, the share-cropper in Mississippi needed songs that would cope with day-to-day problems. Thus, "Revolutionary Tea" is found rarely, though it is found from time to time, which is more than can be said about dozens of similar parables: for example, "Old Granny Wales." Perhaps the fact it is presented as a family squabble has helped. Anyone with a teen-aged daughter must understand what "the old lady over the sea" had to go through.[15]

REVOLUTIONARY TEA.

There was an old lady lived over the sea
And she was an island queen.
Her daughter lived off in a far country
With an ocean of water between.
The old lady's pockets were full of gold,
But never contented was she.
She called on her daughter to pay her a tax
Of three-pence a pound on her tea,
Of three-pence a pound on her tea.

"Now Mother, dear Mother." the daughter replied,
"I can't do the thing that you ask.
I'm willing to pay a fair price for the tea,
But never the three-penny tax."
"You shall," quoth the mother, and reddened with rage,

[14] Stanza 4 of a song called "The Ballad of the Tea Party."

[15] This is the version Edith Fowke and Alan Mills print in their *Canada's Story in Song* (Toronto, 1960), 54-56.

"For you're my own daughter, you see,
And sure 'tis quite proper a daughter should pay
Her mother a tax on her tea,
Her mother a tax on her tea."

And so the old lady her servants called out
And packed up a budget of tea,
And eager for three pence a pound she put in
Enough for a large family.
She ordered her servants to bring home the tax,
Declaring her child should obey,
Or old as she was and almost woman grown,
She'd half whip her life away,
She'd half whip her life away.

The tea was conveyed to the daughter's door
All down by the ocean's side,
And the bouncing girl poured out every pound
In the dark and boiling tide!
And then she called out to the island queen,
"Oh, Mother, dear Mother," quoth she–
"Your tea you may have when it's steeped enough,
But never a tax from me,
No, never a tax from me."

"The Dying British Sergeant," which Laws lists as a ballad of doubtful currency in oral tradition, has always had appeal for me. The variant that Helen Flanders obtained in Montpelier, Vermont is one of its rare appearances in folk repertories The melody was sung by the grandmother of the informant, Mrs. Ellen Nye Lawrence, while the text is one that Mrs. Lawrence "found published in a *Vermont Journal* as taken from an 'old manuscript. The . . . ballad is said to have been written by a brave soldier in the British army in one of the battles of the Revolution, after he received his death wound from a musket ball.' " Mrs. Flanders described the collecting of this song quite vividly when she first published it in the *Springfield (Massachusetts) Sunday Union* on March 6, 1932. [16]

One of the most moving experiences in my folk-song recording was in Montpelier last autumn, when I sat by the bedside of Mrs. Ellen

[16] See Flanders, *The New Green Mountain Songster*, 118-120.

Nye Lawrence, and watched her write as fast has she could think, notes of songs known sixty or seventy years before, which now her feeble voice could now no longer make clear.

She taught music for many years in schools in Lowell and could set down the music as easily as the rest of us write words. The Revolution came a bit nearer to me in hearing her speak of her grandmother who, at the age of 12, came into Vermont (in 1793) in an ox team. Her name was Mrs. Betsey Gray.

THE DYING BRITISH SERGEANT.

Come all you heroes, where'er you be,
That walk by land or sail by sea,
Come hear the words of a dying man
And surely you'll remember them.

In '76 that fatal year
As by our signal doth appear
Our fleet set sail for America
Twas on the fourteenth day of May.

Twas a dark and dismal time
Our fleet set sail for the northern line
Where drums did beat and the trumpet sound
And into Boston we are bound.

And when to Boston we did come
We thought the noise of the British drum
Would drive the rebels from that place
And fill their hearts with sore distress

But to our woful, sad surprise
We saw them like grasshoppers rise
To fight like heroes much in rage—
Which sorely frightened General Gage.

Like lions roaring for their prey
They fear no danger, no not they
True British blood runs in their veins
While them with courage it sustains.

We sailed to York, as you've been told,
With the loss of many a Briton bold,
And there we many a traitor found
False to the land where he belonged.

They told us twas a garden place
And that our armies might with ease
Burn down their towns, lay waste their lands
In spite of all their boasting bands.

A garden place it was indeed
And in it grew many a bitter weed
Which did pull down our brightest hopes
And sorely wounded our British troops.

Tis now December, the seventeenth day,
Since we set sail for America,
Full fifteen thousand have been slain—
Bold British heroes on the plain.

Now I've received my mortal wound.
Adieu unto old English ground.
My wife and children they'll mourn for me
While I lie cold in America.

Fight on, fight on, American boy,
But ne'er heed bold Britain's thundering noise.
Maintain your rights, years after year.
God's on your side, you need not fear.

The glory of Great Britain's soil
Is now eclipsed for a while
But it shall shine bright in meridian year
Although our king is most severe.

His crown shall fade most certainly
A reward for all his cruelty
America shall her rights maintain
While proud cold England sinks with shame.

The ballad is just another broadside piece, and it was thought by Worthington Ford, who locates two copies of it in his list of Massachusetts broadsides, to date from 1776. It does have an appealing theme—the idea of a British soldier giving his life to his country, but his heart to his foe. However, I will have to take issue with the cliché that it was composed by the dying sergeant himself, who I suppose dipped a quill in the blood of his wounds during his final moments. Ford may have been literal and dated the ballad 1776 in that fashion, but actually there is no chance that the sergeant, who most likely was illiterate, composed this story of his demise. For centuries now, broadside printers have published accounts of crimes, warnings from condemned murderers, regrets of sinners supposedly written on the eve of their executions. This is a melodramatic and amazingly successful, commercial ploy that brings immediacy and poignancy to routine cases. It is surprising enough that the public will swallow this fiction year after year, but it is positively staggering that ballad "scholar" after ballad "scholar" has been willing to foster the concept by printing it as fact in the song notes. Sydney Carton, certainly; but a dying British soldier, never.

There are two more songs, both originally British, that are set in Revolutionary times and that are still sung by the folk. One is "Donald Monroe," which is rather violent in its denunciation of the American cause. As one might suspect, it is most often found in Canada, although it is not unknown on this side of the border. There is no particular event behind its story; it is just a typical broadside, originating in Scotland about 1778, with a theme somewhat reminiscent of the old love and honor quandary of the 17th century drama.[17]

DONALD MUNRO

Ye sons of North Britain, you that used to range
In search of foreign countries and lands that was strange,
Amongst this great number was Donald Munro.
Away to America he likewise did go.

Two sons with his brother he caused them to stay
On account of their passage he could not well pay.
When seven long winters were ended and gone,
They went to their uncle one day alone,

To beg his consent to cross o'er the main
In hopes their dear parents to meet with again.
Their uncle replied then, and answered them, "No,
Thou hast no money wherewith thou canst go."

[17] *JAF*, 1912, 124-125. The informant was Alexander Murphy of Cape John, Nova Scotia.

And when they were landed in that country wild,
Surrounded by rebels on every side,
There being two rebels that lurked in the wood,
They pointed their pistols where the two brothers stood.

And lodging a bullet in each brother's breast,
They ran for their prey like two ravenous beasts.
"You cruelest monsters, you bloodthirsty hounds,
How could you have killed us until we hath found,

"Found out our dear parents whom we sought with much care?
I'm sure, when they hear it, they'll die in despair,
For they left us in Scotland seven twelvemonths ago.
Perhaps you might know them; their names were Munro."

"Oh, curse to my hands! Oh, what have I done!
Oh, curse to my hands, I have murdered my sons!"
"Is this you, dear father? How did you come by?
And since I have seen you, contented I'll die."

"I'll sink into sorrow till life it is o'er
In hopes for to meet you on a far brighter shore,
In hopes for to meet you on a far brighter shore,
Where I'll not be able to kill you no more."

Most recent versions obscure this story of Revolutionary woe, and as the song is sung in Canada and the northern States today the father has become a highwayman, not a rebel, and the son is shot as part of a robbery. The change makes little difference to the "emotional impact" of the story, though the bitterness against the American cause does disappear.

The other song is "The Sons of Liberty," and it differs from "Donald Monroe" in its sympathy for the unfortunates caught up in the struggle and for George Washington and his brave men. The ballad is not widely distributed in the States, Laws listing but two Kentucky texts that Cecil Sharp found. However, the Sandgate soldier included a fine version in *The Green Mountain Songster* under the title "O Ireland, Dear Ireland."[18]

[18] *GMS*, 47-48.

O IRELAND, DEAR IRELAND.

O Ireland, dear Ireland, I ne'er shall see thee more,
My very heart is aching, to leave my native shore,
But our king he does command us and we must sail away,
To fight the boys of liberty in North America.

The seventeenth of June boys, by the dawning of the day,
Our fleet quitted their sailing and anchor'd in their bay,
Our sails they were unloosed and spread abroad to dry,
Our Irish heroes landed then, the Lord knows who must die.

The French, the Dutch, the Spaniards, could no more cruel be,
Nor use bold Irish heroes with more barbarity,
For they pored down their grape-shot and cut our men away,
Which was a sad inspection in North America.

Through fields of blood we waded where thundering cannon roar,
And many a bold commander lay bleeding in his gore,
And heaps of mangled soldiers upon the ground did lay,
Which were both kill'd and wounded in North America.

Polly, when you read these verses I have written here,
And as you do peruse the same you can but shed a tear,
To think upon our misery, 'twould grieve your heart full sore
When I relate my sorrows since I have left my native shore.

'Twould grieve your heart with pity to see the soldiers wives,
Looking for their dead husbands with melancholy eyes,
And the children crying mamma, for we do rue the day,
That we come to loose our daddys in North America.

But to conclude my ditty, God bless George Washington,
And all his loyal subjects, their praises we will sing;
God grant him great protection, its both by land and sea,
Success to the boys of liberty in North America.

The name "Sons of Liberty" undoubtedly attaches itself to this song by a simple adaption of the original phrase "boys of liberty." Almost as soon as Colonel Isaac Barre used the phrase "sons of liberty" in a speech of rebuttal directed at Charles Townshend when the Stamp Act of 1765 was introduced in the House of Commons, it became a favorite with the Colonists, and a host of secret societies went under the name in the days before war broke out.

These then are six of the seven ballads in American tradition that can honestly be called folk ballads about our war for freedom. Like all war songs, they impress by their routine nature. When I look over the sections entitled "War Ballads" in Laws' two bibliographies, *Native American Balladry* and *American Ballads from British Broadsides*, I find the same old stories again and again. Here and there is an account of a great, but bloody, victory or a noble defeat; once in a while a tribute to foolhardy daring and courage; but most often everyday sweethearts, sons, fathers enlist, go off to "India's fatal shore," to Sebastapol, to Amerikay, to Texas, lie wounded and dying, coughing out last words for the loved ones at home. The places, the actors, the causes seem completely interchangeable. One can almost see the printer putting the type in storage at the declaration of peace, its sentimentality certain to be fresh when the inevitable next conflict breaks out.

6 New England's God

AN UNSPECTACULAR, BUT NONETHELESS very real, influence that war can have on folk tradition comes through the stimulus it gives to individual energy and genius, mothering invention, not merely by inspiring man to create trite songs and legends, but by inspiring him to create artistic techniques that eventually shape the lore of later times. I am thinking of William Billings, the testy, half-blind tanner, whose interest in the Colonial cause enflamed him, forcing him to develop ways of presenting music to his church choir that were to spread down the Appalachians and out across the Southern states, forming the basis of country religious singing even to the present day.

Born in Boston on the 7th of October in 1746, Billings was the son of a Cornhill shopkeeper and a woman maidenly named Elizabeth Clark. He attended the local common schools until he was 14, when his father died leaving an estate of "1 great and six small chairs, 1 old broken desk, 1 sm. looking glass, 1 old table etc. etc. Total value £5-3-½." His musical education began during these early years, and his only formal instruction seems to have been in one of the church singing schools that were common in most New England towns in those days. He learned under the supervision of John Barry, a choir leader of the Congregationalist New South Church, where Sam Adams was a member.

After William Billings, Sr. died, the boy was apprenticed to a tanner, a profession he followed faithfully in spite of his deep involvement with politics and music. The nickname, "the musical tanner," was well earned, and legends that he chalked tunes on the walls and on handy strips of leather ring accurate. He married Lucy Swan, one of the singers in his music class, who took feminine advantage of her position even though her father Major Robert Swan of Stoughton was vigorously against the match. In one way at least, the marriage was "for worse." The couple lived close to poverty, and several public appeals to support the Billingses were made. On December 8, 1790, *The Columbian Centinel* remarked on "a concert of Sacred Musick for the benefit of Mr. William Billings of this town–whose distress is real. . . ." While in 1792, just before his last work was published, a statement appeared in the *Massachusetts Magazine* saying that "the distressed situation of Mr. Billings' family has so sensibly operated on the minds of the committee as to induce their assistance in the intended publication."[1] Nevertheless, he left an estate of about $1500 to his widow and the six surviving of their nine children.

We know he died in 1800, but his place of burial is in dispute, though it is probably on Boston Common. He was scarcely a candidate for the three other local cemeteries: Copp's Hill, where paupers went; King's Chapel, reserved for Episcopalians; or Granary Burying Ground, for the more prominent like Paul Revere, Sam Adams, John Hancock.

The Reverend William Bentley of Salem described him after his death as "a singular man, of moderate size, short of one leg, with one eye, without any address, and with an uncommon negligence of person." However, he modifies this description by adding, "Still he spoke and sang and thought as a man above the common abilities."[2] One gathers he was cross and given to unpleasantness. Somehow he has always made me think of Alexander Pope and Joseph Dennis'

[1] Cited by John Tasker Howard in *Our American Music* (New York, 1939), 52-53.

[2] Cited by Gilbert Chase in *America's Music from the Pilgrims to the Present* (New York, 1966), 128.

reference that Pope's wit and morals were as warped as his body, but I am probably being unfair.

Exactly how this "musical tanner" got into politics is not hard to guess. 19 years old at the time of the Stamp Act, a member of the same church as Sam Adams, living in Boston during the unrest, he could not have avoided some commitment. In the days leading up to Concord, church choir school gatherings, traditionally an accepted time for flirting, gossip exchange, and political discussion, rapidly became a front for political protest and even rebellious planning, the lessons of the church intertwining with the lessons of the state. Billings had been actively involved in the development of church choir schools similar to the one he attended under John Barry during his youth, and like many Christians he saw God as fully committed to his own views. These views were the views of his close friend Paul Revere, who did the engravings for the 1770 *The New England Psalm-Singer*, and of Revere's mentors, Adams and Dr. Joseph Warren. Thus, Billings, whose crippled body was ill-suited to activism, felt compelled to rewrite old hymns and psalms and to compose new works that he might inspire the more vigorous. Through this fervor, lines such as those opening the 137th Psalm,

> By the rivers of Babylon, there we sat down,
> Yea, we wept, when we remembered Zion.

became,

> By the rivers of Watertown, we sat down;
> Yea we wept as we remembered Boston.

The finest of all these contributions was the political version of his famous hymn, "Chester," which became the most popular march in the Continental Army.[3]

CHESTER.

> Let tyrants shake their iron rod,
> And slavery clank her galling chains.
> We fear them not, we trust in God,
> New England's God forever reigns.
> Howe and Burgoyne and Clinton, too,

[3] From *The Singing Master's Assistant* of 1778, "Billings' Best."

With Prescott and Cornwallis join'd,
Together plot our overthrow,
In one Infernal league combin'd.
When God inspired us for the fight,
Their ranks were broke, their lines were forc'd,
Their Ships were Sheltered in our sight,
Or swiftly driven from our coast.
The Foe comes out with haughty Stride,
Our troops advance with martial noise,
Their Vet'rans flee before our Youth,
And gen'rals yield to beardless boys.
What grateful Off'ring can we bring,
What shall we render to the Lord?
Lord Hallelujahs let us Sing,
And praise His name in ev'ry chord.

The Revolution undoubtedly acted as a major catalyst for Billings' genius, and the popularity of his songs with the troops was outstanding, especially in the South, where New England soldiers who knew them by heart spread them from camp to camp. However, there is no question he would have made a contribution even without the war. By the time Billings had reached his maturity, there was already a growing discontent with the traditional methods of psalm-singing and church music. English Protestants, following the lead of their European forerunners, "lined out" psalms: that is, the leader would intone a verse or phrase, the members of the congregation would follow, each in his own way. The result has been described as "an assemblage of jackasses braying together," and the variety in performance and the stock of tunes was limited. Furthermore, lining out, which had originally been done with a certain amount of vigor and pep, had become dragging and flat through usage, losing what vitality and freshness it once offered. And as no instruments were used, frequent mistakes in holding tunes and keys destroyed much of the emotional effect of the music.

Billings is one of the musicians who made a break with this old way of church singing and began to introduce instruments, new tunes, and practiced harmony. Having grown up in Colonial Boston, he had quite a stock of material to draw on. On the one hand, there was all about him the rich heritage of folk melodies: jigs, ballads, sentimental lyrics that singers like the Sandgate soldier sang; on the other hand, there were the concerts and closet performances that the British military officers and royal governors sponsored from time to time. Some musicologists have treated Billings as though he were laboring without light in a wilderness of unsympathetic barbarians. But this was not the case. Music, even if it were not always the music of classical tradition, was everywhere, and Billings was free to use what he heard as he wished. Murray Barbour has found themes also used in "London Bridge is Falling Down," "Greensleeves," "The Girl I Left Behind Me," "The Campbells Are Coming," and even Jerome Kern's "Old Man River" in his hymns.[4] We know he introduced the pitch-pipe and the bass viol into the church to insure proper performance, and he published all sorts of instructions to teachers of singing schools that were designed to help introduce the rudiments of music to the students. In *The Singing Master's Assistant* of 1778 he stresses that all members sign an agreement requiring punctual attendance and that they conform to the master's judgment with regard to voice placement. In short, Billings was trying to bring freshness, system, and discipline to what had become a rather weary aspect of religion.

His publications were widely known. The first one, in 1770, was entitled *The New England Psalm Singer, or American Chorister.* Containing a Number of Psalm-Tunes, Anthems and Cannons In Four and Five Parts. (Never before published.) Composed by William Billings, A Native of Boston, in New England. This work was engraved by Paul Revere, and its credo is a musical statement of standard 18th century aesthetic philosophy. In Alexander Pope's words,

> First follow nature, and your judgment frame
> By her just standards which is still the same:
> Unerring Nature, still divinely bright,
> One clear, unchanged, and universal light,
> Life, force, and beauty, must to all impart,
> At once the source, and end, and test of art.[5]

[4] Murray J. Barbour, *The Church Music of William Billings* (East Lansing, Michigan, 1960), 430 f.

[5] From "An Essay on Criticism," Part 1, Lines 68-75.

In Billings',

> Perhaps it may be expected by some, that I should say something concerning Rules for Composition; to these I answer that Nature is the best Dictator, for all the hard, dry, studied rules that ever was prescribed, will not enable any person to form an air. . . . It must be Nature, Nature must lay the Foundation, Nature must inspire the Thought. . . . For my own Part, as I don't think myself confin'd to any Rules for composition, laid down by any that went before me, neither should I think (were I to pretend to lay down Rules) that any one who came after me were anyways obligated to adhere to them, any further than they should think proper; so in fact, I think it best for every *Composer* to be his own *Carver*.

More famous, however, was *The Singing Master's Assistant* of 1778, which was known as "Billings' Best". In it he re-wrote much of his earlier material and apologized for what he considered youthful errors. Referring to *The New England Psalm Singer* as his "Reuben," he offered the "Kind Reader" this entertaining commentary—a commentary that reveals Billings to be a man of both objectivity and Augustan wit.

> Kind Reader—
>
> No doubt you (do or ought to) remember that about eight years ago, I published a Book entitled *The New England Psalm Singer, etc.* And truly a most masterly and inimitable performance, I then thought it to be. Oh! how did my foolish heart throb and beat with tumultuous joy! With what impatience did I wait on the Book-Binder, while stitching the sheets and putting on the covers, with what extacy did I snatch the yet unfinished Book out of his hands, and pressing to my bosom, with rapturous delight how lavish was I in encomiums on this infant production of my own Numb-Skull. Welcome, thrice welcome, thou legitimate offspring of my brain, go forth my little book, go forth and immortalize the name of your Author; may our sale be rapid and may you speedily run through ten thousand Editions, may you be a welcome guest in all companies and what will add tenfold to thy dignity, may you find your way into the Libraries of the Learned. Thou art my Reuben, my first born; the beginning of my Strength. . . . Since I have begun to play the Critic, I have discovered that many pieces were never worth my printing or your inspection; therefore in

order to make you amends for my former intrusion, I have selected and corrected some of the Tunes which were most approved of in that book and have added several new pieces which I think to be very good ones. . . .

He also answers those critics who had attacked his earlier tunes as being too simple and lacking in traditional discord. He included a tune entitled "Jargon," which began with the words "Let horrid Jargon split the air, and rive the nerves asunder . . .," with directions for its singing, a *Manifesto* to the Goddess of Discord, which went as follows,

In order to do this piece justice, the concert must be made of vocal and instrumental music. Let it be performed in the following manner, viz: Let an Ass bray the base, let the filing of a saw carry the tenor, let a hog who is extremely weak squeal the counter, and let a cart-wheel, which is heavy-loaded, and that has long been without grease, squeak the treble; and if the concert should appear to be too feeble you may add the cracking of a crow, the howling of a dog, the squalling of a cat, and what would grace the concert yet more, would be the rubbing of a wet finger upon a window glass. This last mentioned instrument no sooner salutes the drum of the ear, but it instantly conveys the sensation to the teeth; and if all these in conjunction should not reach the cause, you may add this most inharmonious of all sounds, "Pay me what thou owest."

This outburst supposedly caused a local wag to hang two live cats by their tails to the sign outside Billings' home which read "Billings' Music," and he is meant to have been asked by a humorous visitor if snoring were to be classed as vocal or instrumental music.

But such is the price of success. Four more collections followed these two: *Music in Miniature* (1779); *The Psalm Singer's Amusement* (1781); *The Suffolk Harmony* (1786); and *The Continental Harmony* (1794). The latter work is typical of the tune-books that have become popular in rural areas since Billings' day. It contains both an exposition of musical theory and the songs themselves. The theoretical introduction is designed for the use of teachers in singing schools. Billings suggests the use of "fa so la mi" as the best means of teaching scales to students. He gives instructions on how to construct a pendulum of heavy wax and a piece of egg-shaped wood to be whitewashed that it might be visible in candlelight. He informs teachers that women will be more receptive to music than men, saying, "I scarcely ever met with one but what was more or less entertained with musical sounds, and I am very positive that nine tenths of them are much more pleased and entertained with a flat, than a sharp sir." Finally, he presents the songs themselves—psalm tunes, what he called fugues, and anthems, songs that were developed from popular sources many of which were to flourish in rural, folk communities. George Pullen Jackson's definition of a folk hymn comes very close to describing these pieces: "songs with old folk-tunes which everybody could sing and with words that spoke from the heart of the devout in the language of the common man."[6] Not unlike Robert Burns and Woody Guthrie, Billings is somewhat hard to define. He is clearly sophisticated, a member of literary tradition, but at the same time he can almost as easily be defined as an unusually talented member of oral tradition—for it is from oral tradition that he gets his inspiration and it is in oral tradition that he has had a fair share of his influence.

Billings loved his fugues, which were in reality little more than rounds, finding in them the best means of releasing that incremental enthusiasm that is so rewarding to the singer of church music. In his introductory remarks to the *Continental Harmony* he makes the following comment,

> It is an old axiom, and I think a very just one, viz. that *variety is always pleasing*, and it is well known that there is more variety in one piece of fuging music, than in twenty pieces of plain song. . . . Each part seems determined by dint of harmony and strength to accent, to drown his competitor in an ocean of harmony, and while each part is thus mutually striving for mastery . . . the audience are most luxuriously entertained. . . . Now the solemn bass demands their attention, now the manly tenor, now the lofty counter, now the volatile treble, now here, now there, now here again.—O enchanting! O ecstatic! Push on, push on ye sons of harmony. . . .

[6] George Pullen Jackson, *Spiritual Folk-Songs of Early America* (New York, 1964), 6.

John S. Dwight, describing what he considered "Our Dark Ages in Music," read this passage and commented, "Indeed, it seems to have been a sort of musical horse-race." A stuffy remark on any terms, but particularly so when one realizes that all incremental matters, musical or otherwise, have the elements of horse- or rat-racing in them. Perhaps, Harriet Beecher Stowe's description of her village choir in Litchfield, Connecticut touches best what Billings loved about the fugue.[7]

> . . . there was a grand, wild freedom, an energy of motion in the old "fuging tunes" of that day that well expressed the heart of the people courageous in combat and unshaken in endurance. . . . Whatever the trained musician might say of such a tune as old Majesty, no person of imagination or sensibility could hear it well rendered by a large choir without deep emotion.

Of course there is no purpose in trying to compare these fuging tunes with the fugues of classical music. The sort of fugue that Billings used developed from psalm and hymn singing in England and on the Continent and is really not related to the fugues of Bach. Billings seems to have learned about this music through his early studies with John Barry and through his contact with the works of William Tans'ur, the English Surreyian composer and teacher, whose *Royal Melody Compleat or New Harmony of Scion* had been printed in Boston during 1767 in the Third, and revised, London edition. A good many of the church choir leaders were using the fuging tunes in America before the Revolution, but Billings appears to have been one of the great popularizers of the form, which was to spread first over New England, then Pennsylvania, and finally the South and West. A study of 268 American collections published before 1810 shows that only 31 are completely without fuging tunes, and half of the collections devote about a quarter of their space to such music.[8]

[7] As cited in Chase, 131.

[8] These figures come from Irving Lowens, "The Origins of the American Fuging Tune," *Journal of the American Musicological Society*, Spring 1953, 51. Lowens' book, *Music and Musicians in Early America* (New York, 1964), Chapter 14, gives a thorough discussion of the fuging tune.

The reaction against this music was violent in the seaboard cities as the United States began to become more urbane. In the urban areas, the singing schools were becoming formal choirs and choral societies, like the Handel and Haydn Society of Boston, and these groups frowned upon all music which was not classical in the European sense. Identified with Colonialism and the rural, the Billings-type fugue was belittled by writer after writer. As early as 1791, Samuel Holyoke wrote in his *Harmonia Americana*,[9]

> Perhaps some may be disappointed that fuging pieces are in general omitted. But the principal reason why few were inserted was the trifling effect produced by that sort of music; for the parts, falling in, one after another, each conveying a different idea, confound the sense, and render the performance a mere jargon of words.

In 1807, Elias Mann commented gruffly in his *Massachusetts Collection*,[10]

> In this collection will be found none of those wild fuges, and rapid and confused movements, which have so long been the disgrace of Congregational psalmody, and the contempt of the judicious and tasteful amateur.

And even as recently as 1939, Carl Lindstrom felt free to write,[11]

> The musical significance of the tunemongers who flourished in the United States at the turn of the 19th century has long ago been dealt with. . . . A paragraph apiece has usually sufficed the investigator for each of these quaint personalities who produced a multitudinous crop of rectangular tune books and during a generation peddled them like tinware along the eastern seaboard, particularly in New England. A handful of biographical facts regarding . . . their motley school is all we know and all we need to know.

[9] Cited by Louis C. Elson, *The National Music of America and Its Sources* (Boston, 1900), 73-74.

[10] Cited by James W. Hall, *The Tune Book in American Culture 1800-1820*, a Ph.D. dissertation (University of Pennsylvania, 1967), 216.

[11] Carl E. Lindstrom, "William Billings and His Times," *Musical Quarterly*, 1939, 479.

"Billings' *Chester* as Sung Today"
from *The Original Sacred Harp*, Denison Revision, Cullman, Alabama, 1966, 479.

But such sophisticated reaction was never even noted by the folk, who continued to sing the "old style" generation after generation.

The spread of the rural singing school and its folk fuging was facilitated by the development of the shape-note songster—a device right in the spirit of Billings' teaching techniques. In these books, which were one of the first of many short-cuts to culture to be fostered in this country, the notes in the "sol, fa" scale were distinguished by their shapes as well as by their positions on the staff. Hundreds of singing teachers, some well known like Andrew Law, some now forgotten, carried the word of God up and down the Appalachians, out across the Deep South, and later into the Southwest, teaching choirs by means of the shape-note system, training persons in the fuging style of William Billings, and writing thousands of new anthems and fuging tunes, many of which were adapted straight from the ballads and reels of the time. Today, rural people still sing these old hymns, particularly in the strip that runs from northern Georgia across Alabama, southern Tennessee, Mississippi, Louisiana, and southern Missouri into East Texas. A modern meeting of people who sing from a "Sacred Harp Songster" would not, I imagine, seem odd to William Billings. Alan Lomax, writing on the cover jacket of one of his *Southern Journey* record albums, has described just such a gathering.[12]

When we arrived at ten o'clock on Saturday morning, the singing had been in progress for an hour. It went on until lunchtime, when all adjourned to a fifty-yard long table set under the post oak trees, laden with chicken, ham, hot rolls and biscuits, corn pone and every kind of cake and pie known to the cooks of northern Alabama. I think the congregation enjoyed watching us stuff ourselves almost as much as they did seeing us run our stereo recording machine. They were a kindly, hospitable group of farmers, small town merchants, school teachers and their wives and children. Singing from the Sacred Harp book is the cultural center of their lives.

Promptly at two o'clock, the chairman called the meeting to order. The "school" assembled in the nave of the church—about forty people

[12] Quoted from the essay by Alan Lomax on the back of the record "All Day Singing from 'The Sacred Harp'" in *Southern Journey*, Prestige/International 25007.

ranged around four sides of a hollow square—trebles, sopranos, tenors and bases—both sexes and all ages in each group. The committee had already drawn up a list of song leaders containing the names of every experienced singer present, and the chairman now called someone forward. Everyone had his "Original Sacred Harp" song book in hand and turned to the page number announced by the leader. In a matter of seconds, everyone had found his place and the older heads in the group had established the pitch. The leader launched immediately into a sol-fa interpretation of the song with the whole group joining in. Thus, every song is rehearsed once with its notes and then one or two verses are sung; another song is announced, found, pitched sol-faed and performed, and another leader is called. Matters proceed so briskly and efficiently that perhaps a hundred songs are sung in one day, and before the week-end singing is over, most of the favorites in the book have been sung.

Every well-practiced Sacred Harper knows all the parts of all the songs in the book and can move from side to side of the hollow square as he wishes. All can conduct capably but when one of the old-timers steps into the leader's place, he is likely to set a more appropriate tempo and to carry his chorus with more swing.

That the harmonies are unconventional at times is due to three causes. First, the influence of the Billings school; second the blessed ignorance of some of the early composers who had more feeling for folk music than knowledge of the "rules of harmony;" and third, the powerful character of some of the old tunes, themselves, which demanded a really fresh treatment. Further, the Sacred Harpers sing in the folk style of the South, adding many interesting embellishments, using tremolo, glissando and attack in traditional folk style and pitching their voices in the old manner of their folk ancestors. This style of vocalizing lends a thrilling quality to their harmony, reminding one faintly of a Ukranian country chorus. Indeed, if the Sacred Harp music is performed by a city choir it loses half of its punch, and one hopes that, when the "Original Sacred Harp" becomes one of the Bibles of the folk song movement, as it certainly will, the singers will take the trouble to learn *how* to sing as well as what to sing.

These singing meetings are intensely emotional. The Sacred Harp folk are deeply religious. When I asked one old gentleman what lay back of his beautiful singing, he slapped his big, country palm down on his book and said, "Every word in that book is true—true as Gospel." One feels this emotion when individuals rise to speak, for their voices often tremble with feeling and tears sometimes course down their cheeks.

The Sacred Harpers feel themselves members of a family, or rather a clan, that will someday be singing in harmony with the angels. Meantime they deeply mourn the passing of each beloved member and they part from one another at the close of the meeting with keen regret. This musical community is also deeply democratic. All chairmen and officers are elected by an open show of hands and these officials run their meetings in accordance with the parliamentary rules of order. Everyone who wishes has an opportunity to lead and every person is treated with a tender respect in regard for his or her feelings.

And Billings' songs are still among those sung. A check of *The Original Sacred Harp*, published in Cullman, Alabama in 1966 shows nine tunes by Billings, including the famous "Chester" printed above.

From our point of view today, it is hard to measure how much the unrest of the days before the Revolution inspired Billings, how active he would have become without the political catalyst, how much less his influence on rural religious singing would have been. There can be no doubt that he was deeply involved in music and singing schools from his earliest years, and there can be no doubt he would have written music and trained choirs whether the Colonies had been dissatisfied or not. But there is also no question the choirs offered him, and his friends Revere and Adams, a wonderful cover for their plots and plans. From such associations, Billings must have gained encouragement and prestige. What's more, the resultant popularity of his work, its significance in furthering the cause, and the fact that the soldiers took up his patriotic hymns and spread them throughout the country, must have had an immeasurable amount to do with the ease by which his followers were able to introduce singing school styles into area after area.

At least for me, this sort of influence of a war upon a culture is far more fascinating than the simple record of a battle between two ships or a description of a tea dumping that has been preserved here and there by the folk. Not that I have any ready answers as to how much influence "New England's God" had on the development of the American folk hymn and the shape-note songster. It is just this sort of thing is so much more subtle, ultimately so much more important, that it makes me wish someone would take the time to do a thorough study of it.

PART TWO Fakelore Goes to War

7 Three Spies

As we begin Part II, I must remind you to re-focus your mind. We are no longer really interested in the folk and what they cherish, but rather in our own, literate society and what we cherish—no longer in folklore, but in fakelore. Part II, using selected historical legends as its laboratory, will analyze how the heroes of modern American society are created, why they manage to survive.

In the introductory chapter you were given the typical professional folklorist's definition of fakelore, with its heavy implication that even though fakelore serves the needs of national unity a folklorist need know about it primarily to stay clear of it. The time has now arrived to approach the subject with a bit more sophistication. Fakelore, I suspect, must be re-assessed by folklorists, who might well start to study it without bias concerning its admittedly artificial nature. After all, we live in an age of print, of mass media, of rapid travel. America as a nation has become for most of us what the local community was for our forebears. We can communicate across it, travel about it, become familiar with it just as easily as a frontiersman could do these things with his Vermont woodlands or Virginia mountains. We are a literate, promotion-oriented people. The old ethnic, regional, and occupational lores are archaic, even to those who embrace them, and are disappearing into industrial urban life.

For while it is true that we can still collect old mountain ballets from displaced Kentuckians in Columbus, Ohio or hear variations of European motifs from auto-workers in Detroit, it is also obvious that the ballet singer and the auto-worker share the same national heritage and identify better with the literary homogeneity it represents than they do with their vestigial mountain or midnight-shift homogeneity. There may be no American folklore in the sense of a true oral tradition, but there is an American printed and visual lore serving the American community much as folklore served the Green Mountains or the Blue Ridge. Furthermore, the word "fakelore" is unfair when it implies that folklore is free from phoniness and promotion. I don't think it is or ever was. I suspect that most witch doctors and quite a few informants would do very well on Madison Avenue today. And if Paul Bunyan, Paul Revere, and Johnny Appleseed are spoon-fed us from the labelled jars of hucksters, I am certain that Anansi, Coyote, and Barbara Allen were the products of similar, if more primitive, opportunisms of yesteryear.

There is also a definite parallel between the way origin, variation, and borrowing operate in the oral tradition of folklore and the literary tradition of fakelore. Writers borrow motifs, adapt old materials, and re-use clichés much in the way the folk do. Historical figures become legendary in one tradition just as they do in the other. People, whether literate or ignorant, are by nature, it seems, trite and given to formula. So an event occurs, a man distinguishes himself, and accounts are told about what he has done. It isn't long before these accounts are shaped along lines that tales of earlier heroes have taken. The hero begins to become what he should have been, not what he was. And once this happens, he will serve as a whirlpool, sucking in narrative flotsam and jetsam from all over.

Thus, neither a folklorist nor a fakelorist is ever dealing with legends about a single, historical hero, but rather with a set of stories that for the moment are circulating around a particular man. An outlaw holds up a stagecoach, but with such courtesy it is a pleasure to be robbed. He comes to a lovely girl. As she pulls the ring from her third-finger, left-hand, she bursts into tears. The outlaw at once returns the ring, wishes the girl "God speed," and remarks how he envies the "lucky fellow." Is the robber Dick Turpin, Jesse James, or Heraclio Bernal? And how many times at the bottom of the page in *The Reader's Digest* have you run across a silly anecdote about the cleverness of some charmer, say Jackie Kennedy, only to see it told about Jane Fonda two months later in *Silver Screen?* When I was young wasn't every clever line (if all the dates at the Yale Prom were laid end to end I wouldn't be surprised) attributed to Dorothy Parker?

Of course, a man's field of endeavor, his life pattern, and history itself provide controls on legend. Jackie Kennedy and Paul Revere aren't likely to share stories, nor are Molly Pitcher and Bess Truman. Every legend, popular or folk, will be a blend of truth and appropriate formula, one often overbalancing the other. If the truth prevails, the figure is almost certain to be non-folk or historical. If the formulaic matter prevails, folk or legendary. For example, in "real life," George Washington and Ethan Allen were both flesh and blood Continentals. However, excepting the Parson Weems stories of the cherry tree and the Rappahannock dollar, his connection with Betsy Ross, and his ability to "have slept" everywhere, Washington is always thought of purely historically. Allen, on the other hand, was both a land speculator who advocated statehood for Vermont, and a legendary leader of Green Mountain boys who appears as a white stallion after his death. While Washington is remembered for being the "Father of Our Country," for being a fine tactician, for his Farewell Address, Allen is remembered for formulaic pranks and for a ghostly return shared by similar figures here and abroad.

Thus, although we must remain aware that some heroes develop in oral tradition and that some spring like Athene full-grown from urban minds, let's, during Part II, do what the mass media does and lump all Revolutionary heroes—folk and fake—together, excluding only those who remain bound in historicity. The legendary figures left, though their actions are formulaic and their personalities stereotyped, have one thing in common: they have developed an aura, and it is this aura, phoney as it can be, that has enabled them to become symbolic for the nation. However, we must take care not to let their symbolic importance deceive us into thinking of them as mythological figures. They are not that, for they have no religious or explanatory purpose of any significance in spite of what commercial hacks and pattern-seeking psychologists may claim. To a folklorist myths deal with figures who actually create the pattern through which a culture evolves physically and ethically; legends are much less remote, dealing with figures that lived or supposedly lived in what one might call the "touchable past." Christian-Jewish America satisfies its urge toward myth through the *Bible*. Revolutionary heroes, folk and fake, are simply more of our time than Jesus or Moses.

Naturally, we can't discuss all the legendary figures which our culture has seen fit to hand down to us from Continental times. However, we will look at enough to understand the processes through which they develop and the final images they attain. Let me begin with a discussion of three spies: one a completely fictitious hero of a widely read novel, whose tale nevertheless was based on the exploits of a real man; two, an historical Yale graduate whose story would be long forgotten had it not been for the efforts of enthusiastic alumni and local historians; three, an historical British major whose story has entered our true folklore, if only in a limited way, where we see it being subjected to the variation and re-creation of oral tradition. From them, we will be able to understand better the similar manner in which literary figures, popular hacks, and folk informants develop legendary history. Then we can consider other heroes against the backdrop so established.

Critics, professors of literature, may look askance at James Fenimore Cooper, but there is no denying he is an established literary figure, a veritable genius when compared with the broadside hucksters and magazine hacks of the 19th century. Born at Burlington, New Jersey in 1789, son of a prominent family for which Cooperstown, New York is named, he is as unpopular today for his belief in the aristocracy of the cultivated mind as he is for his rhetorical style, insipid characters, and idealized situations. Be that as it may, he can tell a good story, and plenty of people here and particularly in Europe continue to put up with his faults to enjoy his adventures.

Every college student knows how he came to be a writer.

Supposedly, he griped to his wife about some English novels he had been reading and was asked why he didn't try to do better. The result was *Precaution*, which isn't "better" than very many books. It didn't exactly succeed, but it did serve to get him started. Shortly after, in 1821, *The Spy* was published, and this historical romance of the Revolution made him famous, opening the way for an incredible flood of 33 novels, a history of the Navy, five travel books, and a host of essays on American customs. He is our first successful novelist and eventually became known as the "American Scott."

Like his contemporary, Washington Irving, Cooper worked hard to establish the reputation of American letters in Europe. Living at Lyon as consul from 1826 to 1833, he did a lot to make Europeans aware of the United States, its nature, weaknesses, and virtues. A bright man, he approached all subjects with real objectivity, whether dealing with the plight of the Loyalists during the Revolution or the tyranny of vulgar standards inherent in Jacksonian democracy. Such detachment brought him respect abroad, but made him suspect at home where blind commitment to the new nation was most popular.

Here, we are concerned with Cooper as a creator of heroic figures like Natty Bumppo, the Hawkeye-Pathfinder-Deerslayer of the Leatherstocking Tales, and Harvey Birch, the hero of *The Spy*. Modelled on woodsmen and secret agents about whom Cooper had read and heard, these figures demonstrate well how a really popular literary figure can create national images out of whole cloth. Sculley Bradley, for instance, refers to Cooper as "the creator of an American hero-myth,"[1] and I suppose it is true that most people's idea of a frontiersman or a Revolutionary agent can be traced back to Bumppo and Birch. Both are sort of incarnations of what we have come to believe a hero should be: Bumppo: noble, capable, cool, kind or hard as the occasion demands; Birch: selfless, resourceful, hero-worshipping, patriotic beyond our fondest expectations. Not that such images wouldn't have come into existence

[1] Sculley Bradley, Richmond C. Beatty, E. Hudson Long (editors), *The American Tradition in Literature*, 2 volumes (New York, 1956), I, 390.

without Cooper. Certainly, Jacksonian political hacks and Western magazine writers would have taken care of things. But their efforts were sporadic and diffused. Cooper's novels were read consistently, generation after generation by millions of Americans and Europeans who grew up believing in Bumppo and Birch, as well as Long Tom Coffin and Uncas, as surely as they believed in Washington, Hamilton, or their own great grandfathers. Bumppo and Birch, then, like Tom Sawyer, Little Orphan Annie, and Scarlett O'Hara become something in our literate, educated world not unlike folk heroes —though, if we insist on a strict, and sensible, definition of folk, it is hard to know what to call them.

As we are discussing the Revolution, let's turn to Harvey Birch—Birch who is certainly known to more Americans than such real Revolutionary spies as John Champe, Enoch Crosby, or Ann Bates. Cooper's wife was born Susan Augusta DeLancey, and her family had been Loyalists who lived in Westchester County, New York (the Neutral Ground) during the Revolution. When Cooper wrote *The Spy*, he dealt with problems people like the DeLanceys had known. In it, Henry Wharton, a young British major, returns to his home behind the American lines in disguise. He is captured by troops under the command of one of his best friends, the American Major Dunwoodie, who also happens to be engaged to Henry's younger sister, Fanny. After a series of ups and downs, during which the older sister Sara is deceived by the already married British officer Wellmere, Henry escapes from the Americans with the aid of the spy, Harvey Birch, and the book and the war conclude. The real hero of the story is Birch, supposedly a British agent, but actually working directly for George Washington, who wanders in and out of the story disguised as a mysterious and wise Mr. Harper. Birch, who is despised by both sides and persecuted by the choleric Captain Lawton of Dunwoodie's Virginia Horse, carries the secret of his unselfish loyalty to the day of his death, which comes as he is shot fighting in the War of 1812 far in advance of all other soldiers. For a final fillip, his secret is discovered by the son of Dunwoodie and Fanny, who has gone to war carrying both Tory and Rebel blood in his veins.

As the Wharton family reflects the DeLanceys, as the house

in which the Whartons supposedly lived could be seen until it gave way to a Holiday Inn Motel a few years back, and as the novel is very accurate historically, it has always been assumed that Harvey Birch is a picture of an actual spy. Thousands of pages have been written trying to identify him, even in face of the fact that Cooper specifically explained his sources for Harvey Birch in the Introduction to the 1849 edition of the book.

The controversy began shortly after the first publication of *The Spy* when Enoch Crosby, a shoemaker who had worked as a secret agent in the Neutral Ground, claimed he was the real Harvey Birch. His case was taken up by H. L. Barnum in 1828 in a volume entitled *The Spy Unmasked: or Memoirs of Enoch Crosby, Alias Harvey Birch.*[2] This book was remarkably successful, convincing local historians and the general public alike. Until about 1930, it was automatically assumed that Crosby was Birch, because one scholar just followed the other like buffalo over a cliff. Crosby made public appearances while he lived and was even invited to be guest of honor at a dramatic version of *The Spy* produced in 1826. The whole thing got so out of proportion that Cooper became disturbed.

In 1850 he wrote the following letter to an unknown person,[3]

Hall, Cooperstown, August 21st, 1850

Sir,

Never having seen the publication of Mr. Barnum, to which you allude, I can give no opinion of its accuracy.

I know nothing of such a man as Enoch Crosby, never having heard his name, until I saw it coupled with the character of the Spy, after my return from Europe.

The history of the book is given in the preface of Putnam's edition, where you will probably find all you desire to know.

Respectfully yours,

J. Fenimore Cooper.

[2] (New York, 1828).

[3] See *The Correspondance of James Fenimore Cooper*, as edited by his grandson, also James Fenimore Cooper (New Haven, 1922), I, 684. The letter is listed "To an Unknown Person."

In the preface of the year before, he tells how he heard an anecdote at "the residence of an illustrious man, who had been employed in various situations of high trust during the darkest days of the American Revolution." The gentleman was John Jay, a fact we know from the following letter written by Cooper's daughter, Susan.[4]

Precaution having been quite as successful as he expected, the writer now planned another book. It was to be thoroughly American, the scene laid in West Chester County, during the Revolution. An anecdote which Governor Jay had told him relating to a spy, who performed his dangerous services out of pure patriotism, was the foundation of the new book.

My Father never knew the name of the Spy; Governor Jay felt himself bound to secrecy on that point. But he never for a moment believed that Enoch Crosby was the man. Various individuals, twenty years later, claimed to have been the original Harvey Birch. One man even asserts that Mr. Cooper used to visit at his house frequently, for the purpose of hearing his adventures and then writing them out in *The Spy*. This is utterly false. From only one person did my Father ever receive any information connected with the life of the Spy who was the dim original of Harvey Birch, and that person was Governor Jay. The conversation on the piazza at Bedford relating to the patriot spy occurred a long time before my Father dreamed of writing a book.

When he had fully made up his mind to write a novel entirely American, whose scene should be laid in West Chester during the Revolution, he amused himself by going among the old farmers of the neighborhood and hearing all the gossip of those old times, about the "Neutral Ground" on which we were then living, the ground between the English in New York, and American forces northward. Frequently he would invite some old farmer to pass the evening in the parlor at Angevine, and while drinking cider and eating hickory nuts, they would talk over the battle of White Plains, and all the skirmishes of the Cow-Boys and Skinners. Many such evenings do I remember, as I sat on a little bench beside my Mother, while Uncle John Hatfield, or George Willis, or one of the Cornells related the stirring adventures of those days of the Revolution. There was a shallow cave in a rocky ledge on the road to Mamaroneck, where a Tory spy had been con-

[4] *The Correspondance of James Fenimore Cooper*, 42-43.

cealed, and was stealthily fed for some time. And on the road to New Rochelle there was a grove where a sharp skirmish had taken place; it was called the Haunted Wood—ghosts had been seen there! The cave and the grove were full of tragic interest to me, whenever we passed them.

Every chapter of *The Spy* was read to my Mother as soon as it was written, and the details of the plot were talked over with her. From the first months of authorship to the last years of his life, my Father generally read what he wrote to my Mother.

The Spy, when it appeared, was brilliantly successful. Never before had an American book attained anything like the same success.

Jay, the first Chief Justice and former Governor of New York, was long a family friend of the Coopers and a sometime neighbor of the author in Westchester County. Related to the DeLanceys by marriage, he had two sons who knew Cooper well, one even having been a classmate at Yale. Cooper's version of what Jay told him follows,[5]

". . . Congress named an especial and a secret committee . . . for the express purpose of defeating this object [internal dissension]. Of this committee Mr. ——, the narrator of the anecdote, was chairman.

In the discharge of the novel duties which now devolved on him, Mr. —— had occasion to employ an agent whose services differed but little from those of a common spy. This man, as will easily be understood, belonged to a condition of life which rendered him the least reluctant to appear in so equivocal a character. He was poor, ignorant, so far as the usual instruction was concerned; but cool, shrewd, and fearless by nature. It was his office to learn in what part of the country the agents of the crown were making their efforts to embody men, to repair to the place, enlist, appear zealous in the cause he affected to serve, and otherwise to get possession of as many secrets of the enemy as possible.

. . . In addition to the danger of discovery, there was the daily risk of falling into the hands of the Americans themselves, who invariably visited sins of this nature more severely on the natives of the country than on the Europeans who fell into their hands. In fact, the agent of Mr. —— was several times arrested by the local authorities; and, in one

[5] See the "Author's Introduction" to the 1849 edition of *The Spy*, printed in the edition by Curtis Dahl (New York, 1946).

instance, he was actually condemned by his exasperated countrymen to the gallows. Speedy and private orders to the jailer alone saved him from an ignominious death. He was permitted to escape; and this seeming and indeed actual peril was of great aid in supporting his assumed character among the English.

. . . Before vacating his seat in Congress, he [Mr. —] reported . . . an outline of the circumstances related, necessarily suppressing the name of his agent, and demanding an appropriation . . . [which] was voted; and its delivery was confided to the chairman of the secret committee. . . . They met in a wood at midnight. Here Mr. — complimented his companion on his fidelity and adroitness; explained the necessity of their communications being closed; and finally tendered the money. The other drew back . . . [saying] 'The country has need of all its means, . . . I can work, or gain a livelihood in various ways.' Persuasion was useless, for patriotism was uppermost in the heart of this remarkable individual. . . ."

Cooper then states flatly that Jay never told him, that he never found out, what the name of this agent was, though such a denial offers no barrier to the scholar, who has learned to claim Cooper was simply lying.

At any rate, Cooper's debt to John Jay for the basic facts from which he created Harvey Birch and his story are apparent enough. Birch, like Jay's spy, operates in the Neutral Ground of Westchester County. This area, infested with brigands who covered their looting by professing loyalty to one side or the other, criss-crossed by British and American patrols, thick with agents, was a hotbed of adventure. Birch, like Jay's spy, had the job of keeping tabs on British activities and reporting them to the Americans. Like Jay's spy he had developed the cover that he was actually a Tory, wanted by the Continental Army. And like Jay's spy, he is sentenced to hang more than once, each time managing to escape under mysterious circumstances. Finally, General Washington confronts Birch, much as Jay confronted his spy, with the offer to pay for his services, only to be refused by the noble patriot. Of course, Cooper dressed all this up with the sure touch of a sentimental novelist, adding the complex love story, the strange Mr. Harper, the raucous Betty Flanagan, the exciting escape of Henry Wharton, and the note from

Washington which Birch always carries, as well as the excellent pictures of the troops, the Skinners, and the local situation.

In 1930, Tremaine McDowell wrote an article in *American Literature*[6] pretty well proving that Enoch Crosby was not John Jay's spy and ending the long-lived hoax for all but the most amateur. What his findings show is that Barnum, using Cooper's work as a model, simply created adventures for Crosby that would make him the obvious source for Harvey Birch. Crosby, who started the whole thing—maybe even in good faith—was willing to go along, probably feeling the end justified any means. One cannot underestimate the influence of all this. Crosby, like most spies and most frauds, had lots of personality, and with Barnum helping him out, he was able to gain a fame that few Revolutionary agents except Nathan Hale and John André can match. Some of the tales about him are still told in New York State oral tradition, and most of them, like the one below from Fishkill, reflect the confusion with Cooper's Birch.[7]

During the American Revolution, both sides used spies to try to get information about the enemy's troop movements. One of the best spies employed by either side was an American named Enoch Crosby. Under his disguise as a travelling peddler, he could pass easily through either side's camps. One day he was caught in a surprise attack on a British camp and was imprisoned by the American forces in a church in Fishkill that had been converted into a prison. None knew of his service to his country save General George Washington who arranged to have Crosby escape. Crosby managed to elude American troops who knew nothing of these facts and hide in a cave in the low, rugged hills between Fishkill and the Hudson River. He stayed there for about a week during which time he was visited many times by General Washington, in disguise, and it is said that the voices of these two great patriots may be heard in serious discussion by anyone who dares enter

[6] "The Identity of Harvey Birch" in *American Literature*, May 1930, 111-120.

[7] Handed in by Gordon R. McLaren as part of an assignment in English 126, General Folklore in the Spring of 1967 at the University of Pennsylvania. McLaren states, "I cannot name any person from whom I heard this tale as I have heard it ever since I was old enough to remember it."

this cave after dark in the month of April during which these events took place.

The voices have been explained by geologists, who point out that as the ground thaws in the spring water collects in a shallow, bowl-shaped depression above the back part of the cave. This bowl is separated from the roof of the cave by surface dirt and a thick layer of sandstone. As the water collects, it begins to seep through the dirt and then the sandstone, eventually dripping through cracks in the cave roof and forming puddles on the floor. The noise of the water falling into the puddles echoes off the walls, sounding like voices at the entrance. Although the sound is audible both day and night, although the dripping frequently begins in March and runs into May, and in spite of McDowell's scholarship, local residents have adjusted the legend to suit their fancies.

Nor are local residents the only persons with fancies. Indisputable as McDowell's scholarship and Cooper's statements may be, they have served to dismiss Crosby merely to create new candidates. It reminds me of the people who insist Shakespeare didn't write Shakespeare's plays. No sooner does Bacon fall than along comes some nut with Oxford or Marlowe. In 1954, James Diemer[8] suggested that John Champe, whom we will encounter shortly in connection with the Arnold-André affair, did things that were strikingly similar to those done by Harvey Birch. Diemer points out that Dunwoodie's Virginia Horse and Dr. Sitgreaves of the book are paralleled by Light-Horse Harry Lee's legion and Alexander Skinner in life. Champe did work directly for Washington, and his staged flight from his own troops during the Arnold affair is not unlike Henry Wharton's escape; but as spying, war, and escapes never differ much, such parallels are not too significant. At any rate, Diemer seems to have convinced almost no one. In 1956, Warren Walker brought out an article[9] that surveyed the history of the whole issue, convincingly eliminating Champe, Crosby, and all other candidates previously presented. Then, he comes up with

[8] "A Model for Harvey Birch" in *American Literature,* May 1954, 242-247.

[9] "The Prototype of Harvey Birch" in *New York History*, October 1956, 399-413.

not one, but two, of his own. These are Abraham Woodhull and Robert Townsend, who worked as a team, signing their letters Samuel Culper, Sr. and Samuel Culper, Jr. respectively. They were recruited as spies by Major Benjamin Tallmadge, a college friend of Nathan Hale, who we will see was really responsible for André's capture, and they make good candidates. They operated in the Westchester area. Townsend was a travelling merchandizer before and during the war, and he used his occupation to cover his spying, working in Loyalist territory constantly in danger from American patrols, Skinners, and Cowboys. Woodhull, who served as a courier between the lines, was also plagued by Skinners and Cowboys. He was robbed on the road, and his neighbor's house was plundered in a way strikingly similar to the disaster that befalls "The Locusts" in *The Spy*. Townsend, particularly, cultivated the popular image of the Tory sympathizer, but neither he nor Woodhull ever had any problems in being thought Tory spies by the Americans and so wanted dead or alive, although one of Townsend's cousins, substituting for him, was taken by the Rebels and would not have been released had not Washington intervened. Moreover, Townsend's house was occupied by British soldiers and his sister, Sarah, did fall in love with Colonel John Simcoe, the British officer in charge, and while Simcoe did not prove to be a bigamist like Colonel Wellmere in the novel, Sarah Townsend, like Sarah Wharton, never married.

Walker has a good case, twenty times as good as Barnum's. He can even clinch it with the fact Major Tallmadge eventually married a cousin of Cooper's wife, which also establishes a connection with Jay. And when one adds to all this the fact that Sir James Jay, John's English brother, had developed the secret ink that the spies under Tallmadge used, he begins to get excited. In short, if anyone without the gift of revelation can discover who Jay's spy really was, I think Walker has done it. Nevertheless, I am inclined to believe that Cooper never did have any notion who the model for Harvey Birch really was, and I think he simply got an idea from Jay, then patched together bits from popular and literary accounts of the Culpers, Champe, Crosby, and others, eventually creating a mongrel spy and mongrel plot that almost any dog can claim.

So facts, filtered through the mind of a fine writer, find their way back into popular imagination and even oral tradition, creating first a spy-hero from what is pretty close to whole-cloth and then breeding legends that place George Washington in hushed conversation with Enoch Crosby in a damp Fishkill cave just as certainly as he had been with General Braddock at Fort Duquesne. The catalyst is the printed page, reaching thousands upon thousands in a literate society, causing them to develop and perpetuate their beliefs, their history, their culture from the Coopers and even the Barnums, where the older folklore no longer reaches and the Walkers and McDowells stand ignored.

Nowhere is this more obvious than in the legend of Nathan Hale, about whom most of us would know no more than we do about Culper Jr. were it not for the industry of the press.[10] Hale was born in Coventry, Connecticut on June 6, 1755. After what appears to be an average youth, he entered Yale at 14, planning to become a minister. When he graduated in 1773, he worked as a teacher in East Haddam and then in New London, Connecticut, enlisting as the war began. He served with Colonel Charles Webb's regiment as a lieutenant and then was made a captain in the Connecticut Rangers under Lt. Colonel Thomas Knowlton. That was in May 1776. He seems to have been sick and out of action most the summer, but in September he was well enough to volunteer to spy on the British in Long Island. Washington, who had retreated after the Battle of Long Island, needed information on the enemy's plans. He asked Knowlton to select a volunteer, and Hale evidently was the only one willing. He went behind the enemy lines about as ill-prepared as a spy can be, with a scarred face that anyone who had ever seen him would recall, cousin of the British Army's deputy commissary of prisoners. He was without training, pre-arranged contacts, secret ink, or experience. In addition, everyone in the Rangers

[10] For references to source material concerning the facts of Hale's life and last days, see the notes on p. 379 of John Bageless' popular study, *Turncoats, Traitors and Heroes* (Philadelphia and New York, 1959). Henry P. Johnston, *Nathan Hale 1776* (New Haven, 1914) also contains many references, and examples.

seems to have known he was going off spying, and he discussed the whole thing with his Yale classmate and fellow officer under Webb Captain William Hull. Hull tried to argue Hale out of the mission, pointing out that no soldier was obligated to spy, but Hale wanted to be of service and felt that spying, by its very necessity, was honorable.

On September 12, Hale landed at Huntington, Long Island, where he assumed the character of a Dutch schoolmaster. He had his Yale diploma along. Exactly what he did behind the lines is not known. He seems to have obtained sketches of the fortifications, made notes on troop numbers and positions, and entered Manhattan after the British, seizing it on the 15th, had driven the Americans to the northern tip. He was arrested on the night of the 21st, and reports differ as to how. One version says that he mistook a boat from a British man-o-war for an American craft sent to take him to safety. This incident is sometimes placed in the East River, sometimes off Long Island. A second version claims that he was betrayed by a Tory who recognized him at the Widow Chichester's Tavern, popularly known as Mother Chich's. And a third version says that his cousin, Samuel Hale, saw him and betrayed him, though Samuel later denied any such thing. Perhaps a combination of the versions is the truth. Perhaps, being recognized, he panicked and so approached the wrong boat. At any rate, he was taken and searched. Found to be carrying incriminating papers, he was sentenced without court martial to be hanged. All sorts of stories have grown up about the cruelties to which Hale was subjected by the provost marshal, William Cunningham. Cunningham is even accused of ripping up a letter the prisoner was writing to his mother the night before the execution. This in face of the fact the "intended recipient" had been dead for four years. Nonetheless, Cunningham was a rough customer. In 1791 he was hanged in London for forgery, and he may well have failed to deliver the notes Hale wrote to his brother Enoch (not his mother) and his commanding officer that last night. Nor is it unlikely he refused Hale a *Bible* and access to a clergyman. Captives had a rough time of it in those days, and spies were treated that much worse.

Hale died on a makeshift gallows, without much ceremony,

September 22. If there is one fact an American knows about him it is that his last words were "I only regret that I have but one life to lose for my country." This is a paraphrase of a speech in Act IV of Joseph Addison's *Cato*: "What a pity is it that we can die but once to save our country!" That Hale knew these lines well enough to paraphrase them is quite likely, for the play was much read by educated Americans, including George Washington himself; but whether or not he paraphrased them at the moment of his death is a moot, moot point. Hale's friend, Captain Hull, quotes Captain John Montresor, chief engineer in the British Army, as describing Hale's last moments to American officers who received him under a flag of truce the night after the execution. Montresor is reported to have told the Americans of Hale's poise, and cited the famous words. However, the diary of Frederick Mackenzie, a British officer present at the hanging, records only that,[11]

> A person named Nathaniel Hales, a lieutenant in the rebel army and a native of Connecticut, was apprehended as a spy last night upon Long Island. And having this day made a full and free confession to the Commander-in-Chief of his being employed by Mr. Washington in that capacity, he was hanged at eleven o'clock in front of the park of artillery. He was about twenty-four years of age and had been educated at the College of New Haven in Connecticut. He behaved with great composure and resolution, saying he thought it the duty of every good officer to obey any orders given him by his Commander-in-Chief, and desired the spectators to be at all times prepared to meet death in whatever shape it might appear.

Nor does Nathan's brother, Enoch Hale, mention the phrase, although Enoch had gone directly to the American lines upon hearing of his brother's death and undoubtedly had spoken with officers who knew what Montresor said. Furthermore, the tombstone placed in the cemetery about 1814 by Hale's family reads only that he "resigned his life a sacrifice to his Country's liberty at New York, September 22d, 1776." My suspicion is he made some reference

[11] Frederick Mackenzie, *Dairy of . . . an officer of the regiment of Royal Welch fusiliers during the years 1775-1781*, 2 volumes (Cambridge, 1930), I, 62-63.

to the Addison lines, even if he didn't paraphrase directly. However, the reference was probably not melodramatic, but rather intermingled with the remarks Mackenzie refers to. Montresor may have recalled it, but it seems not to have been thought significant until Hale became a sort of martyr. References from the *Essex Journal* of Newburyport, Massachusetts in a February 13, 1777 article on Samuel Hale's supposed betrayal of his cousin and from the *Boston Independent Chronicle* of May 17, 1781 back up my supposition. The *Journal* recounts "Hale's last speech" in which he tells the British "that if he had ten thousand lives, he would lay them all down, if called to it, in defense of his injured, bleeding Country." The *Chronicle* says his last words were "I am so satisfied with the cause in which I have engaged, that my only regret is, that I have not more lives than one to offer in its service." Neither article cites its authority, but there is something about the *Chronicle* quotation that rings genuine to me. In 1821, in *The Spy*, Cooper mentions Hale, just after Henry Wharton is condemned. He footnotes the passage as follows:[12]

> [1] An American officer of this name was detected within the British lines, in disguise, in search of military information. He was tried and executed, as stated in the text, as soon as the preparations could be made. It is said that he was reproached under the gallows with dishonoring the rank he held by his fate. "What a death for an officer to die!" said one of his captors. "Gentlemen, any death is honorable when a man dies in a cause like that of America," was his answer.
>
> André was executed amid the tears of his enemies; Hale died unpitied and with reproaches in his ears; and yet one was the victim of ambition, and the other of devotion to his country. Posterity will do justice between them.

There is no doubt that Hale was very earnest in his patriotism. The aphorism that time has fixed upon him is completely appropriate and surely close enough.

Right after his death a pair of poetic tributes were published. One is quite good and may well have been sung as a ballad.[13]

[12] The footnote occurs in Chapter 26.

[13] Quoted from Moore, 131-133.

HALE IN THE BUSH, OR HIS CAPTURE AND DEATH.

The breezes went steadily through the tall pines,
Asaying "Oh! Hu-ush!" asaying "Oh! Hu-ush!"
As stilly stole by a bold legion of horse,
For Hale in the bush, for Hale in the bush.

"Keep still!" said the thrush, as she nestled her young
In a nest by the road, in a nest by the road;
"For the tyrants are near, and with them appear
What bodes us no good, what bodes us no good."

The brave captain heard it, and thought of his home
In a cot by the brook, in a cot by the brook;
With mother and sisters and memories dear,
He so gladly forsook, he so gladly forsook.

Cooling shades of the night were coming apace,
The tatoo had beat, the tatoo had beat;
The noble one sprang from his dark lurking place
To make his retreat, to make his retreat.

He warily trod on the dry rustling leaves
As he passed through the wood, as he passed through
the wood,
And silently gained his rude launch on the shore,
As she played with the flood, as she played with the flood.

The guards of the camp on that dark dreary night,
Had a murderous will, had a murderous will;
They took him and bore him afar from the shore,
To a hut on the hill, to a hut on the hill.

No mother was there, nor a friend who could cheer,
In that little stone cell, in that little stone cell;
But he trusted in love from his Father above–
In his heart all was well, in his heart all was well.

An ominous owl with his solemn bass voice
Sat moaning hard by, sat moaning hard by;
"The tyrant's proud minions most gladly rejoice,
For he must soon die, for he must soon die."

The brave fellow told them, no thing he restrained—
The cruel gen'ral; the cruel gen'ral!
His errand from camp, of the ends to be gained,
And said that was all, and said that was all.

They took him and bound him and bore him away,
Down the hill's grassy side, down the hill's grassy side.
'Twas there as base hirelings, in royal array,
His cause did deride, his cause did deride.

Five minutes were given, short moments, no more,
For him to repent, for him to repent.
He prayed for his mother—he asked not another—
To heaven he went, to heaven he went.

The faith of a martyr the tragedy showed,
As he trod the last stage, as he trod the last stage.
The British still shudder at gallant Hale's blood,
As his words do presage, as his words do presage.

"Thou pale king of terrors, thou life's gloomy foe,
Go frighten the slave, go frighten the slave;
Tell tyrants, to you their allegiance they owe—
No fears for the brave, no fears for the brave."

The other comes 75 lines into Book I of Timothy Dwight's interminable *The Conquest of Canaan.* Dwight had known Hale at college and no doubt was completely sincere in his tribute to an old friend, just dead:

How short his course, the prize how early won,
While weeping Friendship mourns her favorite gone.

But there was no general fuss over this spy who met his conventionalized fate, and one is interested to note that Cooper, writing in 1821, felt obliged to footnote his reference to Hale.

Local historians devoted to Connecticut and Yale University are almost completely responsible for developing the heroic Hale. All the way from an article called "Sketch of Capt. Nathan Hale" in the June 1839 *Yale Literary Magazine* to studies done after the First World War, just about every student of Hale has been a local

Connecticut writer, a graduate of Yale, or an employee of persons interested in Yale. Much of the early work centers on the idea that if the British André were a golden lad, the Americans must have had one every bit as splendid. Citing how "nobly gallant André died" these writers ask, in their various ways, "Doth *freedom* less deserve a tear?"[14] Their works were published in connection with surveys of Yale's role in the Revolution; with centennial celebrations, such as that of the secret college society, Linonian, of which Hale was an early member; and with the erection of monuments such as the one put up in Coventry, Connecticut by the Daughters of Freedom. Most of this poetry and prose looks pretty dated today, but the poem done in 1853 by Francis M. Finch, author of the well-known "The Blue and the Gray," for the centennial celebration of the Linonian Society is not bad. It begins,

> To drum-beat and heart-beat
> A soldier marches by:
> There's color in his cheek,
> There's courage in his eye:
> Yet to drum-beat and heart-beat
> In a moment he must die.

This revival is of course connected with America's 19th century need for national heroes, first as a replacement for the English heroes that had to be discarded, later as a verification for her heritage, local and national, in the face of the Mexican, Civil, Spanish-American, and World Wars.

In 1845 David Trumbull wrote a play called *The Death of Capt. Nathan Hale.* Shortly after, two books appeared which fixed the legend forever. One was an 1846 work by J. R. Simms called *The American Spy or Freedom's Early Sacrifice,*[15] supposedly "founded

[14] These quotations are from an anonymously written poem at the end of a "Sketch of Capt. Nathan Hale" printed in the June 1839 issue of the *Yale Literary Magazine.* See p. 342, Stanza 5.

[15] (Albany, 1846).

on fact." Simms tells us his "desire to interest young readers in the early history of the country, and at the same time do justice. . .to the ennobling virtues of a brave man. . ." The other was the 1856 biography by Isaac Stuart, a resident of Hartford.[16] In his prefatory remarks Stuart points out that "It is indeed 'hard' that a spirit as exalted as was that of Captain Hale – that a life and conduct like his own, so pure, so heroic, so disinterested, and so crowned by an act of martyrdom, one of the most galling and valiant on record – should not have been fitly commemorated hitherto. . . ." He felt it his duty to right this wrong, and taking his lead from the occasional poetry portrayed Hale accordingly. By the time these men had finished, "interest was high" and Hale had been "commemorated," "fitly" or not.

Others followed the now well-marked path. It soon became accepted historical fact that Hale martyred himself, won the hearts of his captors as surely as André had ever done, and passed on leaving a great aphorism that Americans would never forget. By 1886, Benson J. Lossing was able to write in his classic comparison[17] of Hale and André that,

> . . . funds will speedily be forthcoming sufficient to erect a magnificent monument in memory of NATHAN HALE, in the city where he died for his country. I recommend, as a portion of the inscription upon the monument, the subjoined epitaph, written fully thirty years ago, by George Gibbs, the ripe scholar and antiquary, who was at one time the librarian of the New York Historical Society: *
>
> "STRANGER, BENEATH THIS STONE
> LIES THE DUST OF
> A SPY,
> WHO PERISHED UPON THE GIBBETT;
> YET
> THE STORIED MARBLES OF THE GREAT,

[16] *Life of Captain Nathan Hale, the Martyr of the American Revolution* (Hartford, 1856).

[17] *The Two Spies–Nathan Hale and John André* (New York, 1886).

THE SHRINES OF HEROES,
ENTOMBED NOT ONE MORE WORTHY OF
HONOR
THAN HIM WHO HERE
SLEEPS HIS LAST SLEEP.
NATIONS
BOW WITH REVERENCE BEFORE THE DUST
OF HIM WHO DIES
A GLORIOUS DEATH,
URGED ON BY THE SOUND OF THE
TRUMPET
AND THE SHOUTS OF
ADMIRING THOUSANDS.
BUT WHAT REVERENCE, WHAT HONOR,
IS NOT DUE TO ONE
WHO FOR HIS COUNTRY ENCOUNTERED
EVEN AN INFAMOUS DEATH,
SOOTHED BY NO SYMPATHY,
ANIMATED BY NO PRAISE!

* A statue in plaster, modeled from a description of Hale's features and person, has been made by E. S. Wood, sculptor. It represents an athletic young man, with his coat and vest removed, his neck and upper portion of his chest bared by the turning down of the collar of his ruffled shirt, and holding in his right hand, which is resting upon his hip, the rope with which he is about to be suspended from the tree. The face of the martyr is an excellent ideal of the character of the young hero.

By 1899, a prominent playwright, Clyde Fitch, saw profit in choosing Nathan Hale as a subject for a successful play of love and honor, where his duties as a spy are set against his feelings for his historical sweetheart, Alice Adams.

The Fitch play is not a bad one, although it is terribly dated with its open sentimentality and melodramatic emphasis on the "I could not love thee, dear, so much" theme. Yet Nathan Hale was engaged to Alice or Alicia Adams, and she must have felt as other sweethearts and wives have felt about war and death. Alice had known Nathan since they were quite young. Her mother became the second wife of Richard Hale, Nathan's father, and they lived in the same house for awhile. Alice's older sister, Sarah, married Nathan's older brother, John, in 1771. The younger pair started along the same path and were childhood sweethearts, though Alice married an older man, Eleazer Ripley, when she was 16 and Nathan a senior at Yale. Ripley died less than two years after the marriage, leaving Alice a widow with a child at 18. She was engaged to Hale during the early days of the war and lost him when still but 19. Finally, she had some luck, marrying William Lawrence of Hartford and living happily ever after. She died at 88 in 1845. Consistently, she is reported a sweet person, and Fitch didn't have to falsify her to get the appropriate heroine.

William Ordway Partridge did a statue of the spy for Yale University. In researching Hale's story in preparation for the work, he became sufficiently interested to write, in 1902, a full-length biography.[18] In it Hale is depicted as "trustworthy, loyal, thrifty, kind . . ." – as near perfect as a man can be. Partridge informs us that he was asked to do the statue because the Yale alumni ". . . felt Hale was their typical hero . . ." – *Nathan Hale: The Ideal Patriot,* archetype of the Yale man, his legend now suited to those late 19th and early 20th century days when to be a Yale man was to have attained the first significant rung on the ladder of success. Thus, in 1908, when Charles Cushing followed Fitch in dramatizing the story, he was able to introduce the most extravagant climax of all. Hale not only surrenders himself to a British officer, but refuses, even in the face of entreaties by his captors, to effect an escape.

Distinct as such fame was, it was nonetheless a local fame, almost certain to fade as the importance of Yale was undermined by broad educational policies and admission standards based on brains. If it were not for the aphorism, the name Nathan Hale might need a footnote today as it did in Cooper's time. My 16-year-old daughter didn't even react when I asked her who he was the other day. "Haven't you ever heard of the man who had 'but one life to lose for his country'?" I asked, flabbergasted. "Oh yes, I remember, that's who he was!" came the insouciant reply.

Earlier I wrote that Harvey Birch was made up pretty much out of whole cloth. So was Hale, though he is a product of local pride where the other is the product of a novelist's compulsions.

[18] *Nathan Hale: the Ideal Patriot* (New York, 1902).

John André actually develops on the fringes of and in the manner of folk tradition. His name has survived among people who have never heard of Cooper and who wouldn't go to Yale, even today's Yale, if they could get in. True, André is not a well-known folk hero of the sort Davy Crockett or Mike Fink is, but his legend in ballad form, though of restricted distribution, is not contrived or the least bit phoney where it is to be found.

There was something about this Englishman that tugged at the hearts of Colonists and Tories alike. In a war where it was hard to distinguish between treason and loyalty, his fate concerned both sides. Swiss by parentage and education, a person of some poetic and artistic talent, John André was an adjutant-general in the British army and 28 years old in 1779. Ambitious, somewhat egotistical, he had taken on the task of corrupting American leaders. After extensive efforts to bring Samuel Parsons to the British side, he learned in May of that year that an American general, who remained unnamed, was willing to sell out. The general was, of course, Benedict Arnold. Arnold had long been resentful over his treatment by the American military. Difficult to begin with, he had been passed over for promotion and actually court-martialled for improper commercial dealings while American commander in Philadelphia. What's more, he was a social climber with expensive tastes. When he married Peggy Shippen, an attractive, unscrupulous, money-hungry girl with definite Tory connections, circumstances had combined to make treason appealing. After securing the command of West Point, possibly with the idea of betraying it, and entering into long negotiations with André, the stage was set in late summer, 1780. By then Arnold had converted as much of his property as he could to cash, had even transferred some holdings to London, and had been promised a reward from Sir Henry Clinton in New York. He had also done what he could to disperse American forces away from West Point and generally prepared for a fatal split of Colonial strength by means of a simple British takeover of the major barrier to control of the Hudson.

A meeting to work out final details was arranged on neutral ground about fifteen miles below the Beverley Robinson house that served as Arnold's headquarters across from the Point. Before dawn

I *Benedict Arnold Major General* do acknowledge the UNITED STATES of AMERICA to be Free, Independent and Sovereign States, and declare that the people thereof owe no allegiance or obedience to George the Third, King of Great-Britain; and I renounce, refuſe and abjure any allegiance or obedience to him; and I do *Swear* that I will, to the utmoſt of my power, ſupport, maintain and defend the ſaid United States againſt the ſaid King George the Third, his heirs and ſucceſſors, and his or their abettors, aſſiſtants and adherents, and will ſerve the ſaid United States in the office of *Major General* which I now hold, with fidelity, according to the beſt of my ſkill and underſtanding.

Sworn before me this *B Arnold*

30th. May 1778 at the

Artillery Park Valley Forge *Henry Knox*

"The Oath of Allegiance to the United States signed by Benedict Arnold in 1778 at Valley Forge"

on September 22, André was rowed out from the British man-o-war *Vulture* to his fate. He had been instructed by Clinton to remain on the *Vulture* and not to enter the American lines. He had also been told not to disguise himself, not to accept passes, and not to carry papers, but to conduct all negotiations verbally. André couldn't have ignored this mature, fool-proof advice more completely if he had been drunk through the whole affair. He did leave the *Vulture*, met Arnold at the home of Joshua Smith within the American lines, and accepted a pass to assure his safety. When the American forces fired upon the *Vulture* and she had to drop down river, André disguised himself and started his return by land, carrying papers for Clinton. Even then, he surely would have gotten safely back, had he any resourcefulness at all.

Wearing a civilian cloak and travelling under the name of John Anderson, a title he had used throughout his negotiations, he set out with Joshua Smith as guide at sundown the 22nd. After spending the night with a local farmer, the two headed toward White Plains. Fifteen miles from their goal, Smith turned back, leaving John Anderson to travel alone. This was the "Neutral Ground," that dangerous portion of Westchester County where no stranger was safe from the marauding of two renegade groups: the Skinners, who claimed they were patriots, but who were really interested in robbery; and the Cowboys, who claimed they were Loyalists, but who were really interested in robbery.

It is not known whether John Paulding, David Williams, and Isaac Van Wart were affiliated with the Skinners, but they certainly were operating in such a fashion when along came John Anderson, obviously a gentleman, alone and well-heeled. Because Paulding, the most forceful, was wearing part of a stolen British uniform, André thought the men were Cowboys and immediately identified himself as a British officer. Paulding, a former New York militiaman, who had recently escaped from the hardship of a British prison, had no love for the Crown. When André learned the trio were Americans, he said that he was happy to find his original ideas wrong and claimed to be an American himself, producing Arnold's pass as evidence. The three, however, insisted he was a British officer, probably so they could rationalize robbing him under the New

York act which allowed them to claim as prize property taken from a captured enemy. They demanded his money. André, who had none, tried to trade on their avarice for his release, telling them he could get cash from Clinton if they would escort him down river. They were wary of a trick, and, after searching him and finding that he carried nothing but papers, decided to take him to the American commanding officer in the area.

André's fatal mistake was not presenting Arnold's pass to these three renegades as soon as they stopped him. If they really had been British they would have taken him to his own lines for questioning. If they had been Americans they would have been afraid not to honor such a document. Even then, he might have been all right, had it not been for Major Benjamin Tallmadge, Nathan Hale's college friend. Lt. Colonel John Jameson, the Virginia cavalry officer on duty was no genius, but he did what he felt was his job. He sent André, under guard, to Arnold at West Point and the captured papers to Washington. Had André reached West Point, he and Arnold would have escaped together. As luck would have it, however, Tallmadge returned from reconnaissance and, hearing about the capture of the forenoon, became suspicious and persuaded Jameson to have "Anderson" recalled. Tallmadge, who had been in intelligence and had heard rumors of a sell-out by an American general, may well have wanted to seize Arnold also, but Jameson certainly did not follow such advice, if it were offered. In fact, he allowed the report of "Anderson's" capture to go through to the Point, enabling Arnold to escape to New York before Washington could be found. In the meantime, the courier carrying the captured papers to Washington missed connections with the General who was in Connecticut conferring with Rochambeau. Things combined so that Arnold was informed of André's capture while breakfasting with Washington's unsuspecting aides who had come to tell him their commander would be at the Robinson house in about an hour. By the time Washington arrived, his host-to-be was gone, never to return. By the time he learned the reason, Arnold was long since aboard the *Vulture*.

André was hanged on October 2 for his part in the affair. This was military form and was carried out without appetite. The American Board of General Officers seems to have been relatively sympathetic to André's plight and far more disturbed by their peer who had gotten away. Public opinion and feeling throughout the Continental Army was much the same. Nonetheless, the fate of the captured spy was long since fixed. Clinton made an effort to get André, of whom he was sincerely fond, a pardon, but as an exchange for Arnold would have been the only bargain possible, his efforts failed. Arnold himself tried to help, but the messages arrived too late. André was also frustrated in his desire to be shot like an officer instead of hanged like a spy. His final aphorism, more sophisticated than Hale's, emphasizes this wish: "I am reconciled to my death, but I detest the mode."

The ballad, "Major André's Capture," reflects the wide publicity this event received. Paulding and his associates stoutly denied Skinner-like behaviour. They maintained they were offered huge bribes by André, but because of their loyalty and patriotism turned their prisoner, whom they at once suspected, over to Lt. Colonel Jameson. Evidently, their story was believed, probably because it is the kind of story one wants to believe. The three received medals and a cash reward for what they had done, and as the Pauldings later became one of the prominent families in New York City and the Hudson River Valley, nothing was done to undermine popular belief in John Paulding's sterling character. The ballad itself, in which Paulding appears as a bold, young scout; André as a noble victim; and Arnold as a rat, also had a lot to do with the fixing of the image. It was printed in a number of 19th century songsters and has had a steady, if not extensive, folk circulation. Its final lines couldn't be more pointed.[19]

BRAVE PAULDING AND THE SPY.

Come all you brave Americans, and unto me give ear,
And I'll sing you a ditty that will your spirits cheer,
Concerning a young gentleman whose age was twenty-two;
He fought for North America; his heart was just and true.

[19] See Laws, *NAB*, A2. The text below is from Moore, 316-321.

They took him from his dwelling, and they did him confine,
They cast him into prison, and kept him there a time;
But he with resolution resolved not long to stay;
He set himself at liberty, and soon he ran away.

He with a scouting party went down to Tarrytown
Where he met a British officer, a man of high renown,
Who says unto these gentlemen, "You're of the British cheer,
I trust that you can tell me if there's any danger near?"

Then up stepped this young hero, John Paulding was his name,
"Sir, tell us where you're going, and also whence you came?"
"I bear the British flag, sir; I've a pass to go this way,
I'm on an expedition, and have no time to stay."

Then round him came this company, and bid him to dismount;
"Come, tell us where you're going, give us a strict account;
For we are now resolved that you shall ne'er pass by."
Upon examination they found he was a spy.

He begged for his liberty, he plead for his discharge,
And oftentimes he told them, if they'd set him at large,
"Here's all the gold and silver I have laid up in store,
But when I reach the city, I'll give you ten times more."

"I want not the gold and silver you have laid up in store,
And when you get to New York you need not send us more.
But you may take your sword in hand, to gain your liberty,
And if that you do conquer me, O, then you shall be free."

"The time it is improper our valor for to try,
For if we take our swords in hand, then one of us must die;
I am a man of honor, with courage brave and bold,
And I fear not the face of clay, although 'tis clothed in gold."

He saw that his conspiracy would soon be brought to light;
He begged for pen and paper, and asked leave to write
A line to *General Arnold*, to let him know his fate,
And beg for his assistance; but now it was too late.

When the news it came to Arnold, it put him in a fret;
He walked the room in trouble till tears his cheeks did wet;
The story soon went through the camp, and also through the fort.
And he called for the Vulture, and sailed for New York.

Now Arnold to New York has gone, a-fighting for his king,
And left poor Major André on the gallows for to swing;
When he was executed he looked both meek and mild;
He looked on his spectators, and pleasantly he smiled.

It moved each eye with pity, caused each heart to bleed;
And every one wished him released and Arnold in his stead.
He was a man of honor, in Britain he was born;
To die upon the gallows most highly he did scorn.

A bumper to John Paulding! now let your voices sound;
Fill up your flowing glasses, and drink his health around;
Also to those gentlemen who bore him company;
Success to North America, ye sons of Liberty!

The original, clearly an American "come ye all" ballad, can be found in such publications as *The Forget Me Not Songster* of Philadelphia (no date) and *The New American Songster* (Philadelphia, 1817). There is no question that the folk texts derive directly from such semi-literary sources, and we can see the process of oral variation just beginning to work in a text like the one Herbert Halpert found in New Jersey in the 1930s.[20] The loss of detail, the corruption of André's name, the concentration of action all show that this songster ballad is on its way to becoming a genuine folksong.

MAJOR ANDROW.

I'll sing you a small ditty that will your spirits cheer,
Concerning a young gentleman whose age were twenty-two,
And he fought for North Americay with a heart both just and true.

The English they did taken him and kep' him close confined,
They put him into prison and kep' him for some time.

By his been bold and valiant, resolved not there to stay,
He set himself at liberty and so he come away,
He set himself at liberty and so he come away.

'Twas of the scoutin' party which rode from Tarrytown,
A meeting this young officer, a man of high renown.
"I think by your experience, sir, you are the British force,
I'll trust to you to tell to me the danger I a-roar."

[20] *JAF*, 1939, 62, as sung by Stacey Bozorth of Buddtown, N. J.

"Come tell to me your business, sir and when from hence you came,
Or I'll have you well-ed search-ed sir before you do pass by,"
By strict examination, found him to be a spy.

When he found his projects would soon be brought to light
He asked for ink and paper, and liberty to write
A line to traitor Arnold to let him know his fate,
He begged on his desistance, till last it was too late.

When traitor Arnold read those lines it put him in a fright,
He called for men and ba-argey, and sailed for New York straight;
And now he goes a-cruiting and fighting for a king,
He left poor Major Androw on the gallows for to swing.

On the day of execution he looked both meek and mild,
He looked on his spectatons, and gave a pleasant smile,
Which filled each mind with horrow, and caused each heart to bleed.
And every man wished Androw clear, and Arnold in his stead.

John André has always reminded me of Mary Hamilton—young, vibrant, appealing, "the golden lads and girls" who must "like chimney sweepers come to dust." Her words,

Little did me mither kin
The day she cradled me
The paths I was to wander in
The death I was to dee.

fit his story too, and I can envision them entering his ballad. The song concentrates on one of those universal themes the folk treasure, and should it continue to be sung the tragic fact of youth cut off in its prime must ultimately transcend historical fact, reducing actuality to formula, obliterating the real André as surely as it has obliterated some unhappy girl in Mary of Scotland's court.

The story of this spy doesn't end with his execution and ballad, however. Washington was particularly bitter towards Arnold, and there is no doubt that he offered to spare André if Clinton would just let the Americans place "Arnold in his stead." Clinton, fond as he was of the Major, couldn't really do this, for he had to consider Arnold not as a traitor, but as a rebel who had finally seen the error of his ways. The result was that all overtures of this sort were turned down, and the Americans not only had to execute André, but had to come up with some plan for abducting Arnold if they were to get the chance to hang him. The plan that was concocted is one of the great spy stories of history.

Light Horse Harry Lee, the father of the great Civil War general, was given the job of selecting the man. He chose Sergeant-Major John Champe, a fellow Virginian, about 23 years old. Champe was to desert to the British, join their forces in New York City, and gaining Arnold's confidence through prepared letters abduct him. Under no conditions was Arnold to be killed. The Americans were determined to try him and hang him as a public example. Originally, this abduction was to enable Washington to negotiate for André's life, but things didn't work out that way. Champe didn't even arrive in Manhattan until October 19, more than two weeks after the execution. He nearly didn't make it at all.

It had been agreed that Champe was to stage his own desertion, as Lee wanted no one else in on the plot. Stealing a headquarters orderly book to make things look real, he decided to ride through the patrols in northern New Jersey and cross to Staten Island from Paulus Hook. His desertion was spotted almost at once, and Lee, in spite of delaying in every way he could think of, finally had to order him pursued. Unfortunately, it was raining and Champe's horse left a simple trail of footprints. Near Bergen, where the pursuers got within a half-mile of him, Champe decided to make straight for the Hudson and to gain haven in two British galleys that were anchored there. He just made it, dismounting and splashing through the marshes until he could swim toward the ships. The British saw the "escape," drove the rebel pursuers off with gun-fire, and sent a boat out to rescue him. There was no suspicion. Champe and his orderly book were given a warm welcome, and within twenty-four hours Lee's agent was interviewed by Clinton himself.

Champe nearly pulled off the abduction. He contacted Arnold, gained his confidence, and was offered his rebel rank of Sergeant-Major in the General's new troop unit, the "American Legion." With two other agents in New York, he arranged to abduct Arnold from his garden where he had the habit of urinating when he came home late at night. The idea was to tie and gag him, then walk him as though drunk through the back streets of the city, and row him across the River to Hoboken before dawn. Washington and Lee were informed, and the latter was to be at the riverbank to await Champe and his prisoner.

Lee showed up with a cavalry detachment and extra mounts for Champe and Arnold, but no one ever came. It wasn't until January 2, 1781 that he learned what had happened. Champe, as a member of the American Legion, had been ordered to embark for Virginia. He spent the night set for his great coup aboard a transport which he could not leave until he and his intended victim were both in the South. Once in Virginia he escaped from the British and joined Nathanael Greene's forces on the Congaree River in South Carolina. Greene sent him back to Washington and Lee, who discharged him, fearing his fate were he to be captured. The Americans tried to abduct Arnold again on the Chesapeake Bay shore, but without success, and the traitor was never to be punished, except by his unpopularity, even in England, and the equation of infamy with his name.

A ballad of Champe's adventure was composed around 1781 and sung fairly widely to the tune of "Barbara Allen." It is clearly a popular song and has no oral tradition to speak of. Laws doesn't include it in his *Native American Balladry*, even as a piece of "doubtful currency," and I don't know that it has been collected from the folk. However, it undoubtedly did its bit to fix the image of Arnold as a dastard and André as an unfortunate victim of chance. It is cut from the same cloth as "Major André's Capture."[21]

SERGEANT CHAMPE.

Come, sheathe your swords! My gallant boys,
And listen to my story,
How Sergeant Champe, one gloomy night,
Set off to catch the Tory.

You see the general had got mad,
To think his plans were thwarted,
And swore by all, both good and bad,
That Arnold should be carted.

[21] From Moore, 322-328.

So unto Lee he sent a line,
And told him all his sorrow,
And said that he must start the hunt,
Before the coming morrow.

Lee found a sergeant in his camp,
Made up of bone and muscle,
Who ne'er knew fear, and many a year
With Tories had a tussle.

Bold Champe, when mounted on old Rip,
All button'd up from weather,
Sang out, "Good-bye!" crack'd off his whip,
And soon was in the heather.

He gallop'd on towards Paulus Hook,
Improving every instant—
Until a patrol, wide awake,
Descried him in the distance.

On coming up, the guard call'd out
And ask'd him where he's going—
To which he answer'd with his spur,
And left him in the mowing.

The bushes pass'd him like the wind,
And pebbles flew asunder.
The guard was left far, far behind,
All mix'd with mud and wonder.

Lee's troops paraded, all alive,
Although 'twas one the morning,
And counting o'er a dozen or more,
One sergeant is found wanting.

A little hero, full of spunk,
But not so full of judgment,
Press'd Major Lee to let him go,
With the bravest of his reg'ment.

Lee summon'd cornet Middleton,
Expressed what was urgent,
And gave him orders how to go
To catch the rambling sergeant.

Then forty troopers, more or less,
Set off across the meader;
'Bout thirty-nine went jogging on
A-following their leader.

At early morn, adown a hill
They saw the sergeant sliding;
So fast he went, it was not ken't,
Whether he's rode, or riding.

None looked back, but on they spurr'd,
A-gaining every minute.
To see them go, 'twould done you good,
You'd thought old Satan in it.

The sergeant miss'd 'em, by good luck,
And took another tracing,
He turn'd his horse from Paulus Hook,
Elizabethtown facing.

It was the custom of Sir Hal
To send his galleys cruising,
And so it happened just then,
That two were at Van Deusen's.

Strait unto these the sergeant went,
And left old Rip, all standing,
A waiting for the blown cornet,
At Squire Van Deusen's landing.

The troopers didn't gallop home,
But rested from their labors;
And some 'tis said took gingerbread
And cider from the neighbors.

'Twas just at eve the trooper reach'd
The camp they left that morning.
Champe's empty saddle, unto Lee,
Gave an unwelcome warning.

"If Champe has suffered, 'tis my fault";
So thought the generous major:
"I would not have his garment touch'd,
For millions on a wager!"

The cornet told him all he knew,
Excepting of the cider.
"The troopers, all, spurr'd very well
But Champe was the best rider!"

And so it happen'd that brave Champe
Unto Sir Hal deserted,
Deceiving him, and you, and me,
And into York was flirted.

He saw base Arnold in his camp,
Surrounded by the legion,
And told him of the recent prank
That threw him in that region.

Then Arnold grinn'd, and rubb'd his hands,
And e'enmost chok'd with pleasure,
Not thinking Champe was all the while
A "taking of his measure."

"Come now," says he, "my bold soldier,
As you're within our borders,
Let's drink our fill, old care to kill,
To-morrow you'll have orders."

Full soon the British fleet set sail!
Say! wasn't that a pity?
For thus it was brave Sergeant Champe
Was taken from the city.

To southern climes the shipping flew,
And anchored in Virginia,
When Champe escaped and join'd his friends
Among the picininni.

Base Arnold's head, by luck, was sav'd,
Poor André's was gibbeted,
Arnold's to blame for André's fame,
And André's to be pitied.

These, then, are the ways in which legendary heroes are created. Why, after their births, some are set adrift and some are fostered by the more educated portion of this nation is our last pressing question. We shall confront it by looking at four representative case histories: first, that of Timothy Murphy, a genuine folk hero, if only to see that the most appropriate sort of Revolutionary legend may not survive in fakelore; second, that of Ethan Allen, also a genuine and appropriate folk hero, if only to see the power of the West in our legendary history; finally, those of Paul Revere and Ben Franklin, neither of whom have much claim to being genuine folk heroes, but whose stories every educated American finds himself "married to" for better or for worse. If these four chapters prove nothing else, they will prove the role that print plays in the flowering of fakelore.

8 "The Man Who Shot General Fraser"

Timothy Murphy, Indian-hater, is said to have been born in Minisink, New Jersey in 1751 of parents who had emigrated from Ireland. In view of his name, the last fact seems likely. The other two are less certain, though they tend to have become fixed because his first biographer, William Sigsby, a law clerk in Schoharie, New York, set them down as fact in an 1839 volume entitled *The Life and Adventures of Timothy Murphy, the Benefactor of Schoharie*. He probably grew up in Pennsylvania. There is a legend that he appeared in New York State in his youth with a company of rafters who were returning from a trip down the Delaware River, and that he married and lived at Stamford and Harpersfield. His hate of Indians is supposed to date from this period, for one day he returned from a trip for supplies to find his young wife and babies slaughtered. But the fact is we know little about his youth. For one thing, his name is too common. For another, records just weren't kept at his level of society.[1]

[1] The definitive life of Tim Murphy is Michael J. O'Brien's *Timothy Murphy, Hero of the American Revolution* (New York, 1941). This is a thorough, if a bit gullible, study of a career now well obscured by the mists of time.

In July 1775 Murphy is known to have joined the group that was to become the First Pennsylvania Regiment of the Continental Line and in July 1777 to have gone north with Captain Gabriel Long in one of two companies of Morgan's Riflemen. These riflemen were invaluable to General Gates as he got ready to confront Burgoyne at Saratoga. Men like Murphy were little more than white Indians, and a good bit more manageable than the red variety. They were used as scouts and spies. They loved to fight and were well-versed in guerilla methods. Murphy, for example, is said to have slipped behind the British lines, discovered an officer in his tent, and brought him at knife-point to the American camp. However, his great moment came on October 7, 1777 when General Simon Fraser, Burgoyne's top commander, was shot from his horse at the second battle of Freeman's Farm, also called the Battle of Bemis Heights or Stillwater. Murphy has been given credit for pulling the trigger.

Fraser was a favorite in the British Army. Mrs. General Riedesel, as she is called, describes his death in the *Letters and Journals* she wrote as she travelled with her German husband through this and other campaigns.[2]

. . . they cried out to me, "War! war!" which meant that they were going to fight. This completely overwhelmed me, and I had scarcely got back to my quarters when I heard skirmishing and firing, which by degrees became constantly heavier, until finally the noises became frightful. It was a terrible cannonade, and I was more dead than alive.

About three o'clock in the afternoon, in place of the guests who were to have dined with me, they brought in to me, upon a litter, poor General Frazer (one of my expected guests), mortally wounded. Our dining table, which was already spread, was taken away, and in its place they fixed up a bed for the General. I sat in a corner of the room trembling and quaking. The noises grew continually louder. The thought that they might bring in my husband in the same manner was to me dreadful, and tormented me incessantly. The general said to the surgeon, "Do not conceal anything from me. Must I die?" The ball had gone through his bowels, precisely as in the case of Major

[2] See *Letters and Journals relating to the War of the American Revolution and the Capture of the German troops at Saratoga. By Mrs. General Riedesel*, as edited by William Leeke Stone, Jr. (Albany, 1867), 196-197.

Harnage. Unfortunately, however, the General had eaten a hearty breakfast, by reason of which the intestines were distended, and the ball, so the surgeon said, had not gone, as in the case of Major Harnage, between the intestines, but through them. I heard him often, amidst his groans, exclaim, "Oh, fatal ambition! Poor General Burgoyne! My poor wife!" Prayers were read to him. He then sent a message to General Burgoyne, begging that he would have him buried the following day at six o'clock in the evening, on the top of a hill, which was a sort of a redoubt.

I knew no longer which way to turn. The whole entry and the other rooms were filled with the sick, who were suffering with the camp sickness, a kind of dysentery. Finally, toward evening, I saw my husband coming, upon which I forgot all my sufferings, and thanked God that he had spared him to me. He ate in great haste with me and his adjutant, behind the house. We had been told that we had gained an advantage over the enemy, but the sorrowful and downcast faces which I beheld bore witness to the contrary, and before my husband again went away, he drew me to one side and told me that everything might go very badly, and that I must keep myself in constant readiness for departure, but by no means to give anyone the least inkling of what I was doing. I therefore pretended that I wished to move into my new house the next morning, and I had everything packed up.

My Lady Ackland occupied a tent not far from our house. In this she slept, but during the day was in camp. Suddenly one came to tell her that her husband was mortally wounded, and had been taken prisoner. At this she became very wretched. We comforted her by saying that it was only a slight wound, but as no one could nurse him as well as herself, we counseled her to go at once to him, to do which she could certainly obtain permission. She loved him very much, although he was a plain, rough man, and was almost daily intoxicated; with this exception, however, he was an excellent officer. She was the loveliest of women. I spent the night in this manner—at one time comforting her, and at another looking after my children, whom I had put to bed. As for myself, I could not go to sleep, as I had General Frazer and all the other gentlmen in my room, and was constantly afraid that my children would wake up and cry, and thus disturb the poor dying man, who often sent to beg my pardon for making me so much trouble.

About three o'clock in the morning, they told me that he could not last much longer. I had desired to be apprised of the approach of this moment. I accordingly wrapped up the children in the bed coverings, and went with them into the entry. Early in the morning, at eight o'clock, he expired. After they had washed the corpse, they wrapped it in a sheet and laid it on a bedstead. We then again came into the room, and had this sad sight before us the whole day. At every instant, also, wounded officers of my acquaintance arrived, and the cannonade again began. A retreat was spoken of, but there was not the least movement made toward it. About four o'clock in the afternoon, I saw the new house which had been built for me, in flames; the enemy, therefore, were not far from us. We learned that General Burgoyne intended to fulfill the last wish of General Frazer, and to have him buried at six o'clock, in the place designated by him. This occasioned an unnecessary delay, to which a part of the misfortunes of the army was owing. Precisely at six o'clock the corpse was brought out, and we saw the entire body of generals with their retinues on the hill assisting at the obsequies.

Whether Murphy fired the shot that caused this consternation in the British ranks can never be settled short of revelation. First legend and then written history have given him credit so consistently that most formal students of the Revolution, if they know nothing about Murphy, know that he killed Fraser at Saratoga. It is interesting to note that Sigsby, the first biographer, fails to mention the fact. The story appears to originate on pages 259-260 in Jeptha R. Simms' *History of Schoharie County and the Border Wars of New York* published in Albany in 1845. Simms' claimed to have interviewed Murphy's son, who insisted that his father had shot Fraser. Later historians, probably agreeing that Murphy certainly should have been the one to shoot Fraser even if he weren't, accepted Simms' statement as gospel. In 1860, Benson Lossing in his widely read *Pictorial Field-Book of the Revolution* wrote,[3]

The name of the rifleman who killed General Fraser was Timothy Murphy. He took sure aim from a small tree in which he was posted, and saw Fraser fall on the discharge of his rifle. Fraser told his friends before he died that he saw the man who shot him, and that he was in a tree.

[3] (New York, 1860), I, 62, Footnote 2.

"The Death of General Fraser" (from a 1794 London engraving)

In 1895, William Leeke Stone, Jr. in his *Visits to the Saratoga Battlegrounds* "followed the leader,"

> Brigadier-General Fraser, who, up to this time, had been stationed on the right, noticed the critical situation of the centre, and hurried to its succor with the twenty-fourth Regiment. Conspicuously mounted on an iron-gray horse, he was all activity and vigilance, riding from one part of the division to another, and animating his troops by his example. Perceiving that the fate of the day rested upon that officer, Morgan, who with his riflemen, was immediately opposed to Fraser's corps, took a few of his sharpshooters aside, among them whom was the celebrated marksman "Tim" Murphy—men on whose precision of aim he could rely—and said to them, "that gallant officer yonder is General Fraser. I admire and respect him, but it is necessary for our good that he should die. Take your station in that cluster of bushes and do your duty." Within a few moments a rifle-ball cut through the crupper of Fraser's horse, and another passed through his horse's mane. Calling attention to this, Fraser's aid said, "It is evident that you are marked out for particular aim; would it not be prudent for you to retire from this place." Fraser replied, "My duty forbids me to fly from danger." The next moment he fell mortally wounded by a ball from the rifle of Murphy, and was carried off the field by two grenadiers. Upon the fall of Fraser, dismay seized the British.

Stone's book, however, also includes an account of the battle by Ebenezer Mattoon, who was in the midst of the fighting, and who claimed that an old man with a long hunting gun fired the famous shot. This man who is called "Daddy" could not have been Murphy, for Murphy would have been 26 at the time. The man is meant to have fired, then asked Mattoon whom he had killed and been told, "Fraser." Stone faithfully thinks the old man shot some officer, but not Fraser.[4]

Although Henry Cabot Lodge states in his 1898 *The Story of the Revolution* that Fraser was killed by "a Virginia rifleman,"[5] the deed has remained Murphy's. Michael J. O'Brien in his 1941 "definitive" biography of the scout says that Murphy was known to the

[4] (Albany, 1895), 31 and 244-246.

[5] (New York, 1898), I, 256.

general public for this shot and even cites the indignation Murphy would express when asked how many times he fired to make the hit. Murphy was renowned for his ability with a rifle, accounts such as the following clustering about his name.[6]

Then, too, when Tim was a little fellow, my grandad said, his old man used to take little white marbles, about as small as a kernel of pop corn and have Tim pop them off as he tossed them into the air. Then his old man had so much confidence in young Tim that he'd show off to the neighbors by putting a clay pipe in his mouth, while the boy took aim and knocked it out from between his teeth. No wonder Tim spent his life a-killin' the Indians off the way he did.

* * * *

If you are a hunter, you may wish to know how expert the best shot in Morgan's Rifles was. Well, General Fraser didn't have a chance. In 1781, after he had brought in a fine lot of deerskins and cured them, Tim conducted a competition for marksmen who were to receive a hide as prize. In the shooting for the skins Tim was barred—he had already been paid by the competitors. Afterwards he proposed an additional competition for a gallon of rum, a super-extra-shoot in which the Old Master could compete. A small piece of paper was affixed by a brass nail to a blazed tree. Pacing off one hundred yards, he rested his rifle on his hat, as he always did when he took pains, and at the first shot drove the nail right into the tree.

* * * *

Then there was the day in 1799 when the four best marksmen in Schoharie County, including Tim's old scouting partner, David Elerson, took turns holding between their knees a target made of a little piece of white paper fastened to a board two feet long. At one hundred yards the other three champions cut the edge of the paper; when Tim fired, the paper fell from the board—his bullet had driven the *pin* through the wood.

[6] The last two anecdotes are from Harold Thompson, *Body, Boots and Britches* (New York, 1940), 61-62. The first is in the personal files of the late Dr. Thompson at the Cooperstown Folklore Archives. Material from this file, some of which appears below, was sent me by Louis C. Jones, Director of the New York State Historical Association, with the permission of Mrs. Thompson. Much of it was collected by students as part of class assignments.

Nevertheless, I am quite cynical about the whole matter. A friend of mine, David Winslow is an authority on New York State. He wrote the following comment for me, after having visited the battlefield.

. . . it is difficult to see, if the markers are in the correct locations, how Murphy could have fired over the hill. Although there are no trees now at the spot, it is very likely that Murphy was posted in a tree, for even yet in this part of New York State, and probably elsewhere, this is a popular method of hunting deer. But it is still hard to see how anybody could have fired over a hill.

Harold Thompson, in *Body, Boots, and Britches* cites the same difficulty.[7] But that problem doesn't force me toward disbelief as surely as my general instincts about legend. I will concede that the markers are wrongly placed, that the tree was very high, that Murphy had moved to a spot where he could have taken unobstructed aim, but I can't get away from the fact that Murphy was locally known for his marksmanship, that he assumed heroic stature, and that later, when in politics, he was colored by what we call "promotion"—factors which would naturally sweep an event like the shooting of Fraser toward him.

Furthermore, the shot that killed Fraser was nowhere near as unusual as it is made to look. No doubt a number of Morgan's riflemen could hit almost anything they could see. A description of frontier hunters, taken from the *Virginia Gazette* of 1775, appears in the Blair and Meine biography of Mike Fink.[8]

On Friday last there arrived at Lancaster, Pennsylvania Captain Crescap's company of riflemen consisting of 130 active and brave young fellows, many of whom were in the late expedition of Lord Dunmore against the Indians. These men have been bred in the woods to hardships and danger from their infancy. With their rifles in their hands they assume a kind of omnipotence over their enemies. Two brothers in the company took a piece of board 5 inches by 7 inches

[7] See *Body, Boots, and Britches*, 58.

[8] Quoted from Walter Blair and Franklin J. Meine, *Half Horse, Half Alligator* (Chicago, 1956), 6.

with a bit of white paper the size of a dollar nailed in the center, and while one held the board upright gripped between his knees, the other at 60 yards without any kind of rest shot 8 balls through it successfully and spared his brother's thighs. Another . . . held a barrel stave close against his body perpendicularly while one of his comrades at the same distance shot several bullets through it. The spectators were told that there were upwards of 50 persons in the company who could do the same.

Three of Crescap's men, it was reported elsewhere, "fired simultaneously at a buzzard flying overhead. The bird fell . . . and . . . examination proved that all three bullets had hit their mark."

Stories of frontier marksmanship, before and after the war, are numerous and in many cases authenticated. They hold that from forty paces, shooting at the head of a nail, a good shot could hit the nail squarely; that from fifty yards on a dark night many a settler could fan a candle flame by hitting the tip, without extinguishing it. At fifty yards up to ninety yards, Daniel Boone and others of his day could "bark" squirrels—knock the animals off branches by clipping the bark from beneath their feet.

At first glance, such descriptions may seem fabulous. I recall Mark Twain's skeptical reaction to the description of a frontier shooting contest in "Fenimore Cooper's Literary Offenses."

The reader will find some examples of Cooper's high talent for inaccurate observation in the account of the shooting-match in *The Pathfinder*.

"A common wrought nail was driven lightly into the target, its head having been first touched with paint."

The color of the paint is not stated—an important omission, but Cooper deals freely in important omissions. No, after all, it was not an important omission; for this nailhead is a *hundred yards from* the marksmen, and could not be seen by them at that distance, no matter what its color might be. How far can the best eyes see a common house-fly? A hundred yards? It is quite impossible. Very well; eyes that cannot see a house-fly that is a hundred yards away cannot see an ordinary nail head at that distance, for the size of the two objects is the same. It takes a keen eye to see a fly or a nail-head at fifty yards—one hundred and fifty feet. Can the reader do it?

The nail was lightly driven, its head painted, and game called.

Then the Cooper miracles began. The bullet of the first marksman chipped an edge of the nail-head; the next man's bullet drove the nail a little way into the target—and removed all the paint. Haven't the miracles gone far enough now? Not to suit Cooper; for the purpose of this whole scheme is to show off his prodigy, Deerslayer-Hawkeye-Long-Rifle-Leather-Stocking-Pathfinder-Bumppo before the ladies.

" 'Be all ready to clench it, boys!' cried out Pathfinder, stepping into his friend's tracks the instant they were vacant. 'Never mind a new nail; I can see that, though the paint is gone, and what I can see I can hit at a hundred yards, though it were only a mosquito's eye. Be ready to clench!'

" The rifle cracked, the bullet sped its way, and the head of the nail was buried in the wood, covered by the piece of flattened lead."

There, you see, is a man who could hunt flies with a rifle, and command a ducal salary in a Wild West show today if we had him back with us.

Yet if one recalls what fantastic accuracy an ordinary athlete can develop in shooting a basketball or throwing a baseball, he must be quite ready to accept as routine spectacular shots by any fellow who grew up with a gun in his hands. Brilliant markmanship is not a convincing argument for Murphy.

At any rate, the scouts were invaluable to the generals fighting the wars of the American forests, and Murphy, whether he shot Fraser or not, was no doubt one of the best. After Saratoga, he spent most of the time with the New York militia, fighting under Sullivan and Clinton along the Mohawk, in the West, and around Schoharie. His reputation continued to grow, for the Tories put a price on his head and the Indians began to think of him as a kind of magician, partly because of his spectacular escapes and partly because he owned a double-barrelled grooved-gun (probably a forerunner to those made by James Golcher of Easton, Pa.) that appeared to fire without re-loading. His life during these years is vivid enough—without exaggeration.

In the winter of 1778, a group of Loyalists and Seneca Indians had descended on the Wyoming Valley in Pennsylvania and on the Cherry Valley in New York slaughtering settlers and ravaging the land. Washington had retaliated by ordering General John Sullivan and 5000 men into Seneca country to lay waste crops and, if possible, to assault Niagara. Sullivan went as far as the Genesee River, meeting few foes, but destroying a good many orchards and food supplies. Murphy was along.[9] At one point in the campaign, he and nineteen Colonials are reported to have been surrounded by Joseph Brant, the part-White Mohawk, and his savages. Fifteen were slain, but Murphy got away, hiding behind a brush fence while in best movie serial fashion a redskin searching after him stood right beside his concealed body.

In the fall of 1780, Indians and Tories under the leadership of Brant and Sir John Johnson struck back in answer to Sullivan's campaign, which had given the Seneca a winter of famine and hardship. They came down the Scholhaire Valley 800 strong to wipe out Dutch settlements. There were three forts in the Valley, named imaginatively the Upper Fort, at Fultonville; the Middle Fort, at Middleburg; and the Lower Fort, now a museum, at Schoharie. The principal attack was on the Lower Fort (Old Stone Fort) in the late afternoon of October 17. You can still see a hole made by a cannon ball that Johnson's men fired through the roof. However, Tim Murphy was involved in an incident that occurred at the Middle Fort. Harold Thompson has described it somewhat melodramatically[10]

> The fort's garrison of one hundred and fifty regular troops and one hundred militia was commanded by a cowardly Major named Wolsey, who was quite willing to strike his colors, especially after a cannonball had spoiled a perfectly good mattress where another not very valiant person was hiding. A white flag of truce was approaching, greatly to the relief of the Major and much to the unease of Tim and the valiant Dutch settler, Colonel Vroman.
>
> As usual, Tim made a quick decision and acted upon it immediately

[9] See G. S. Conover, ed., *Journals of the Military Expedition of Major General John Sullivan . . .* (Auburn, New York, 1887), 162 where Lt. Col. Adam Hubley of the 11th Pennsylvania mentions Murphy in his entry for Sept. 13, 1779. Murphy had evidently "killed and scalped that morning . . . an Indian; which makes the three and thirtieth man of the enemy he has killed as is well known to his Officers, this War." This was near Kanaghsas, N. Y.

[10] *Body, Boots, and Britches*, 59.

—regardless of the rules of civilized warfare. (After all, the rules had not been observed by his enemies at Cherry Vally and a dozen other ravaged settlements; he was fighting Indians and a dispossessed Tory.) Murphy fired toward the flag of truce. When his Major ordered his arrest, nobody stirred. Again the enemy sent a flag of truce; again Tim fired. After this symbolical rejection of surrender had been repeated a third time, two angry men faced each other in the little beleaguered fort: the Major with a pistol pointed at Tim's heart, Tim with a rifle which slowly rose to cover an officer unworthy of obedience. Tim's eyes didn't waver; the Major's did. In fact, Wolsey went to bed, Colonel Vroman took over the command, and there was no surrender at Schoharie that day—or on any other day. Sir John Johnson marched off, burning crops and cursing Tim Murphy; to keep the score even, Tim burned the houses of several Tories.

This dauntless frontiersman seems to have understood womanship as well as woodsmanship. Besides the young girl who was murdered by Indians, Murphy married two others. His biographers have spared no cliché in telling this side of his adventures, and the accounts of his union with the Dutch charmer, Peggy Feeck, are both neo-classic and unlikely. Sigsby's version is presented in full-blown, 18th century pastoral style, with poetic interspersions.[11]

Tim first sees Peggy one spring morning, when his attention is "arrested by

> —A rose complexioned lass,
> Nimbly tripping through the grass,

with a milkpail on her arm." Her dress is plain, but in true Arcadian style serves best to display her beauty and insinuate her charms. According to Sigsby, Murphy "tho't almost audibly" when he saw her, "J---s, what a swate creature!" Soon, the two are in pleasant conversation, and Peggy invites her new suitor home to a Dutch breakfast and to meet the folks. Murphy, who is completely smitten, uses every excuse he can to see more and more of this girl, but as the affair becomes serious Peggy's parents begin to object, finally banning all communication. Murphy suspects this is because of his poverty. No matter, the lovers meet in secret and finally plan an

[11] See Sigsby, 15-19.

elopement. At the chosen time, Peggy flees "through the window in her best petticoat and short gown." The marriage takes place at Duanesburgh, and the couple returns to the fort where Tim's fellow soldiers and their families celebrate the occasion. The father, noting his daughter's disappearance, becomes frantic and turns up at the fort greatly disturbed. However, when he learns he is "a day after the fair," he quietly submits to what Sigsby points out Virgil sang two thousand years earlier: "*Omnia vincit amor; et nos cedamus amori.*"

Perfect as Sigsby's scenario may seem, it is not accepted by all. One of Harold Thompson's students, Catherine Shafer, interviewed Mott Lawyer of Fultonham in the spring of 1941. Lawyer owned a large collection of relics: deeds, guns, books, arrowheads that dated back to Revolutionary days. He claimed to be descended from Murphy and had set up a marker to show where Tim used to live in Fultonham. A self-styled authority on the War and his ancestor's life, he insisted that Sigsby had the story wrong and that the correct version was to be found in Simms.[12]

Simms' text which is entitled "*An affair of love:* for Cupid was unchained even in perilous times" is not so very different from Sigsby's, although more words are spent on the machinations of both the love affair and the family reunion. Simms agrees Murphy first saw Miss Margaret, as he calls her, when she was carrying her milk-pails. "She," he writes, "had just passed 'sweet seventeen,' and was entering her eighteenth year; a period in the life of woman peculiarly calculated to convey and receive tender impressions. She was rather tall, and slim; possessing a genteel form, with a full bust; and features, if not handsome, at least pretty and very insinuating. Her hair was rich and auburn; her eyes a dark hazel, peering from beneath beautiful eyelashes; her teeth clean and well-set; her nose—but alas! that was large, and altogether too prominent a nasal organ to grace the visage of a perfect beauty. Her ruby lips and peach-colored cheeks, however, contrasted charmingly with her clear white skin,

[12] See Simms, 388-397. The information on Mott Lawyer and the letter from Mildred Murphy below are from the Thompson files.

besides nature had given her, what all men like to see, a neatly turned ankle."

According to Simms, Murphy was twelve years older than this country charmer, though not quite as tall, and among other things "indulged too much in profane levity." Margaret's family did everything they could to prevent interviews. Margaret was even required to do her milking in the company of a cousin. Still *omnia vincit amor*, and through one Maria Teabout Tim and Margaret were able to exchange verbal messages, written ones being useless as Tim could neither read nor write.

Finally, about October 1, 1780, Murphy and Margaret were ready to elope. Tim sent the message, "Come, for all things are now ready." Margaret replied, "Tell him, I will meet him near the river at the time appointed." That evening she milked the cows with her cousin as usual, but after the cousin left, spilled some of the milk and hurried home. There she told her mother that she had failed to milk one of the cows, knowing she would be sent back to finish her job. Once out of sight of the house, she hung her milk pail on a post and stole off to the tryst by the river.

When she got to the river, Tim was not there, so she forded the cold stream and set out for the Middle Fort where she expected to find her lover. Tim, in the meantime, had been at the trysting spot, but missed Margaret, and thinking something had happened to the plan, started back to the Fort calling the name of his sweetheart as he went. Much to his surprise, as he neared a spot just below the sight of the present Middleburgh bridge, he heard Margaret reply.

The next day they went to Schenectada and were married, Margaret, who had hurried off without a wardrobe, in borrowed clothes. After the ceremony, the couple returned to Schoharie where a party was held for them. Margaret's parents were furious, but could do nothing as the marriage proved completely legal. Tim had even taken the precaution of having the bans read the required number of times in church. Margaret's new husband was not allowed in the family home, and Margaret refused to enter without him, for, as she declared, "he was just as good as she was." A reconciliation didn't take place until Tim was offered a commission in Pennsylvania some months later. At that point, the parents relented, rather than lose their daughter for good.

You can take your pick between Sigsby and Simms. Both versions read like pulp-novels, and if the date October 1, 1780 is correct, Tim and Peggy had a rocky honeymoon, what with the intrusions of Sir John Johnson et al.

The rest of Murphy's military career, which eventually led him to Virginia, is unrewarding to trace. After the War is over, facts are just as hard to come by. In 1784, he seems to have gone to the rescue of his neighbor, John Adam Brown, when Brown's house was washed away in a March flood. Murphy is credited with saving two sons and the wife though Brown and his daughter, Maria, were lost. In 1807, Peggy died, leaving her fertile mate with nine children. About 1812, he married Mary Robertson, and also had several children with her.

Small in stature, perhaps about 5′ 6″, he was a wiry, firey man, easily excited. Although he could neither read nor write, he is supposed to have had a ready Irish wit and a quick tongue. The watchword attributed to him, "My boys, every ball was not moulded to hit" is a worthy aphorism. It is not hard to believe its author was influential in the local political campaigns and that he was helpful in projecting William C. Bouck, Schoharie County's only governor, into public notice.

In June 1818 he died, of "a cancer of the throat" that had troubled him for some time. Whether this disease resulted from injuries incurred in rescuing the Brown family, from the recoil of his famous rifle against his neck, or from a virus is lost to medical history. But it did the little Irishman in, where Indians, Tories, and irate parents had failed. In Harold Thompson's personal files is a letter from Miss Mildred H. Murphy of Oneonta, Tim's great-great granddaughter, written in 1940. At the end, it reads,

> One of the old milestones [of the Catskill turnpike] is only a few rods from my home in Treadwell, and until recent years one of the old toll gate houses was still standing less than half a mile from my home.
>
> I discovered in some of my historical notes that I had some concerning this old road, the mail service, etc. I have also heard my grandmother, Sally Treadwell Smith, tell stories of her father's trips

on horseback from Treadwell to Catskill, carrying grain there to be ground into flour.

. . . If you have never visited Timothy Murphy's grave on the hillside in Middleburgh cemetery, I think you would find it worth your while to stand there, overlooking that beautiful valley, as you picture to yourself his part in saving it.

At this gravesite, in 1910, a shaft was raised to Tim Murphy's memory. The monument, sculptured by Evelyn Longman, is granite, eight feet high, three feet wide, and ten inches deep. It is set on a broad base. On the shaft there stands a bas-relief in bronze of the patriot scout, showing him as a slim, athletic man, clothed in buckskin, jacket belted down at the waist, trousers fringed on the side, coonskin cap on the head. In his right hand is a musket, the butt of which is resting on the ground. His left hand rests on the hunting knife in his belt. He is looking out into the distance, though his left foot rests on a tomahawk and an arrow is embedded in the earth behind his right leg. The relief is bordered with tracings of pine needles and acorns. The inscription reads as follows,

TO THE MEMORY OF
1751 TIMOTHY MURPHY 1818
PATRIOT, SOLDIER, SCOUT, CITIZEN,
WHO SERVED IN MORGAN'S RIFLE CORPS,
FOUGHT AT SARATOGA AND MONMOUTH
AND WHOSE BRAVERY REPELLED THE ATTACK OF
BRITISH AND THEIR INDIAN ALLIES
UPON THE MIDDLE FORT
OCTOBER 17, 1780,
AND SAVED THE COLONISTS OF THE
SCHOHARIE VALLEY

Give or take a few details, this is what we know about the historical Murphy. He is just another in a long series of real-life Natty Bumppos who flourished in the forests from the French-Indian wars to the closing of the American West. The lives of these men are all strikingly similar, even to the entrance into politics that frequently characterizes the later years. Around the facts, which are usually dressed up a bit, circulate a series of folk motifs that are used again and again. To these motifs, as they have gravitated toward Murphy, we shall now turn.

It is not hard for a folklorist to believe in the outline of Murphy's life given above. One only questions the "window dressing." However, it is impossible for a folklorist to take seriously the mass of stories about him as a woodsman and Indian fighter, almost all of which are variants of tales previously attached to other adventurers and tricksters the world across. The motifs of these tales, like the shooting of General Fraser, may catch the spirit of Murphy's obvious talents, but they also remove him from the realm of history into the realm of folk fiction.[13]

For one thing the characters in the folktales that are built from such motifs tend to divide themselves most simply, and unreally, into good guys and bad guys who act with clear-cut, naive motivation. The Indians against whom Murphy vents his irritation have become such characters, vicious, but easily duped, of indeterminate tribe, indistinguishable from Tory, Moor, Jew, Western badman. Murphy, on the other hand, is imperturbable, resourceful, without any uncertainty at all, similar to Horatio at the Bridge, the Lone Ranger, Superman. The events occur nowhere in particular, except that the setting is the wooded frontier and the place names are those of the Schoharie Valley. A standard example is the "Claw in Split Tree."

Murphy is out splitting rails. Along comes a band of Indians, looking for him, but not recognizing him as they stop to ask directions. Murphy says he will help them locate their enemy, if they'll just give him a hand with the rails. Arranging some on one side of a wedged log and some on the other, he instructs them to pull with all their might, so he can free the wedge. They do this.

[13] The "handbook" (though its six volumes are anything but 'handy") that a folklorist uses for matters concerning folk fiction is Stith Thompson's *Motif-Index of Folk Literature*. This book is a listing and labelling of the narrative kernels from which the folktales of the world have grown. It is a fascinating thing to page through and is full of flotsam and jetsam that circulate around the legendary heroes who have assumed permanent positions in this or that folklore. See the revised edition published in 1955 at Bloomington, Indiana.

Murphy then releases the wedge and the log snaps together on their fingers, holding the whole party fast. He scalps them, telling them they have found the man they are looking for.

The story dates back a few years before Murphy's birth in 1751. It has been told about Tom Quick, another New York State scout, about Daniel Boone, Davy Crockett, and many others. Stith Thompson numbers it 38 in his descriptive index, *The Types of the Folktale*,[14] and cites texts of it from all over Scandinavia, northern and Slavic Europe, Spanish-speaking areas, the United States, and even Oceania. Usually the trickster is a fox, who dupes a bear.

Murphy also outwits the Indians by means of the spider web gimmick, listed by Thompson under the number 967. Murphy is pursued by redskins and is forced to hide in a hollow log. The Indians think he may be hiding in the very spot he has chosen, but look no farther when they see an unbroken spider web he has placed over the open end. Christ, Mohammed, Robert Bruce, as well as some Japanese and Eastern Indians, have been saved by this device. Nor is there anything particularly unique about many of his other adventures. When he puts skates on his feet on the dead run so that he can glide out onto the frozen river and outdistance his pursuers; when he pretends not to be able to handle skates, falling down continually, but steadily using the ruse to put distance between him and the redskins who are laughing at him; when he leaps over a fence on the dead run, then hides up against it so that the Indians on his trail jump over him without knowing he's there, he is performing standard tall tale escapes. Nor is any tale about him more trite than the "Bent Gun" story mentioned in the Introduction.

No one in his right mind can consider such anecdotes as historical, as things that really happened. However, it is more difficult to be sure about some of the others. One tells how Murphy, out scouting, had his leggings torn to shreds by bull-briars and blackberry. Hunting down an Indian, he shot the unlucky fellow, skinned him from knee to ankle, and made himself leggings. The heat was intolerable that day, and as Tim worked his way home the

[14] (Helsinki, 1961).

Indian's skin shrank, cutting off his circulation and causing him to be bed-ridden for a couple of weeks. Such a tale may not be all fiction. Anyone who looks into the lives of the frontiersmen encounters a pretty barbaric, often sadistic bunch, who sincerely believed the Indian to be a lower order of life than the White. Tales of Germans making lampshades from the skin of despised Jews horrify us, but our woodland heroes thought nothing of using Indian skin for bullet pouches, Indian teeth for jewels, Indian scalps for trophies. Such men eliminated the Indians by any means, fair or foul, the slogan "a good Indian is a dead Indian" covering morality. So Murphy, unarmed, clearing land, can trick a passing redskin into a shooting contest. It is to his credit that he gives the Indian the first shot, then, borrowing the rifle to take his turn, kills the fellow in cold blood. Or he can find an Indian relieving himself in the woods, shoot him in the rear-end, and laugh with his friends over the fact the dying Indian's bowels explode an answer even louder than the gun report.

His many escapes, some of which must have been close are likely to have an aura of truth about them, though they couldn't have happened quite as dramatically as they are told. Emelyn Gardner[15] knew a stage driver who in 1912 pointed out to her a cave where Murphy is supposed to have eluded pursuing Indians. It seems a branch grew near the entrance, which Murphy had discovered but of which the Indians were ignorant. Pressed by the redskins, he leaped from the cliff above, grabbed the branch, and disappeared into the cave, the Indians of course thinking him dead on the rocks below. Another time he is supposed to have been walking down a mountain with a huge load of wheat on his back, when the ever-present redskins attacked. He chose to leap from a cliff and landed on a projection a hundred feet below. His weight, combining with the weight of the wheat, forced him knee deep into the rock. The Indians, assuming him dead, went on. Murphy then hurried down into the valley, got a pick, and returned to dig himself out. Possibly both these stories are essentially true. Of course, the second one has been adorned with the old European motif of the man who falls

[15] See *Folklore from the Schoharie Hills* (Ann Arbor, Michigan, 1937), 26.

out of a balloon and, buried in the soil, gets a shovel to free himself.[16] But Murphy may have used the trick of seeming to leap from a cliff to escape more than once. Others have done it.

The Schoharie area abounds in this sort of anecdote. The notes in the late Harold Thompson's files contain papers from a collecting assignment on Murphy given around 30 years ago at what was then Albany State College. Much of what was brought in hovers between that which appears to be history and that which is surely folklore.

In 1938 Eleanor Ribley, an Albany State College student, interviewed Mr. Samuel I. Brown, a "life-long resident of Stamford." He was then in his eighties and claimed to have known in his boyhood, St. Leger Crowley, who according to Miss Ribley, "in 1792 erected the first grist mill on the west branch of the Delaware near the present site of Stamford." From Crowley, Mr. Brown learned much about the frontier. Mr. Brown referred to the hero of his tales as "Jim Murphy who had a farm near Harpersfield," but obviously Jim and Tim are the same man. The following is taken from Miss Ribley's retelling of Brown's recollections:

"Murphy enlisted in the colonial Army, and after the surrender of Burgoyne, brought his company to Schoharie to track down Tories in that vicinity. Murphy had a narrow escape near Charlottville while trying to capture a man named Service.

"Because he knew the Indian language, he was able to lead successfully many expeditions, and went among the Indians disguised as one of them. He had unfailing courage and infallible judgment.

"Once he was captured with Colonel Harper by a dozen Indians. During the second day, they procured enough rum to make sure the Indians would spend the night in deep slumber. During the night Murphy and his companions escaped after using the Indians' weapons to tomahawk the sleepers. All but one were killed. This one surviving quickly spread the news, and when Murphy and Harper returned home they found their wives and babies cruelly murdered. The bodies of Harper's wife and baby had been left for the wolves to tear apart. Mrs. Murphy and her two children had been brutally beaten.

"These acts led the men to seek vengeance at every opportunity, and as a result Fort Schoharie was built to house the wives and families

[16] Motif X 917. See also X 1731.2.1.

of the settlers, to protect them as they were sure further trouble would result. They were right; the battle took place about half a mile from Lake Utsayantha. Murphy tricked the one escaping Indian away from his comrades by calling out his name in the Indian language. When the Indian stepped from the bushes, Murphy, who was hiding behind a big pine tree shot him. Four white men and about thirty Indians were killed. The surviving Indians fled down the valley toward Charlottville, but Murphy followed. He came near enough that night to learn that their band was composed of less than thirty. He organized an attack and killed all but six.

"One day Murphy came upon a settlement where a girl had been kidnapped by four Indians. He found them camped and asleep. The girl was bound to a tree. After releasing her, he killed three of the Indians, and the fourth nearly killed him.

"Later, at Harpersfield, Murphy organized a rescue party to go after two men who had been taken by the Indians. They arrived at the Indian camp just as the two men were about to be burned alive. The Indians were killed and the men freed.

"Another story tells that Murphy came upon an Indian skinning a deer near Summit Lake. He shot the Indian and stretched the deer skin over the body. He concealed himself behind a tree and there he waited. Three Indians appeared at the sound of gun fire but seeing the deer shot at it, only to find that they had shot their companion. From his hiding place Murphy shot two of the Indians, and the third hid behind a big tree. As each waited for the other to produce a head to shoot at, Murphy held his hat out and the Indian saw it drop at his shot. He rushed out to scalp his victim, only to be shot down himself.

"On another escapade, Murphy became surrounded by a band of Indians and fired his gun in such rapid succession that the Indians fled.

"Once he is supposed to have removed the skin from the feet of a dead Indian and to have drawn it over his own skin. He was nearly captured by pursuing Indians because as the skin dried, it contracted and hampered his speed so his followers caught up to him. His deftness with his fists was all that saved him.

"Murphy died a natural death near Harpersfield at the age of sixty-seven."

This account may contain a folk recollection of the massacre that befell Murphy's first family, though certainly the chronology has been confused. Everything in it is perfectly believable, including the leggings motif which crops up again. However, one of the other accounts in Thompson's files seems to have Tim Murphy confused with a different historical figure, perhaps also named Murphy.

Another Albany student, Helen Roickle, in 1940 collected a beautifully garbled account of Murphy. . . :

"Some of the stories that I shall include I obtained from my grandmother, Keza Young Veeder. She is now 76, and looks and acts 60. She was born and brought up in and near Cobleskill, in Schoharie County. One of her forebears, either her grandfather or her great grandfather, was the first white child born in Schoharie County. These stories are bits of tales that she had heard told when she was a child.

"There seems to be a series of tales about a Tory named Murphy. Some of these are like those told about Tim Murphy, but this particular Murphy, Grandma said was a Tory. He was constantly in fights with Indians, whom he hated apparently, and the Indians seemed to have little love for him.

"One time the Indians had made a raid on a settlement over in Schoharie, and killed off most of the people. In one of the cabins was a tiny baby. The Indians killed and scalped the mother and father, and one of the braves was about to kill the sleeping baby, when it awoke. It opened its very beautiful blue eyes, smiled very happily at the savage and stretched out its hands for the raised tomahawk. This was too much for even a savage, so the life of the child was spared by the Indians. Apparently Murphy had witnessed this scene, for as soon as the Indians had departed, he came forward and killed and scalped the baby. Some time later, in town, he bragged about the fact that he had done something that the Indians could not do. Some of these Indians learned about it, and swore eternal vengeance on Murphy, for he had not only killed a child which to them had something of the supernatural protecting it, but he had tried to ridicule the braves.

"There seems to have been a number of tales about Murphy after this, but my Grandmother couldn't remember them well. One other story is similar to the railsplitting story of Tom Quick. In my Grandmother's version, it seems that some Indians were going through a woods in search of Murphy, when they came upon a man splitting a huge log by means of a wedge. They inquired if he knew where they could find Murphy. He said he did, and that he would take them there if they would help him split the log first. He got them to insert their hands in the split, and then he knocked out the wedge, and had the

Indians captive. He then told them he was Murphy, and proceeded to exterminate them with the axe.

"Another of his exploits is slightly vague. He either induced a number of Indians to drink, or else he found them already drunk. He then got them into a house (or perhaps he found them already in the house) and while they were in a drunken stupor, he set fire to the house and burned them alive.

"He must have had numerous experiences after that, but the final thing that my Grandmother remembered was that he was ultimately captured by the Redskins, and after horrible torture was burned at the stake. The Indians taunted him with the reply that he might have done something that the Indians couldn't, but he was afraid to die.

"Then my Grandma told me a story about some good Indians. . . ."

This may well be an attempt by a more civilized age to "correct" the cruelties attributed to a frontier Indian-hater by making him a Tory of whom such conduct might be expected.

At any rate, whatever fame came to Tim Murphy was quite limited. Neither my wife nor my college-age daughter had ever heard of him until I began this book. To historians he has never been of importance, and today his legend is all but forgotten even in New York. It may seem strange that a fellow who so symbolizes the guerilla side of our struggle for independence has never become a national popular hero. Perhaps, Murphy was just too local. But far more likely we ignore him because he never wrote an autobiography like Crockett or never had a "press-agent" like Longfellow to bring him to wide public attention. Yet such explanations don't account for the fact we ignore Ethan Allen, whose reputation was far less parochial than that of Murphy, and who did write a colorful account of his own life.

9 Green Mountain Boy

I am not the only person who has been fascinated by the fact that Revolutionary heroes like Ethan Allen haven't developed as national heroes. Almost everyone who discusses the problem suspects that it has something to do with the West. America has certainly identified with the West, and there is no doubt that Western frontier figures like Davy Crockett, Mike Fink, and Johnny Appleseed relegate Tim Murphy and Ethan Allen to local lore during the 19th century. If you embrace Frederick Jackson Turner's famous thesis, which of course has a lot of truth in it, you have a ready-made answer: the West accounts for the uniqueness of our country and naturally Western heroes are more appropriate, even more typical, than those of the Eastern seaboard. But certainly that is not all there is to it. Print has much to do with things. Our national heroes are products of popular, mass media tradition, not of folk tradition, and the figures whose stories had the widest circulation in 19th and 20th century print are the ones we think of as national "folk" heroes today. When cities began to expand and markets for printed literature began to develop, the Revolution was no longer big news, particularly the Schoharie raids and the quibbling over the New Hampshire grants. The big news of the days was the opening of the West, and not only were American readers fascinated, but so were Europeans.

To me, it has always seemed painfully obvious that America was nothing but a cultural colony until the age of Jackson. In spite of our political independence and the efforts of Cooper and Washington Irving to establish a national literature, it is only with the opening of the West, with the importance of the West in national politics, and with the Turner-like "backwash" of the frontier over the East that America moves free of Europe into an orbit of its own. America gains her identity from the West, and she knows it, and she promotes the West because it makes her different. So Walt Whitman, Mark Twain, Bret Harte, Joaquin Miller, Artemus Ward, Abraham Lincoln were embraced by Europe as fresh new voices in the world, while at the sub-literary level tales of Mike Fink, Appleseed, and the rest were gobbled up. Without a Longfellow to champion him, like Paul Revere, or without an autobiography that remained pertinent as, say Franklin's guideline to wealth in a bourgeoise society, with his glory tied to the entrance of a New England state into the Union, Ethan Allen was certain to be overwhelmed. It is sort of a shame, for his role in the Revolution is no less dramatic than Revere's, his personality no less colorful than Fink's, his political career no less significant than Crockett's. Ethan Allen was, in truth, a natural.

The Green Mountain boy was born at Litchfield, Connecticut on January 10, 1738 of English stock. He grew up in Cornwall on the Housatonic. After obscurity as a soldier in the French-Indian wars, as a miner, and as a manager of a furnace, he came to public notice during the disputes between New York State and the "New Hampshire Grants." Allen was 26 years old when he moved near what is now Bennington, Vermont on land that had been opened for settlement by the Peace of Paris and that was claimed by both New York and New Hampshire. The Board of Trade had allotted the area to New York, but the Governor of New Hampshire continued to grant townships in the district. Allen, with his brothers and a cousin, Remember Baker, had formed the Onion River Company and speculated heavily in the area. When New York grantees began to press their claims to the same region, things became crucial. In 1770, Allen was selected to plead the New Hampshire cause in Albany. He had no luck, and the result of his failure was the organization of the Green Mountain Boys. Allen led this group of vigilantes in efforts to force the Yorkers out of the disputed region, and so became a marked man in Albany.

He was, and there seems to be no dispute on this point, an obstinate, showy, unpredictable soul. Hearing of a $750 reward posted for his capture, he is meant to have ridden up to Albany, entered a crowded tavern, and ordered a bowl of punch. Having drunk at leisure, he rose, slammed his fists on the table, and hands on hips said, "Now then, my name is Allen! Who wants that reward?" Later he offered a counter-reward for the capture of the New York Attorney-General and put up a defiant block fort. Such a fellow, strong of limb and language, clever, foolhardy, might well become legendary in his own time.

And the times were right. A hero needs a dispute in which he represents the underdog, against whom some powerful, unreasonable force is discriminating. Jesse James continues the guerilla aspects of the Civil War after the Union has won; Pretty Boy Floyd represents the farmers against the foreclosing banks; Heraclio Bernal fights the battles of the outlanders against Porfirio Díaz. Allen's reputation grew in such soil, and to Green Mountain settlers struggling against New York, he was a champion, if a most local one, before the Revolution began.

The early days of the war did little to change all this. Soon after the battle of Lexington, on May 10 to be exact, the event for which he is best known occurred. The Americans, embarking on their trip toward freedom, were in desperate need of arms. Benedict Arnold, then a Captain, knew that about eighty cannon, twenty brass guns, a dozen or so mortars, and some small arms were kept at the rotting, old British fort, Ticonderoga, located near the lower tip of Lake Champlain. Although the fort was in New York territory, Joseph Warren and the rest could not wait to get at the arms. They secretly commissioned Arnold to enlist about 400 men in Western Massachusetts, take the fort, leave a garrison there, and bring the arms south. He set out at once, only to discover when he got to Stockbridge that his idea had been borrowed by some Hartford patriots who had commissioned Ethan Allen and his band of Green Mountain Boys to do the same thing. Allen was more than eager, for with war threatening, Ticonderoga looked dangerously close to his Onion River Company's land holdings. He was already en route, and Arnold who saw his plan and his glory being usurped by a rural outlaw sped north on the trail of the Boys. He caught up with them in a taproom at Castleton, 20 miles below Ticonderoga, where they were passing the time waiting to join their leader Allen who had gone on ahead. Arnold demanded recognition as commander of the force. The dispute that followed is typical of "great" men, who invariably have great egos. Eventually, it was resolved by the childish arrangement of having the two march side by side at the head of the troop, although Arnold was not to issue orders.

Ticonderoga, which was not in good shape anyhow, was manned by forty-five redcoats, some of whom were old and weary, others of whom were sick. There were also twenty-four women and children. Allen and Arnold planned to surprise this garrison by crossing the stormy waters of Lake Champlain at night in commandeered boats. However, when the men sent to get the boats were delayed in returning and the dawn of May 10 was drawing near, the incompatible leaders and 83 men crossed in the two available vessels. The rest of the original 230 were left on the east shore with Allen's side-kick, Seth Warner. The 83 quickly approached the fort through the forest. Almost everyone at Ticonderoga was asleep. The sentry was surprised and his gun mis-fired. Although he shrieked an alarm, the Green Mountain Boys stormed into the fort through an open wicket gate. The commander, Captain Delaplace, was slow in waking up and slower in dressing himself. Active leadership was taken by Lieutenant Jocelyn Feltham, who tried to arouse his superior and tried to rally the men. But it all happened too quickly, and the Fort was surrendered before either Delaplace or Feltham were fully clothed. Although the Americans also captured Crown Point and under Arnold took St. John's shortly after, success did not end the quibbling. In the squabble over command and glory, Allen won out. Arnold, difficult enough in good times, was resentful, a resentment that, fanned by Saratoga and Peggy Shippen among other things, matured into treason at West Point.

About four years after this, Allen published his autobiographical account, *A Narrative of Colonel Ethan Allen's Captivity* . . .

"Ethan Allen Captures Ticonderoga" (from an old wood-cut)

Containing His Voyages and Travels,[1] in which the Ticonderoga escapade is more or less accurately described. The book, which was originally serialized in the *Pennsylvania Packet,* went through eight editions within two years, and did much to secure Allen's fame. His account of the surrender fails to mention Arnold, but gives the only phrase for which the author is remembered. He claims to have ordered the Fort delivered to him instantly. When asked by what authority, he says he replied, "In the Name of the Great Jehovah and the Continental Congress." Feltham's report[2] of the debacle received by General Gage in Boston does not mention this phrase. One Israel Harris, claiming to have been present, says the remark was actually "Come out of here you damned old rat."[3] It doesn't really matter. Allen may well have said both these things and a good bit more. Participants, reporters, and historians alike are at best moderately trustworthy in such matters. What four or five letters, after all, do you suppose General "Nuts" McAuliffe really used when replying to German demands for surrender at the Battle of the Bulge in 1945?

Ticonderoga proved to be the bloom of Allen's glory. He was part of the ill-starred expeditions connected with the hope that Canada would join the war, and, though one gets a different impression from reading his *Narrative,* he made a headstrong fool of himself at Montreal and was captured while fleeing the British. After five weeks in shackles in one of the incredible prison ships used in those days, he was taken to England, eventually to be exchanged for a British colonel. From the time he was released until the end of his life, his fame was somewhat tarnished by suspicions that he was pro-British or at least not in complete accord with the American cause.

Allen was held by the British for two years. When he got home in 1779, he was warmly received by General Washington and the Continental Congress. Vermont had just declared herself independent

[1] The text used is the reprint of 1779, by Draper & Folsom.

[2] See Allen French, *The Taking of Ticonderoga in 1775* in Cambridge, 1928) for a full account.

[3] See William C. Todd, "Lord Timothy Dexter" in *The New England Historical and Genealogical Register,* 1886, 380.

of New York, and the Onion River land looked more valuable than ever. Probably because it involved his own economic future, but also because of local loyalties, Allen at once concerned himself with the sticky question of the sovereignty of this new area and the possibilities of its being accepted into the union of colonies. These were difficult days, and the stability of the American government was not the best. Allen, without doubt, seems to have been more interested in his own investments and the future of the old New Hampshire grants as they related to those investments than he was in the revolutionary cause. He had limited faith in the Continental Congress, partially because they refused to supply a separate Vermont militia, and consequently was willing to consider the value of return to British rule, ideas which he put on paper in a written refutation of New Hampshire and Massachusetts claims on independent Vermont. Moreover, he was the sort of person the British, in their search for malcontents among the Americans, were wont to pick out.

In March 1780, he was in close enough contact with the Tories to warn the people of Skeneboro of a British raid. In July, he received a letter from a Tory, Colonel Beverley Robinson, who wrote, "I have often been informed that you and most of the inhabitants of Vermont are opposed to the wild and chimerical scheme of the Americans in attempting to separate the continent from Great Britain . . . and that you would willingly assist in uniting America again with Great Britain . . ."[4] Robinson, who was an agent for General Henry Clinton, was interested to know if Allen could be bought. Allen reported this incident to his governor and the assembly, yet he wrote to the Continental Congress that Vermont was not a part of the confederacy and that it could choose its own destiny, with them or with the British.

During this period, Governor Chittenden granted all Tories safe passage through Vermont to Canada. Some of the Vermonters did not approve this plan and even attacked a group of Tories passing north. Allen broke up this mob action, a moral move, but one which convinced a good many that he did indeed have Tory leanings. He

[4] See John Pell, *Ethan Allen* (Boston and New York, 1929), 192.

was also in correspondence with an old Tory friend, Justus Sherwood, who had gone to Canada to live. On the surface, these letters concerned an exchange of prisoners, but they got into other matters. One thing led to another and Allen entered negotiations with the British for a truce involving upper New York, Vermont, and the British. In 1781, he was a party to an agreement to allow British letters to pass through Vermont to and from Canada. During these years, he falls under suspicion as a Tory sympathizer in both the Vermont Assembly and the Continental Congress, but he seems to have countered charges of being seen with British officers in Quebec, hoarding grain, and raising Tory regiments successfully. At one time he even wrote that he would not be a part of "no damned Arnold plan to sell his country and his honor by betraying the trust reposed in him."[5]

It all boils down to the fact that Allen was opportunistic, more interested in his land holdings and the future of Vermont than in the total American cause. He seems to have been willing to use any means short of outright treason to obtain what he felt was best for his and his region's future. Some of his defenders feel that he was trapped by the fact that the Continental Congress was not defending Vermont and that it was vulnerable to a British takeover. That may have been so, but Allen surely was using Vermont's precarious position to gain sympathy from the other colonies, and the British undoubtedly suspected they were being manipulated in just such a fashion.

When the War was over, he continued his campaign to have Vermont enter the union, and served as a delegate to the Continental Congress working hard for this cause. He died at 52 in 1789, two years before his dream was realized—a man whose name cannot be separated from those chapters that make up the story of the New Hampshire Grants: the New York feuds, the Revolution, and the struggle for statehood.

The legends that cluster about Ethan Allen are pretty much what one would expect. Some are clearly literary, some are not. If there is any distinction to them, it is in their urban nature, their

[5] See Pell, 199.

being set in and near towns rather than in the forests. They focus on his virility, ingenuity, boldness, and his capacity for liquor. Originally, there must have been some that dealt with his sexual prowess, though these are not available now. Thus, we find Allen having a healthy tooth pulled to show a scared woman that the operation doesn't hurt, mistaking olives for green gages at a fashionable English dinner, offering to be hung himself rather than see a mob angered by a postponed execution go off disappointed. His own *Narrative* did much to foster this sort of image. At one point, he tells how he bit off a nail with his teeth causing one of his captors on the ship *Gaspee* to exclaim "Damn him, he can eat iron!"[6] Typical of such stories is the one concerning some pranksters who attempt to frighten him at night on a lonely road. They dressed as ghosts and hid beneath a bridge. As Ethan, slightly drunk, came along, the whole group suddenly leaped out. Allen's horse shied, but he reined in, shouting, "If you are angels of light, I'm glad to meet you. And if you are devils, then come along home with me. I married your sister!" Such tales are not unbelievable, some of them are probably based on actual events that have been dramatized and polished. But none of them are really legendary matter, variants of the sort of lore that survives in oral tradition. These are the "Reader's Digest type" anecdotes and probably have never been widely known to people who do not see books.

They are mixed with others that are much more genuinely folk. When Allen pulls a catamount from his back and kills it with his bare hands, when he imitates an owl's hoot so well he is attacked by jealous male owls who think he is cutting in on their territory, when he runs a deer into the ground instead of shooting it, when his ghost comes back to whinny on the Vermont hills in the form of a great white stallion, you are dealing with the sort of tales that have been told about folk heroes by the folk for centuries. Many of the anecdotes which include his associate, Seth Warner, and his cousin, Remember Baker, are built of widely used motifs.

Allen and Warner are fishing on Lake Champlain, when Seth's powder-horn falls into the water. Allen volunteers to retrieve it and dives overboard. When he doesn't come up for several minutes,

[6] *A Narrative of Ethan Allen's Captivity*, 10.

Warner dives in too. At the bottom of the lake he finds Allen trying to pour some of Seth's powder into his own horn.

Allen and Remember are hiking across the mountains after a hard night of drinking. They fall asleep in a hollow. While they are sleeping a five-foot rattler crawls onto Allen's chest. The snake makes enough noise to awaken Remember, who startled watches it strike Allen again and again. Baker leaps up, grabs his gun, and the snake slips off. Allen sleeps on, while Baker watches the snake weave from side to side, turn cross-eyed, belch, and fall stunned, obviously drunk on the liquor from Allen's veins. Pretty soon Allen wakes up, griping about the damn mosquitoes that won't leave a tired man alone.

These are old stories and have been told before.[7] Soon they were to be told again as they went west like the pioneers and attached themselves to fresh heroes who were involved in the working out of America's manifest destiny. After mid-century the hunger for such fresh heroes and the story matter that goes with them became great indeed. The Mexican War, the Civil War, the Indian Wars, the Spanish-American War, the World Wars all forced this country to explain itself at home and abroad, and genuine folklore simply could not do the whole job. It proved itself too parochial, too Colonial, too unsuited to the new-found national unity and industrial might. So America was forced to turn to its writers, literary and hack. These men, perfectly happy to re-use and re-model the legends of Murphy or Allen or anyone else, responded nobly. Magazines, newspapers, lecturers, schoolteachers spread the names and anecdotes of their adaptions and creations across the world. As Robert Seager wrote in a significant, but well buried, essay in *Midwest Folklore:*[8]

[7] Benjamin A. Botkin, *A Treasury of New England Folklore,* 235 cites the powder-horn story with Jonathan Timbertoes and his Uncle Zekiel as participants from the 1836 *The Farmer's Almanack.* For a parallel to the snake-bite story, see Ernest W. Baughmon, *Type and Motif Index of the Folktales of England and North America* (Bloomington, Indiana, 1966), X 1321.4.6* (c).

[8] See 1951, 220-221. The quotation in the passage is from the essay on "Estonian Folklore" in the Funk & Wagnall's *Standard Dictionary of Folklore, Mythology, and Legend,* I, 349.

Nationalism has outlived its historical usefulness, and its continued existence reflects one of the most obvious culture lags of the modern period. Yet nationalism has lost few of its charms for the historian and fewer still for the man in the street. American history is still largely written from a nationalistic and egocentric point of view. To be sure, American nationalism has served a useful function in that it has provided, among other things, a workable substitute for a national folk tradition. A heterogeneous people achieved an element of cultural cohesion and a focal point for group loyalty in their emotional identification with national heroes. These heroes were created almost overnight, and their creation, as manifested in the history of their times, had conscious aims and ends. Parson Weems' treatment of George Washington was paralleled by the various biographers of Patrick Henry, Nathan Hale, Andrew Jackson, Davy Crockett, Abraham Lincoln, Robert E. Lee, William Jennings Bryan, and Theodore Roosevelt, to mention but a few. Nor does the process appear to have any logical end. While the critical historiography of one generation mortalizes the national deities of an earlier period, it at the same time creates a new set of culture heroes for its own use. Franklin D. Roosevelt is a contemporary case in point.

While pursued more subtly, the overall aim of historians in the United States was not too dissimilar from that followed by F. R. Faelmann, founder of the Estonian Learned Society, who, we are told,

> fabricated some deities and splendid myths. [Faelmann] was eager to furnish a substitute for the national epos. . . . [This contributed to] . . . a widespread national movement by the Estonians . . . [who] were delighted with the traditions of their folk. The gathering of folklore was regarded not as an amusement of rich people but as a national task in which the whole people took pride.

Actually, many, if not most, of the "deities and splendid myths" created by American historians in the interests of American nationality were relatively harmless. Washington and the cherry tree, Patrick Henry's "Give me liberty or give me death," and the alleged off-hand composition of Lincoln's Gettysburg Address served their usefulness as construction materials in the erection of culture heroes as symbols of national unity. Today, no longer taken seriously, their primary value is pedagogical. . . .

Other myths, however, were and continue to be extremely dangerous. The belief that the Pilgrim Fathers invented Democracy and Free Enterprise, that God has a direct and personal interest in the United States, or that the American Constitution is a perfect and infallible document contributes a narrowness, self-righteousness, and wholly unrealistic quality to the American outlook. To the extent that historians aid in the perpetuation of such concepts, they are engaged in the conscious creation of that myth and legend for which Americans will presumably fight.

The mass media hacks and literary historians who created this pap are pretty well committed to thinking of history as Thomas Carlyle did, as a parade of great personalities who fashion the future. There is no better way to make history arresting. There may be a certain grandeur in the idea that civilizations move like vast rivers, the undercurrents sweeping inevitably on, carrying little swirls and eddies of human effort toward oceanic conclusions, but a propagandist can do a good bit more with the idea that a great man can shift currents, vary banks, even influence the point to which rivers flow. Ever since America has asserted her national identity, her river has been the West and the moral, ethical and personal codes the West symbolized best. Thus, the heroes have had to go about their task of literally causing the West to happen and then giving the Western standards to Easterners and the rest of the world. Murphy bogged down in the forest wars of the Revolution, Allen, struggling to gain independence for the New Hampshire Grants, have no role in this. They are forgotten, replaced by men like Johnny "Appleseed" Chapman, who tramps the Muskingum with a *Bible* under his arm and seedlings in his pack; by Mike Fink, who deserts the East when he can no longer travel a day without seeing a farmhouse and dies across the wide Missouri; by Crockett, who fought for freedom as surely as Murphy or Allen did and what's more did it in Tennessee and Texas where the future was coming to pass. It's only the special case: Paul Revere, whose story is told by the most popular poet of our history in a form that everyone can memorize; or Ben Franklin, a real-life Horatio Alger hero, author of a handbook to success, who can survive a Colonial, Atlantic seaboard identity.

10 Midnight Message

FOLKLORISTS ARE WELL AWARE that genuine narrators of genuine folk legends distort what actually happened, fitting real events and real personalities to formulas inherited in the culture of which they are a part. What they sometimes forget is that the literary hack does the same thing. When a popular writer decides to tell the story of a Paul Revere, he is almost automatically committed to certain characterizations and plot patterns. If he is original enough to transcend such conventionality, he may well lose his popular audience just as a folk narrator may lose his listeners if he fails to give them the sort of thing they have come to expect. A man like Revere, middle-class, confused, quite normal as he may have been historically is ordained to uniqueness, brilliance, triumph by the very fact his story is to be told. No one cares that he never reached Concord, no one cares if Dawes and Prescott shouldered the same work, no one cares which side of the Charles he was on when the two lanterns shone forth, because Revere has ceased to function as an historical man and has begun to function as a symbol. This is the way of the hero in all times, in all places—and it matters little whether we are dealing with the folk or the more fortunate.

This is why we cannot dismiss something like "Paul Revere's Ride" as mere fakelore, belittling it as phoney and inaccurate, forgetting it because it has been thrust down our throats by career Americanists. Today, when one travels the route Paul Revere rode, he can barely visualize the farmhouses and old taverns that once stood on the sites of shopping centers, asphalt speedways, and Little League ballparks. He is made to realize the folklore that served a semi-ignorant, long-vanished Middlesex farmer will not serve the educated, industrial present. In an industrial world where the rural is giving away to the urban, where people no longer grow up on family land, where one no longer marries the girl he went to school with, and where a man no longer feels close to another, not because he likes him, but because he shared the same youth—in such an industrial world, local homogeneity has broken down and has had to be replaced by a national, artificial homogeneity. The lore of this world may be phoney, may be pre-packaged, but it serves the old purpose.

So hardly a man is now alive who hasn't heard that on the 18th of April 1775, Paul Revere rode madly out of Boston to warn every Middlesex village and farm that the British were coming to Concord. It had all started two weeks earlier. General Thomas Gage, in command of the British troops in Boston, knew that the Rebels had collected arms and ammunition at both Worcester and Concord. As such caches were directly contrary to King George's orders, he sent Lt. Colonel Francis Smith and Private John Howe, disguised as locals, out to look into the situation and to advise him on the possibilities of a successful raid. Smith, who was recognized by a Negro serving girl in Watertown, proved of little use, but John Howe learned what the General wanted to know. Because of Howe's advice, Gage decided to raid Concord instead of Worcester. Concord, he felt, would be safer, as his troops could move part of the way by water. Moreover, there was the additional chance that John Hancock and Sam Adams, whom the British were anxious to arrest, could be taken in or near Concord before they went south to Philadelphia and the Second Continental Congress. It was known they had attended the Massachusetts Provincial Congress in Lexington and were still in the area. Actually, they were visiting at the parsonage of the Reverend Jonas Clark, whose wife was Hancock's cousin.

"An Engraving of Sam Adams by Paul Revere"

Paul Revere, in addition to doing his regular work of engraving and smithing, had for many months served as a courier for those Bostonians who kept a close eye on British military activities in the area. These "secret agents" or "mechanics," led by Adams, Hancock, and Joseph Warren, met regularly at the Green Dragon Tavern where they discussed information they had picked up and planned harassment activities, stealing guns, destroying equipment, and throwing cannon in near-by ponds. They also kept a close check on troop movements. By April 15, it was quite obvious Gage was planning a raid somewhere, and it wasn't hard to guess that either Concord or Worcester would be the target. Small boats were lowered from the transports into the Charles River and were being checked out. Some of the light infantry, troops especially trained for skirmishing and reconnaissance, as well as some heavier, supporting grenadiers, were withdrawn from their regiments, supposedly for special training. Warren and his friends noticed these things, and Revere was called in and dispatched to Lexington to warn Adams and Hancock of the possibility of their being picked up. His message was spread about the environs, and the people in Concord began to move their stores and artillery to new hiding places and to secret their bullets in sacks buried in swamps. What was really lacking was precise information, whether the British were going to descend on Concord or Worcester and when.

Revere returned to Boston by Charlestown. He was afraid Gage might make it impossible for couriers to leave town just before the troops departed, and he wanted to make sure that warnings would still go forth. So he stopped in Charlestown to make an agreement with Colonel William Conant, a prominent citizen and Son of Liberty. If the British were to leave the town by water, what Longfellow was to call "sea," Revere would show two lanterns in the steeple of Christ Church. If they were to march by land, that is across Boston Neck, he would show one. The steeple of Boston's Christ Church, later known as Old North Church, was easy to see on Charlestown Neck, and the signal was a quick and efficient device, much more certain than trying to slip a messenger across the Charles or down Boston Neck which was but 60 yards wide.

By the 17th, everyone in Boston knew something was afoot.

Many of the houses had British officers billeted in them and others had the wives of soldiers working in them. People talk, and it was plain the troops were being made active. The war-ship *Somerset* was moved into the mouth of the Charles River, making it difficult for anyone to cross to Charlestown Neck at that point. The sentinels at Boston Neck were alerted. Picked officers were dispatched to patrol all routes leading to Concord. Warren, Revere, and the other vigilantes were ready and completely informed, although they had not learned about the patrols on the roads leading north. By evening, Gage was also completely informed, having been told by his spies that Hancock and Adams, as well as the towns of Worcester and Concord, had been more or less alerted. He decided to give it a try anyhow.

The Rebels awaited accurate information as to which route the British would take. Plans had been carefully laid for Robert Newman, the sexton of Christ Church, to show the lanterns. Obviously, these lanterns would not be seen by Revere "on the opposite shore," for he was in Boston and they were signals to Conant and his associates on Charlestown Neck. Revere's job was to try to row past the *Somerset* and then ride north along the Mystic River warning the countryside. William Dawes, a second courier and also from a family of silversmiths, was to try to get through the sentries at Boston Neck. When Warren got the information he wanted, everything was carried out. Newman, slipping from bed in his mother's house where British officers were quartered, climbed through a back window, crossed a roof, and got to the church. He met Revere there, and with vestreyman John Pulling and a friend of Revere's named Thomas Barnard set two lanterns indicating that the water route was the one. Newman got home safely. Interrogated later, he blamed vestreyman Pulling who had fled town for ordering him to open the church and was exonerated. Revere also went home, before leaving to try to slip by the *Somerset.* After some difficulty in eluding British troops, he met Joshua Bentley and Thomas Richardson, who were to row him over, at the riverside. Suddenly, the trio remembered they would need cloth to muffle the oars, but none of them had it. One, however, knew a local girl, and attracting her to a window with a special whistle, he got her to throw down a petticoat. Revere used to insist the garment was still warm. At any rate, it served its purpose and the rowboat got across to Charlestown without being detected. When he arrived safely in Charlestown, the citizens had already attempted to get word to Hancock and Adams at Clark's parsonage in Lexington. One of Conant's friends, Richard Devens, had seen the British patrols and had even been asked where a "Clark's tavern" was. But no one had got through. Revere, who had crossed unaware these patrols would be out, decided to try it himself. Joseph Larkin gave him a good horse, a Narragansett pacer. "So," as Esther Forbes says in her definitive book on all this, "away, down the moonlit road, goes Paul Revere and the Larkin horse, galloping into history, art, editorials, folklore, poetry; the beat of those hooves never to be forgotten."[1]

Revere rode up Charlestown Neck to the mainland with the Mystic River to the north and the Charles River to the south. An encounter with two mounted British officers forced him to cross above the Mystic near Medford, and he didn't come south again till he was beyond Alewife Brook. From Medford on, he alarmed the countryside, literally house by house till he got to Lexington. There he informed Hancock and Adams that the Regulars were out and coming in force. Hancock, who was never noted for his poise, wanted to join the Minutemen with a rifle. Adams had spent about half an hour arguing with him that they could serve the cause better by less direct means, when in came William Dawes, who had left by Boston Neck. It seemed one of the sentries was an old acquaintance, so he was passed through and came north via Roxbury and Cambridge. Revere and Dawes decided to ride on the remaining six miles to Concord. As they left, they were joined by Dr. Samuel Prescott, a young Concord doctor, who had been in Lexington courting his sweetheart, Miss Milliken. Prescott was the one who was fated to get through. Revere describes what happened as follows:[2]

. . . when we had got about half way from Lexington to Concord, the other two, stopped at a House to awake the man. I kept along. when I had got about 200 yards ahead of them, I saw two officers under a tree as before, [not far from Hartwell Farm, North Lincoln.]

[1] Esther Forbes, *Paul Revere and the Times He Lived In* (Boston, 1942), 257-258.

[2] As quoted in Forbes, 262-263.

I immediately called to my company to come up, saying here was two of them. (for I had told them what Mr. Devens told me, and of my being stopped) in an instant I saw four officers, who rode up to me, with their pistols in their hands & said G – D d – m you stop, if you go an inch further you are a dead Man. Immeditly Mr. Prescot came up he turned the butt of his whipp we attempted to git thro them, but they kept before us, and swore if we did not turn into that pasture, they would blow our brains out. They had placed themselves opposite a pair of Barrs, and had taken the Barrs down. They forced us in. The Doctor jumped his horse over a low stone wall, and got to Concord. I observed a wood at a small distance and made for that intending when I gained that to jump my Horse & run afoot, just as I reached it out started six officers, siesed my bridle, put their pistols to my Breast, ordered me to dismount, which I did. One of them, who appeared to have command there, and much of a Gentleman. asked where I came from; I told him. he asked what time I left it; I told him, he seemed much supprised, He said Sir may I crave your name? I answered my name is Revere. What said he Paul Revere? I answered yes; the others abused me much; but he told me not to be afraid, no one should hurt me. I told him they would miss their Aim. [This seems to have been a common catch-phrase that night.] He said they should not, they were only after some Deserters they expected down the Road. I told them I knew better, I knew what they were after; that I had alarumed the country all the way up, that their Boats had catch'd aground, and I should have 500 men here soon; one of them said they had 1500 coming. . . . Major Mitchel of the 5th Reg't clap'd a pistol to my head and said if I did not tell the truth, he would blow my brains out. . . . I gave him much the same answers; after he and two more had spoke together in a low voice he then ordered me to mount, and the Major rode up to me and took the reins. G – d sir you are not to ride with reins I assure you; and gave them to the officer on my right to lead me. I asked him to let me have the reins & I would not run from him, he said he would not trust me. He then Ordered 4 men out of the Bushes, and to mount their horses they were country men which they had stopped who were going home; they ordered us to march. He came up to me and said 'We are now going towards your friends, and if you attempt to run, or we are insulted, we will blow your Brains out.' I told him he might do as he pleased.

Dawes, as well as Prescott, escaped, though Dawes fell from his horse and lost both the mount and his watch in the process. Revere and the four other captives were marshalled along toward Lexington. As they drew near the town, a gun was fired. Revere, who had already upset the patrol by telling them the countryside was up in arms, the British boats had run aground, and that 500 militiamen lay in wait at Lexington, said that it was "to alarm the country." Figuring that their prisoners were too much an encumberance, the soldiers ordered all but Revere to dismount, drove off their horses, and told them to walk home. Shortly after they took Larkin's horse from Revere and set him free on foot. Revere walked across a graveyard and the fields to the parsonage, where Hancock and Adams were still in some disagreement over plans for that April morning to follow. In the meantime, other men and other couriers were criss-crossing the land north of Boston: forgotten men, without their Longfellows, Browns, Halls, Dorrs, doing their part in crying the alarm. The stage had been set for the shot, heard round the world, to be fired.

The account above is, I am sure, a pretty accurate reconstruction of what really went on near Boston in mid-April 1775. It was but the final incident in events leading up to that Lexington skirmish of which British Major Pitcairn seems to have lost control and Concord where the Revolution really began. Caught up in the affairs of Brandywine, West Point, and Yorktown, people soon forgot about it. Dr. Warren died at Bunker Hill. Conant, Devens, Dawes, Prescott slipped back into obscurity. Even Paul Revere, who we like to feel was one of the really vital figures in our struggle for freedom, also faded into middle-class oblivion. Dixon Wecter points out that prior "to Longfellow's poem Revere's name was not included in a single dictionary of American biography. . . ."[3]

In 1795, Ebenezer Stiles composed a tribute to Revere and the men who stood with "their flag to the April breeze unfurled." For obvious reasons, the poem has never been widely read, although it

[3] Dixon Wecter, *The Hero in America* (New York, 1941), 87.

has been preserved in the archives of the Massachusetts Historical Society. Spelling and all, it goes as follows:[4]

March 15/1795

Story of the Battle of Concord and
Lexinton and Revear's ride
Twenty years ago

He speard neither horse nor whip nor spur
As he galloped through mud and mire
He thought of nought but "Liberty"
And the lantern that hung from the spire
He raced his steed through field and wood
Nor turned to ford the river
But faced his horse to the foaming flood
They swam across togather

2

He madly dashed o'er mountain and moor
Never slacked spur nor rein
Untill with shout he stood by the door
Of the church by Concord green
"They come They come" he loudly cried
"They are marching their Legions this way
Prepar to meet them ye true and tried
They'l be hear by Break of day"

3

The bells were rung the drums were beat
The Melitia attended the roll
Every face we meet in the street
Wears a determined Scoul
For this is the day all men expected
Yet none of us wanted to see
But now it had come no one rejected
Our Country's call for Liberty

[4] This poem has been preserved in the archives of the Massachusetts Historical Society. It was sent me through the kindness of the Director, Stephen T. Riley. Neither Riley nor I is aware that it has been printed before.

4

Youngmen and old ansured the call
To defend the land of their sire
The brought with them some powder and ball
To return the British fire
For well they knew the Blood thirsty troops
Would do their best endevour
To ruin their homes destroy their crops
And bind them slaves for ever

5

The morning dawned the Sun arose
The birds sang loud with glee
All nature seemed to strife opposed
And the river Rolled on Merrylie
But Hush! the tramp the gleam of steel
See, See, their waving plums
As slowly they come o'er the fields
Marching to beat of drums

6

Fall in, attention the captain cried
Look well to your guns my men
But do not fire till I give the word
Leave the opening shot to them
E'en as he spoke a shot was heard
And a patriot fell on the green
And again they fired without speaking a word
The assassins what do they mean

7

Unable to stand their withering fire
We're reluctantly foreced to obay
The word from our Captain to gently retire
And meet e'er the close of the day
The foe passed on to his work of blood
And to search for hidden stors
With a laugh and a jest that boaded no good
To the women we left within doors.

Part Second

What sound is that said a ploughman strong
As he stoped his horse in the field
And looked to his wife who sat under the tree
She had brought him his morning meal,
What sound is that and he turned his ear
To list to the far off hum
By Heavens that's a shot I hear
And that's the sound of a drum

2

He reached his gun from the side of the plough
Where he kept it in case of need
And his powder horn he took from a bough
And his Horse became a steed
He turned to his wife she'd a tear in her eye
But she spoke like a matron of greace
As fondly he kissed her a last good bye
She bade to never spare the foe untill they craved for peace

3

He rode down the lane at a breakneck pace
So anxious was he for the fight
That he saw not a youth with unshaven face
Who was running with all his might
To the scene of bloodshed carnage and woe
That the soldiers delt out with joy
His mother said go fight the foe
Although you'r my only boy

4

Go take thy Father's gun she said
That he used in the indian wars
And do not return untill they'r all dead
Or driven from off these shores
Be brave like him whose name you bare
Like him defend the right
Of snars and pitfalls my son beware
And keep thy scutcheon bright

5

Now the patriot captain's voice
Is heard below the ridge
Fall in men quick we have no choice
We must defend the bridge
The little band despersed that morn
Now sweled to thrice their number
Stood no longer like the timed fawn
But a lion roused from slumber

6

The British troops with victory flushed
In wars by sea and land
Scorned ther foe the often crushed
Deened naught could them withstand
They'd fain repet to their farmer foe
The lesson taught that morn
That George's vengance is never slow
To who treat his laws with scorn

7

The Patriots gathered from Hill and Dale
They come from cottage and farm
By Highway and Stream from Hamlet and Vale
Each bringing his polished arm
They form in companys on the hill
Where the plough was latly used
The vandals troops are lacking still
The scene new courage infused

8

With steady step and scowling brow
Each man his rifle grasped
And down the hill to meet the foe
Five hundred patriots passed
With five hundred guns and powder horns
To brave great Britains power
Her trained Brutes her statemens scorn
And the threatened trators dower

9

They marched with firm determined tread
As did ever greek or Trojen
And scorned to think of fear or dread
The steel of the British leigon
One volley from their guns they fired
With true and steady aim
Duble quick the troops retired
And left the bridge to them

10

On we pushed across the stream
The Redcoats before us flew
As though they waked from horred dream
Retreat their bugles blew
Their Flag that never knew defeat
Tho oft in Foregne wars tried
Is trampled now beneath our feet
With Blood the ground is dyed

11

They tried to rally–scatered, fled
With panic stricken feer
Tho ground is covered with their dead
No reinforcements near
For every tree contains a gun
Behind each fence a foe
The Wiley fox's race is run
The Tyrant's got to go

Eb. Stiles

After this poetic effort, not much is heard of Revere's exploit for 65 years, well over two generations. During this time, the event was kept alive only as a family and town legend–the concern of few but local raconteurs and local historians. One of the latter, Jeremy Belknap, a founder of the Massachusetts Historical Society, persuaded Revere to write out his first hand account of the days leading up to and away from Lexington. Revere did this in 1798, basing his remarks on an earlier account he had prepared for his own use.

Three versions of this account, a rough draft, a more polished version for his family, and a polite, extensive text for the Historical Society can still be seen.

But the really important date in Paul Revere's "life" came long after he was dead. It was April 5, 1860, when Henry Wadsworth Longfellow climbed the tower of what was then called Old North Church, the Christ Church of Revere's day, and in that "home of innumerable pigeons" day-dreamed of the rider, the lanterns, and the cause of romantic times gone by.

Longfellow is an interesting figure. A descendant of John Alden on his mother's side; son of a prominent Portland, Maine lawyer; fellow student of Nathaniel Hawthorne and Franklin Pierce at Bowdoin, he became the best known and best loved American poet of his generation here and abroad. And Longfellow was a good poet. Today we think of him as intellectually shallow, as sentimental, even maudlin, a sort of high-class Edgar Guest. But guilty as he may have been of such faults, one also has to remember the age was more naive than ours, that it was a period when sentimentality was cherished, and that a host of writers we rate above Longfellow today may well seem the lesser when our vogues, for example social protest, have passed. Certainly no American poet, before or since, has mastered prosody or proved his versatility the way Longfellow did. He may have had trite, sugary things to say, but he knew his craft absolutely. Who else in the history of American literature can match his successful control of all the standard forms: blank verse, sonnet, ballad, lyric quatrain, horseback meter, etc. or his ability to experiment at length with dactylic hexameter or the *Kalevala* rhythm? Like Tennyson, his English counterpart, Longfellow is unfavorably belittled beside writers whose ideas have more substance, but whose technique and versatility are far inferior. And he did reach the public. He was a "best-selling" writer in the days when poets were still best-sellers. Do you realize his *Miles Standish* sold 10,000 copies in London alone on the day of its publication; 5000 copies in Boston before noon? This would be fantastic, even for a novel in these days of mass promotion, heavy population, and high literacy.

Tales of a Wayside Inn was Longfellow's first undertaking after *Miles Standish.* It is not surprising, therefore, that the first tale in it, "The Landlord's Tale," should return to the theme of popular legend and tell the story of Revere's ride. Nor is it an accident that Longfellow, with his fingers on the pulse of American taste, selected this national, patriotic subject during the Civil War. Modelled on such masterpieces as Chaucer's *Canterbury Tales* and Boccacio's *Decameron, Tales of a Wayside Inn* came out in three parts from late 1863 to 1873. It was first entitled *Sudbury Tales* and the Inn was the old Red Horse Inn at Sudbury, twenty miles out of Boston. Lyman Howe, whose family had kept the Inn for nearly 200 years, knew Longfellow well. He is the Landlord who tells of Revere's ride. About Howe, Longfellow gathered a group of his own friends: a violinist, the Norwegian Ole Bull; a student, Henry Ware Wales; a Sicilian, Luigi Monti; a Spanish Jew and Boston merchant, Israel Edrehi; a theologian, Professor Daniel Treadwell of Harvard; and a poet, T. W. Parsons.

The poem opens,[5]

PRELUDE

THE WAYSIDE INN.

ONE autumn night, in Sudbury town,
Across the meadows bare and brown,
The windows of the wayside inn
Gleamed red with firelight through the leaves
Of woodbine, hanging from the eaves
Their crimson curtains rent and thin.

As ancient is this hostelry
As any in the land may be,
Built in the old Colonial day,
When men lived in a grander way,
With ampler hospitality;

A kind of old Hobgoblin Hall,
Now somewhat fallen to decay,
With weather-stains upon the wall,
And stairways worn, and crazy doors,
And creaking and uneven floors,
And chimneys huge, and tiled and tall.

[5] Lines 1-16.

There follows a description of each of the "group of friends" who cluster "around the fireside at their ease." The musician, Bull, is described last. He is playing his violin. As the music ceases, the applause is loud. The violinist bows and smiles.[6]

Then silence followed; then began
A clamor for the Landlord's tale,—
The story promised them of old,
They said, but always left untold;
And he, although a bashful man,
And all his courage seemed to fail,
Finding excuse of no avail,
Yielded; and thus the story ran.

THE LANDLORD'S TALE

PAUL REVERE'S RIDE.

Listen, my children, and you shall hear
Of the midnight ride of Paul Revere,
On the eighteenth of April, in Seventy-five;
Hardly a man is now alive
Who remembers that famous day and year.

He said to his friend, "If the British march
By land or sea from the town tonight,
Hang a lantern aloft in the belfry arch
Of the North Church tower as a signal light,—
One, if by land, and two, if by sea;
And I on the opposite shore will be,
Ready to ride and spread the alarm
Through every Middlesex village and farm,
For the country folk to be up and to arm."

Then he said, "Good night!" and with muffled oar
Silently rowed to the Charlestown shore,
Just as the moon rose over the bay,
Where swinging wide at her moorings lay
The *Somerset*, British man-of-war;
A phantom ship, with each mast and spar

[6] Lines 303 f.

Across the moon like a prison bar,
And a huge black hulk that was magnified
By its own reflection in the tide.

Meanwhile, his friend, through alley and street,
Wanders and watches with eager ears,
Till in the silence around him he hears
The muster of men at the barrack door,
The sound of arms, and the tramp of feet,
And the measured tread of the grenadiers,
Marching down to their boats on the shore.

Then he climbed the tower of the Old North Church,
Church,
By the wooden stairs, with stealthy tread,
To the belfry chamber overhead,
And startled the pigeons from their perch
On the somber rafters, that round him made
Masses and moving shapes of shade,–
By the trembling ladder, steep and tall,
To the highest window in the wall,
Where he paused to listen and look down
A moment on the roofs of the town,
And the moonlight flowing over all.

Beneath, in the churchyard, lay the dead,
In their night-encampment on the hill,
Wrapped in silence so deep and still
That he could hear, like a sentinel's tread,
The watchful night-wind, as it went
Creeping along from tent to tent,
And seeming to whisper, "All is well!"
A moment only he feels the spell
Of the place and the hour, and the secret dread
Of the lonely belfry and the dead;
For suddenly all his thoughts are bent
On a shadowy something far away,
Where the river widens to meet the bay,–
A line of black that bends and floats
On the rising tide, like a bridge of boats.

Meanwhile, impatient to mount and ride,
Booted and spurred, with a heavy stride
On the opposite shore walked Paul Revere.
Now he patted his horse's side,
Now gazed at the landscape far and near,
Then, impetuous, stamped the earth,
And turned and tightened his saddle-girth;
But mostly he watched with eager search
The belfry-tower of the Old North Church,
As it rose above the graves on the hill,
Lonely and spectral and somber and still.
And lo! as he looks, on the belfry's height
A glimmer, and then a gleam of light!
He springs to the saddle, the bridle he turns,
But lingers and gazes, till full on his sight
A second lamp in the belfry burns!

A hurry of hoofs in a village street,
A shape in the moonlight, a bulk in the dark,
And beneath, from the pebbles, in passing, a spark
Struck out by a steed flying fearless and fleet.
That was all! And yet, through the gloom and
the light,
The fate of a nation was riding that night;
And the spark struck out by that steed, in his
flight,
Kindled the land into flame with its heat.

He has left the village and mounted the steep,
And beneath him, tranquil and broad and deep,
Is the Mystic, meeting the ocean tides;
And under the alders, that skirt its edge,
Now soft on the sand, now loud on the ledge,
Is heard the tramp of his steed as he rides.

It was twelve by the village clock
When he crossed the bridge into Medford town.
He heard the crowing of the cock,
And the barking of the farmer's dogs,
And felt the damp of the river fog,
That rises after the sun goes down.

It was one by the village clock
When he galloped into Lexington.
He saw the gilded weathercock
Swim in the moonlight as he passed,
And the meetinghouse windows, blank and bare,
Gaze at him with a spectral glare,
As if they already stood aghast
At the bloody work they would look upon.

It was two by the village clock
When he came to the bridge in Concord town.
He heard the bleating of the flock,
And the twitter of birds among the trees,
And felt the breath of the morning breeze
Blowing over the meadows brown.
And one was safe and asleep in his bed
Who at the bridge would be first to fall,
Who that day would be lying dead,
Pierced by a British musket-ball.

You know the rest. In the books you have read,
How the British Regulars fired and fled,–
How the farmers gave them ball for ball,
From behind each fence and farmyard wall,
Chasing the red-coats down the lane,
Then crossing the fields to emerge again
Under the trees at the turn of the road,
And only pausing to fire and load.

So through the night rode Paul Revere;
And so through the night went his cry of alarm
To every Middlesex village and farm,–
A cry of defiance and not of fear,
A voice in the darkness, a knock at the door,
And a word that shall echo forevermore!
For, borne on the night-wind of the Past,
Through all our history, to the last,
In the hour of darkness and peril and need,
The people will waken and listen to hear
The hurrying hoof-beats of that steed,
And the midnight message of Paul Revere.

From this moment on it matters little what Revere or Dawes or Prescott actually did. From this moment on, Longfellow's version has become history, to Americans and Europeans alike.

This is the way it always happens. Some singer of tales, a glorious or inglorious Milton, phrases something or organizes something in a way that is accepted without question by succeeding generations. Such genius never originates anything; it simply arranges matters the way people know they ought to be, making "right or wrong," "phoney or genuine" inconsequential and "should have been" "was."

So Paul Revere did stand on "the opposite shore" and waited for the "midnight message" that read "by sea," and he did ride off alone, carrying "the fate of a nation" in "defiance" not "fear" to first Lexington, and then Concord. It's true, because hardly a man is now alive who remembers differently.

11 "The Father of all the Yankees"

BUT ALL HEROES ARE NOT HEROES of the moment. There is the day by day side of life, as well, and it is in the everyday routine that the New England Yankee flourishes, eventually broadening his range beyond the Hudson to the frontier until he is "westernized" into a stock American figure. The Yankee is, of course, a trickster, where figures like Tim Murphy, Ethan Allen, and even Paul Revere are heroes of prowess. The prowess hero is always physically, if not mentally, exceptional. The Yankee is championed because of his mind, which not only enables him to survive with a mediocre or weak body, but also enables him to dupe slower thinkers, play pranks on greenhorns, and make money where there seems none to be had.

As mentioned in the chapter on "Yankee Doodle," the word "yankee" had come, by the time of the American Revolution, to mean to cheat or to complete a clever trade. It was originally Scottish and exactly how a Scottish term for trickery got itself attached to the New Englander is not clear. Whether this term and the Dutch term of derision, Jan Kees, fused or whether one caused the other to develop, I am at a loss to say. All I am sure of is that the New England trader and village wit who "yankeed" his fellow citizens developed into a stock type by the end of the 18th century. Then, with the aid of magazines, dramas, and newspapers became a standard American trickster. The Christian world has long thought of the Jew as the archetypical sharp merchant, but the Scotchman, the Quaker, and others have had their days in this questionable sun. The American 19th century was the day of the Yankee.

Originally, the sharp Yankee merchant was a development of the green countryman, who in his English form is Hodge from Yorkshire and a real rogue under his naive exterior. He is a type whose ancestors go well back into Western European and Eastern lore, and who is not unlike the rabbits, spiders, and coyotes of West African and American Indian mythology. However, his role does not involve creation and the ordering of the universe as the role of the trickster so often does in primitive lore; his role lies in that part of the world where the urban and the rural come in contact, where trade and sales determine a man's ability, and where bargaining is the area through which one demonstrates his intellectual capacity.

Many of the early Yankee tales center around a local inn or tavern, where the "in" group gathers to listen to accounts of gulls long since deceived and coneys yet to be caught. The material of such yankeeisms is well-known to us all: it is the material out of which grows the snipe-hunt at the boy's camp; the plots of Ring Lardner's "Haircut," Thomas Nash's *The Gull's Hornbook*, Mark Twain's "The Celebrated Jumping Frog of Calaveras County." There is nothing particularly unique or American in such material. Loafers and city newcomers have been duped throughout history, petty thieves and greedy churchmen have been cured, horse races and games have been fixed before. The stories never die, never really vary, told today in the lounges of jetliners and after bourgeoise dinners or yesterday in pubs and Pullman car washrooms. The one below, involving a stand-off between two Yorkshiremen, is typical. The antagonists might just as well be a Jew and a Protestant, a Quaker and a customer, a Northern Negro and a Georgia Cracker, a travelling salesman and the farmer himself.

One day a Yorkshireman was ploughing his field when his horse dropped dead in the furrow. The Yorkshireman left him lying there and went right over to the house of a friend who lived down the road.

Walking up to the house, he asked for his friend, sat around talking politics a bit, passing the time of day. Finally, he said,

"By the way, remember my white horse?"

"Fine animal," the other said. "One of the best about."

"How will you trade your bay for him?"

"Even," came the reply. "It'll be a good deal."

"Shake hands on it." They shook and talked a while longer.

"Well, I got to be going," the Yorkshireman remarked, "and don't forget to pick my horse up out of the furrow where he dropped dead ploughing this morning."

"Right," said his friend, "and you will find the skin of my bay hanging in the barn, though I'll have to give you a hand getting the entrails back from the crows."

Everyone has heard hundreds of these stories, and they prove but one thing. The Yankee is a world type. He is American only in that our literary hacks have embraced him so wholeheartedly, identified him so completely with our image of ourselves, throughout our national history.

Royall Tyler's figure, Jonathan, in the comic drama, *The Contrast* of 1787 is sometimes considered the first fictional Yankee. He was followed by Jonathan Ploughboy, Hiram Dodge, Solomon Swap, Sam Patch, and a host of others. Writers like Thomas Halliburton, the Nova Scotia judge, and Seba Smith, a Turner, Maine newsman, developed full biographical accounts of peddler Sam Slick and country politician Jack Downing. The Yankee or Yankee-like character became a vogue, flourishing in print, and eventually moving out to the western and southwestern frontiers where he matched wits with the roarers and braggers developed there. Used by politicians, hucksters, and pulp-writers for immediate needs, he became through sheer volume a national symbol that is still with us. Josh Billings, the late 19th century proverb writer and local colorist, sums up his full-blown character as follows:[1]

LIVE Yankees are chuck full of karakter and sissing hot with enterprize and curiosity.

[1] See *Josh Billings on Ice, and Other Things,* 20-22.

In bild we find them az lean az a hunter's dorg, with a parched countenance, reddy for a grin, or for a sorrow; ov elaastick step: thortful, but not abstrakted; pashunt, bekauze cunnin; ever watchful; slo to anger; avoiding a fight; but rezolute at bay.

In dress alwuz silk, but not stuck up; their harness alwuz betrays them wherever they go.

The oil ov their langwidge iz their dezire tew pleze, and their greezy words foreshadder a proffit.

They are natral mechanicks; the histry ov man's necessitys iz the histry ov their invenshuns.

The Live Yankee haz no hum; hiz luv ov invenshun breeds a luv ov change, and wharever a human trail shows itself we find him pantin on the trak.

He never gits sick at the stummuk in a furrin land, or grows sentermental; the buty ov a river tew him iz its capacity for a steambote; its sloping banks checker into bildin lots, and its poetry waters might do the drudgery ov a cottin mill.

He looks at a marble pyramid, guesses at its height, calkulates the stone by the perch, and sells the magnifisent relick in Boston at a proffit.

He climbs the Alpin hights, crossed by conkerin heroes, and iz struk with the proprierty ov tunneling it.

He sits, cross-legged, beneath the sheltring vine and listens to the oneazy sea, sees the warm promise ov the grape, and forgettin the holy memrys ov the land ov song, grinds the smilin vintage into wine and maiks a happy bargin.

You can meet him in Constanternopel, makin up in grimace what he lacks in langwidge, spreadin a plaster with hiz tounge, for the man ov Mahomet.

Go where you will, from the numb palsied North tew the swetting limberness ov the South, from the top ov earth's mornin tew half past eleven at night, and the everlastin Yankee you will find, either vehement in an argue, or purswazive in a swop.

Hiz religion iz praktikal; he mourns over the heathen, and iz reddy tew save them by the job.

He luvs liberty with a red pepper enthuziasm, and fully beleafs Nu England kan whip the universe.

If the phlegmatick Englishman brags about roast beef and hiz ansesters, Joanthan haz a pumpkin pie and a grandpop tew match them.

If the Frenchman grows crazy over a fragazee ov frog's hind legs, Jonathan pulls out a donut and a Rhode Island greening.

If the dusky Italian talks about the mad vomits ov vesuvius, Jonathan turns in the water power ov Niagara.

In argument alwuz ernest, and in reazoning alwuz specius, this progressive phenomena tramps the world with the skeleton ov a pattent right in hiz carpet bag, and, in his ever open hand and face a pleasant "Heow air yer?"

If you would save your pride from being sandpapered, risk it not in a dicker with Jonathan.

His razor is the true Damascus, strapped on the wand ov Midas for a golden harvest; hiz sanctity iz often shrewdness, and hiz sweet savor is often the reflekted halo ov the comin shillin.

Constitushunaly and by edukashun honest, he iz alwuz reddy tew cry for the deeds dun in the boddy; hiz hospitalitys and charities are ceremonial duty, and if hiz religion iz sometimes only the severitys ov a sabbath, it iz bekauze hiz bias iz the thursting impulse of a creatin genius chained tew the more sordid pashun for lucre.

For better or for worse, Americans like to think of themselves as being "live Yankees": not perfect, mind you, but interesting, different—really something, and without flies; perhaps given to cutting a corner or two, but only as sort of a game; basically honest, even sentimental, sure to come through when the chips are down—and just naturally s-h-a-r-p!"

A few years back, when I was asked to write a short definition of the word "yankee" for the *Encyclopedia Americana*, I concluded my remarks with the following paragraph.

Sam Hyde, the Indian half-breed from Dedhan, Mass., is a true folk figure about whom Yankee tales once accumulated. More famous, but clearly known only through their popularity in early 19th century magazines and newspapers, are Sam Slick . . . and Jack Downing. . . . However, to the average person, Ben Franklin, who preached his gospel of industry and frugality and who wangled his way to fame and fortune, is as Thomas Carlyle called him "the father of all the Yankees."

I quote this passage here because it enables me to point up two things: one, that Franklin is forever associated with the concept of the Yankee in the popular mind: and, two, that this association is not a folk association, but a literary, popular one, taught in school and learned from writings, many of them Franklin's own, many of them created long after Franklin was dead.

Franklin had reason to want to associate himself with the image of the Yankee. At home, it meant money in the bank. He was one of the first of the newspaper and magazine writers to capitalize on the appetite for Yankee wisdom and Yankee acumen that was to be fed so enthusiastically by the 19th century. Abroad, it gave him a means of convincing first the British and then the French that the Colonists were interesting, worthy, and able to hold their own in the civilized world. After his death, as he became a symbol of the way to wealth in a mercantile nation, his admirers fostered this association further, stressing the Yankee practicality, Yankee opportunism, Yankee sagacity of Franklin's life as the model for any young American worth his salt.

Somehow, unfairly I know, I always think of Franklin as an arch fiend who has gained control of this entire land—Franklin the culture hero of the nation described by William Faulkner, a nation of[2]

> . . . the cheap shoddy dishonest music, the cheap flash baseless overvalued money, the glittering edifice of publicity foundationed on nothing like a cardhouse over an abyss and all of the noisy muddle of political activity which used to be our minor national industry and is now our national amateur pastime—all the spurious uproar produced by men deliberately fostering and then getting rich on our national passion for the mediocre: who will accept the best provided it is debased and befouled before being fed to us: who are the only people on earth who brag publicly of being second-rate, i.e., lowbrows.

I see a Franklin who lays down this ethic, verifies the American's desire to measure himself and others by cost alone, and glorifies the necessity of a practical purpose for everything one does. At its worst, *ars gratia argentis*, from the learning of one's style by practicing against Addison to attendance at church when one couldn't care less. Even today, at the University of Pennsylvania (Founded by Benjamin Franklin) where his statue sits outside College Hall, the old humanities building, looking across to the new University

[2] From *Intruder in the Dust.* See Gavin Stevens' remarks in Chapter 7.

library complex, he strikes me as the profit-oriented trustee keeping his efficiency eye on the cost account of the institution's learning, a latter-day saint, conquering the thought of a nation with a religion called Cola.

It's overwhelming. I can remember driving down the Rhode Island shore towards Westerly in September 1962 with my then 13-year-old son, Mark. He was nearly in tears in the backseat because he had forgotten his copy of Benjamin Franklin's *Autobiography*. That was his main summer reading, and he was to be tested on it in Philadelphia the next day. Since June, he had scarcely opened it, finding it excruciatingly dull every time he tried. My younger son, Jock, is 13 as I write the first draft of this. He too has been assigned Benjamin Franklin's *Autobiography* for summer reading. When the teacher announced the fact, Jock was bold enough to say he had heard it was "really dull." The teacher was confused. "It is one of the finest books ever written," he felt compelled to reply. "You should study it. Maybe then you too will be a great American someday."

The teen-aged boy who sits before his rude desk, studying by lamplight under the picture of President Lincoln, is far more likely to emulate Benjamin Franklin than Honest Abe. For Franklin is the one who conquered the Calvinistic, penny-earned, penny-saved world in which today's youth must find its way. Franklin's story is a fairy story, with the Yankee merchant as hero, the plot beginning in the Colonial home of a tallow chandler where a fifteenth son with no prospects sets forth, and ending 84 years later with its hero one of the best known and most honored citizens of the civilized world.

Ben's father, Josiah Franklin, migrated to the Colonies from Ecton, Northamptonshire, England in 1685 when he was 30 years old. He was anxious to escape persecution for his strong Puritan, Protestant beliefs. Settling in Boston, he became a chandler, married twice, and produced 17 children of whom Benjamin, born in 1706, was the fifteenth. As Benjamin was the tenth son, his father, in what now seems a veritable fit of generosity, planned to tithe him to the university. However, money for this noble venture was lacking, and Benjamin was removed from school at the age of 10 and put to work cutting wicks and filling candle moulds. The youth hated this work and might well have made good his threat to run off to sea had not his father apprenticed him at the age of 12 to his older brother, James, a printer.

Ben was a precocious boy. He could read early (he claimed for as long as he could remember), and he read the standard volumes of his day, *Pilgrim's Progress, Robinson Crusoe*, Plutarch, Locke, Addison and Steele. There is little point dwelling on his exaggeration of how he learned to write prose from trying to reconstruct Addison's essays. The fact is he taught himself to write well, and when his brother began the *New England Courant* in 1751, the 15-year-old Ben was able to contribute the *Do-good Papers,* anonymously and successfully. But whether because of natural independence, because his brother was not treating him fairly, or because local authorities were disturbed by his political and religious views, he chose to leave Boston. In 1753, 17 years old, Franklin sold his books, and with the money took passage to New York en route to Philadelphia and fame.

I didn't learn Franklin sailed to New York until I read his *Autobiography* while studying for my PhD. And learning this fact destroyed one of the private legends of my youth. I grew up in Wakefield, Rhode Island, not far from a building since torn down known as The Old Tavern. It was a mile south of the town on what is now called Old Post Road. Even though the Post Road of Franklin's day did not go by the Old Tavern, I had always heard that Benjamin Franklin spent the night there on his long walk to Philadelphia, and the anecdotes I knew about wily Ben always seemed appropriate to its low, dark rooms and narrow halls.

I remember the one that tells how he got a seat at the fireplace one blustery night, when all the chairs were occupied. He called the landlord, and in a loud voice demanded that a peck of raw oysters be served to his hungry horse outside. Everyone was curious to see a horse that ate oysters, so the travellers got up from the fire and followed the host into the cold. When they returned, Franklin was comfortable in the best chair, close to the blaze. Told his horse had refused the oysters, he said, "He has no idea what's good. Bring them to me and see if I refuse them!"

Today I know that the story appears in Thomas R. "Shepherd Tom" Hazard's *Recollections of Olden Times*, where it is set in New London,[3] but when I was ten and my brother and I used to go up to The Old Tavern to buy "Old Nick" candy bars, I had never heard of Shepherd Tom. As we walked home I always felt close to Franklin. I had bought Old Nicks, rather than Baby Ruths or O Henrys or Milky Ways, specifically because the word "old" was in the name, and somehow those candy bars took me back to Colonial times. Later I learned what Old Nick stood for, that Franklin's scalp itched, even that Babe Ruth drank, but for awhile I knew that intimacy with important things that lies behind all local legends—the cliffs where lovers leaped, the house where Washington slept, the flag that Betsy Ross sewed together.

Franklin arrived in Philadelphia, appropriately on a Sunday morning, with one Dutch dollar in his pocket, munching on a loaf of dry bread, watched from the doorway of her father's house by his future wife in a scene quite suitable for framing. As he knew the printing business well, he soon got employment.

Now the axiom that you don't get good literature until you get good journalism, and you don't get good journalism until you get cities and towns may not be 100% true, but it applies pretty well since the invention of the printing press. Franklin came to Philadelphia just as it was beginning to develop sufficient size and sophistication to support magazines and papers. Through his excellent training and his opportunism he was able to capitalize on this situation. His first big break came when Sir William Keith, Governor of the Colony, offered him the governmental printing if he would set up his own business. Franklin leaped at this chance and set out for London to buy type and presses. Letters from Keith were to follow and establish his credit. They never arrived, and Franklin, stranded in London, was forced to take employment as a printer in order to eat. He stayed a year and a half, learning things about both England and printing that were later to prove useful. In the autumn of 1726 he had returned to Philadelphia.

By 1730, at the age of 24, Franklin had become the manager

[3] See p. 38.

of his own printing house. Before long he had established himself as the most accurate, reliable, and generally capable printer about. In 1729 he purchased the *Pennsylvania Gazette*, a weekly newspaper, which he converted into the top-flight journal he was to edit for more than 35 years. In 1732, he began the now almost fabulous *Poor Richard's Almanac*, which he ran for a quarter of a century. The latter reached an annual circulation of 10,000 copies, became the best-known publication in the Colonies, serving to make Franklin's name widely known. He discusses the *Almanac* in the 1758 edition, first published in 1757.[4]

I have heard that nothing gives an Author so great Pleasure, as to find his Works respectfully quoted by other learned Authors. This Pleasure I have seldom enjoyed; for tho' I have been, if I may say it without Vanity, an eminent Author of Almanacks annually now a full Quarter of a Century, my Brother Authors in the same Way, for what Reason I know not, have ever been very sparing in their Applauses; and no other Author has taken the least Notice of me, so that did not my Writings produce me some solid Pudding, the great Deficiency of Praise would have quite discouraged me.

I concluded at length, that the People were the best Judges of my Merit; for they buy my Works; and besides, in my Rambles, where I am not personally known, I have frequently heard one or other of my Adages repeated, with, as Poor Richard says, at the End on't; this gave me some Satisfaction, as it showed not only that my Instructions were regarded, but discovered likewise some Respect for my Authority; and I own, that to encourage the Practice of remembering and repeating those wise Sentences, I have sometimes quoted myself with great Gravity.

The Deistic thinking that had swept across Europe in the 17th and 18th centuries found its way to America. Basic to it is the idea that God can come directly to each and any individual without the aid of minister, priest, or even scripture. Not only is this a great equalizer, eventually resulting in democratic government, the emancipation of women and Negroes, as well as an emphasis on enthusiasm and reliance on one's own conscience in religion, but also it tends

[4] These are the opening lines of "The Way to Wealth."

to imply that education, society's conventions, in fact civilization itself, is inferior to direct, unconfused contact with the wisdom of the Lord. "Paul et Virginie" besport themselves on a desert isle wise in their proximity to Nature, Wordsworth assures us that the uncomplicated Child is Father of the Man, and the savage in his wilderness appears most noble of all. "God made the country; man made the town," William Cowper writes, and if we believe this the cracker-barrel philosopher certainly has something important, almost divine, to tell us.

Among a people who are in the process of evolving a nation according to Deistic principles, readers are bound to be attracted to country wisdom and rural aphorism. Thus Americans have always been suckers for anyone pretending to be a native wit and uneducated sage. Davy Crockett, Jack Downing, Josh Billings, Will Rogers, Sut Lovingood, Abe Martin, Hank Morgan – these are just a few, fictional or real, of the parade of simple pundits that has marched through our literature. Franklin sensed this appetite early and utilized it crassly and commercially. Walter Blair has said,[5]

> Poor Richard was uneducated but so acute and experienced in the ways of the world that he could make witty comments which a nation, worshipping what he called "horse sense," vastly appreciated.

In the Preface to the 1758 *Almanac*, Franklin assembled over one hundred of these comments into a discourse by a wise old fellow to the people assembled at an auction. This preface was entitled "The Way to Wealth" and was reprinted all over the Colonies as well as on broadsides and in newspapers in Britain. Eventually, it was translated into fifteen other languages. Franklin began "The Way to Wealth" by implying that his maxims were folk proverbs, and therefore the wisdom of the ages. However, this seems largely a commercial device, for a study of the material shows very little of it to be from oral tradition and Franklin's usual contribution to consist of making a literary aphorism appear like a folk product. The bulk of the wise old man's remarks are from

[5] See Robert Spiller (editor), *A Time of Harvest* (New York, 1962), 34.

foreign writers whom Franklin either had read or had been interested in seeing translated. Stuart Gallacher has done a study of "The Way to Wealth" in *The Journal of English and Germanic Philology*[6] in which he surveys these maxims. Gallacher lists 82 that appeared in earlier sources, 19 that he feels Franklin originated, and four on which he has no opinion. Some of the ones Franklin borrowed, he borrowed without change. For example, his "We may give Advice, but we cannot give Conduct" is a literal translation of La Rochefoucauld's "*On donne des conseils, mais on n'inspire point de conduite.*" Others he improved, or at least changed to his satisfaction. Samuel Richardson wrote in the "Moral and Instructive Sentiments" in *Clarissa*, "No one is out of the reach of Misfortune. No one should therefore glory in his prosperity." Franklin's version is "King's have long arms, but Misfortune longer. Let none think themselves out of her reach." The sources are numerous and distinguished, but Thomas Fuller's *Gnomologia*, published in 1732, and John Ray's *Proverbs*, published in 1670, seem to have been particularly useable. The chances are Franklin owned both. Fuller wrote, "Creditors have better memories than debtors, and are great observers of days and times." Franklin merely split it down the middle: "Creditors have better Memories than Debtors" and "Creditors are a superstitious Sect, great Observers of set Days and Times." It's disillusioning, but his most famous saying, "Early to Bed, early to rise, makes a Man healthy, wealthy and wise" is also in Fuller, and was certainly not new even then.

However, Franklin did re-popularize or convert to fresh proverbial form a good many sayings that were dropping out of use. Frank C. Brown and his co-workers came up with 26 proverbs from North Carolina folk tradition that are in "The Way to Wealth".[7] There is no telling how many of these would have survived had it not been for the boost given them by the wide distribution of Franklin's writings. Three, for sure, owe their very existence to Franklin as he coined them: "Three removes is as bad as a fire"; "there will

[6] 1949, 229-251.

[7] See *Frank C. Brown Collection of North Carolina Folklore* (Durham, 1952), I, 331-501. Bartlett J. Whiting edited this material.

always be sleeping enough in the grave"; and "always taking out of the meal-tub, and never putting in, soon comes to the bottom." Certainly others, like "constant dropping wears away stones"; "when you run in debt you give another power over your liberty"; and "the sleeping fox catches no poultry" are extremely common today. Such proverbs and such maxims, re-worked or not, popular or forgotten, served Franklin's purposes well, and the country has never been the worse for his commercial use of the old wisdom.

Some writers feel obligated to gloss over the way Franklin made his money from publishing, but there seems little point in such kindness. He made it the way anyone makes it in a competitive, business situation—by being a bit sharper than the next fellow, by placing profit before charity, breeding, or true honesty, and by working incredibly long hours. "Early to bed and early to rise" made Franklin wealthy; he was no doubt born healthy and wise. Like all men on the way up, he devoted all his energies toward the one goal money, and he promoted himself and his products without cease, picturing his life and publications as guides to success. So he felt compelled to leave his light on after he went to sleep hoping people would think he had worked even harder than he actually had; so he ruined his journalistic rivals, destroying them with the same efficiency that John Rockefeller used in nipping other buds that his Standard Oil might blossom; so he raised money for Christ Church and held a pew there even though he made jokes on religion as man's "doxy."

Like many Americans who have followed this path, once he had arrived he became generous. The wealthy Franklin, contrary to his advice in the *Autobiography* and "The Way to Wealth," seems to have found frugality a bore, to have become a soft touch for loans, and to have enjoyed the fruits of his mercantile labors to the fullest. This is one of the great paradoxes of American life, a facet that, as much as his grind to success, makes Franklin so representative of our country. The church-going American merchant connives, eradicates competition, cheats, slaves to make his fortune, then, almost with the fear of the Lord, spends his declining years in helping the poor, often the very ones he has exploited on his way up, giving to causes, and serving his community.

Franklin's "arrival" was most rapid, for he had calculated the advantages of controlling the press well. Through the *Gazette* and the *Almanac* he began to exert an influence in Philadelphia and the Colonies and to open the way for those things that have since reflected glory upon him. The list of his activities from his return from London in 1726 until he became Deputy-Postmaster General of the Colonies in 1753 is remarkable to say the least: 1731, founded the Philadelphia Library Company, the first subscription library in the Colonies; 1736, established the Union Fire Company; 1741, began publication of the *General Magazine and Historical Chronicle*, the second magazine to be published in the Colonies; 1744, established the American Philosophical Society; 1749, founded the Philadelphia Academy; 1752, performed the famous experiment that accidentally established the electrical identity of lightning and invented the lightning rod. Such a list is a delight to our modern business world where junior executives are forced to give their "fair share" to community causes, join a church as well as a country club, and enter into local management of schools, libraries, and politics. What's more, glossing this list of "do-good" activities is Franklin's scientific turn, which links him to the laboratory and its services in the interests of "a better world for better living"—the only part of academia most business men can comprehend anyhow. Dixon Wecter's description of such purposeful brilliance is worth repeating,[8]

> . . . He invented the Franklin stove and the lightning rod and bifocal spectacles, tested the heat absorption of white and colored fabrics, introduced the cabbage turnip to America, speculated sensibly on ventilation and the common cold, studied the Gulf Stream on his voyages across the Atlantic, contrived a mechanical arm to fetch down books from his shelves, devised a musical instrument, and when at last the gout and stone laid him low played with the fancy of "a balloon sufficiently large to raise me from the ground . . . being led by a string held by a man walking on the ground."

His most celebrated experiment, that of the kite in an electrical storm, held such dangerous possibilities that it might have made him

[8] Dixon Wecter, *The Hero in America* (New York, 1941), 63.

a martyr to science rather than allowed him to survive as the apostle of prudence. His son, the only witness of the discovery, by a curious quirk of folklore is shown in innumerable woodcuts and engravings as a small boy, although William was twenty-one at the time. On the other hand, Benjamin West's famous painting of "Franklin and the Lightning," made about 1805, portrays the kite-flyer of 1752 not as a vigorous man of forty-six but as a wrinkled, fat patriarch, his white locks streaming to the wind like Lear's, while cupids and aëry sprites flutter about his electrical apparatus. Franklin showed a casual modesty about his exploit which legend has chosen to ignore: he told no one about it until four months later, upon learning of similar experiments in France, and left no written account whatever. When his practical corollary of the lightning rod drew the applause of French scientists and praise from Louis XV, Franklin wrote in 1753 to a friend that he felt like the girl described in *The Tatler* "who was observed to grow suddenly proud, and none could guess the reason, till it came to be known that she had got on a new pair of garters." It is plain that Franklin enjoyed his part on the world's stage–of being a Yankee handy-andy about whose head the great of Europe had hung the halo of a Solomon or Merlin. He loved parlor tricks slightly tinged with sacrilege, such as stilling the waves by flourishing his bamboo cane filled with oil. His reputation as a wizard enhanced his career as a diplomat. Turgot's too familiar epigram, that "he snatched the lightning from the sky, and the sceptre from tyrants," was echoed even by Franklin's enemies.

And all this from a man who was able to retire at the age of 42! What merchant can resist the idealization of a person who rises so early and works so hard that he can retire to a life of public service, scientific experiment, and international fame at the age when most are just beginning to smell success.

Of course, Franklin didn't retire at all. He simply changed his profession from well-paid printer to well-paid public servant. The Deputy-postmaster, the Colonial Agent for Pennsylvania, the Agent for the Colonies in England and France may well have let his light burn into the morning hours simply because he needed it to see the work that kept him up all night. Nor had he forgotten any of his promotional tricks. Franklin, wily as ever, sensed quickly that the Colonies were considered too remote, too boorish, too uncivilized to gain serious audiences among the parliamentarians and courtiers of first England and then France. Where his job had once been to convince Philadelphians that he was the best printer or the best citizen about, it now became to convince Europeans that he, and by implication the Colonies or the new nation, was sophisticated, witty, of grace. He had to play this game by European rules, and his training in Addison, Steele, and the other 18th century essayists stood him in good stead. The letters and essays he wrote to these ends are well known. His *Rules by Which a Great Empire May be Reduced to a Small One*, relevant to the Colonial policies of 1773; the *Dialogue Between Franklin and the Gout;* the notes to Mme. Helvetius, et al, are *tours de force* demonstrating concretely that Europe was not the only place polite satire and genteel brilliance could appear.

When in London in 1765 as an agent for the Province of Pennsylvania, he had the job of lobbying before the Privy Council for the Colonial commercial interests then hamstrung by the disadvantageous British regulations. He drafted an anonymous letter "To the Editor of a Newspaper," in which he satirized the British reports unfavorable to the Colonial position. He lamented that people no longer believed what they read in print, assuring his readers that "all the Articles of News that seem improbable are not mere inventions." To those who believe that the Colonists could not compete with British producers because of the high cost of Colonial labor and the inferior quality of Colonial wool, he says,

> Dear Sir, do not let us suffer ourselves to be amus'd with such groundless Objections. The very Tails of the American Sheep are so laden with Wooll, that each has a little Car or Waggon on four little Wheels, to support & keep it from trailing on the Ground. Would they caulk their Ships, would they fill their Beds, would they even litter their Horses with Wooll, if it were not both plenty and cheap?

He also gives a report on the status of America's fishing industry.[9]

[9] See Albert H. Smyth, *The Writings of Benjamin Franklin* (New York. 1905-1907), 368-369.

"To the Genius of Franklin," by Fragonard

> . . . the account said to be from Quebec, in all the Papers last Week, that the Inhabitants of Canada are making Preparation for a Cod and Whale Fishery this 'Summer in the upper Lakes' [is true]. Ignorant People may object that the upper Lakes are fresh, and that Cod and Whale are Salt Water Fish: But let them know, Sir, that Cod, like other Fish when attacked by their Enemies, fly into any Water where they can be safest; that Whales, when they have a mind to eat Cod, pursue them wherever they fly; and that the grand Leap of the Whale in that Chase up the Fall of Niagara is esteemed, by all who have seen it, one of the finest Spectacles in Nature.

Such stories are not original. Motifs similar to the sheep with wagons to support their wooly tails are world-wide, as one can see by checking Thompson's *Motif-Index of Folk Literature* under the number X 1202.1. The story of the flying whale seems to have been imitated from early accounts of Colonial flora and fauna composed by such wide-eyed explorers as John Lawson and John Josselyn.[10] But this is not the point. The point is that such satire was esteemed in London and Paris, and was just not expected from the pen of a provincial.

It is convenient to ignore the fact that right up to the outbreak of the Revolution, Franklin was not certain where his allegiance lay. No Sam Adams, he seems to have hovered between the desire to be well thought of in America and to continue to hold his office as agent for four Colonies in London. There is evidence that the Crown sounded him out about better jobs and that he listened, and it is certain that he was still negotiating with the British government over his western land scheme called Vandalia (Queen Charlotte was supposedly descended from the Vandals) while Adams and Hancock and Revere were in near open revolt. Franklin was, it appears, just too sophisticated to be a good revolutionary. Like others, he was irritated by the way the British government and the British merchants wanted to abuse the Colonies, but he had enough perspective to see the disadvantages of rebellion and war. He favored com-

[10] X 1202.1 involves a crippled sow who uses a small cart for back legs. See also X 1243. For lies about fish, see X 1300.

promise, and only joined the Continental cause when it became clear he had reached a fork in the road. Thomas Jefferson noted that "it was one of the rules which, above all others, made Doctor Franklin the most amiable of men in society, never to contradict anybody."[11] Once decided, though, he threw all his wit, shrewdness, and experience against the British, organizing plans for Colonial union, wooing Canada to join the rebellion, and travelling to France to convince another court of the worthiness of remote causes.

Franklin got along well in France. What he had learned from English politics was invaluable, and, even more important, he knew how to accomplish things through women. Lord Chesterfield once wrote,[12]

> . . . a man who thinks of living in the great world, must be gallant, polite, and attentive to please the women. They have, from the weakness of men, more or less influence in all Courts: they absolutely stamp every man's character in the *beau monde*, and make it either current, or cry it down, and stop it in payments. It is, therefore, absolutely necessary to manage, please, and flatter them; and never to discover the least marks of contempt, which is what they never forgive. . . .

Franklin followed such advice instinctively. Certainly not a handsome man, especially with a fur cap hiding his scaly scalp, he was attentive and clever, particularly to older and uglier ladies who, as he observes in his *Advice to a Young Man on the Choice of a Mistress*, are more grateful for one's favors. Almost at once, he was able to establish himself as a living symbol of "sagacity from the primeval forests"—an incarnation of the ideas of Jean Jacques Rousseau. Even the fur cap helped him along these lines, as did his natural fastidiousness and natural dignity, which made contact with this "primitive" appropriate to the *chambre* and *salle de manger*.

For close to ten years he was to charm the French, becoming a member of their *Academie*, negotiating a sixty million dollar loan, shaping the Treaty of Alliance, and helping bring about the Treaty of Paris which ended the War. In 1785, he returned to Pennsylvania

[11] As quoted in Wecter, 53.

[12] See the Letter of September 5 from London (O.S. 1748).

deservedly a hero and was elected President of the State three times. His national prestige was immense, and when he died in 1790, after a twilight of activity in national politics, anti-slavery movements, and educational reforms, his funeral was attended by 20,000 or so mourners. Freneau compared him to "some tall tree that long hath stood the glory of its native wood."[13]

This was a remarkable life; no one can take that from the man. However, it is a painfully American life in which the hero selected the image that would meet his pragmatic ends and then promoted that image relentlessly, successfully obscuring himself behind pages and pages of propaganda. One can say the real hero is always obscured by what he must seem and that it little matters whether a man like Franklin does it for himself or has it done for him by a political party or a popular poet. That's true, but there is something fascinating in a man's promoting an image for mercantile and political purposes in a nation that is later to become the mercantile and political ogre of the world, especially when that nation adapts his promotion as the symbol of its own success. Yet this is what happened, partly because of the popularity of the *Autobiography*, partly because Parson Mason Locke Weems wrote a biography of him, and partly because scores of "Franklin Almanacs" were published in the 19th century, but mostly because time proved his ideas on what a man should be to be the ideas that America was fated to embrace. His work seems absolutely apocryphal in retrospect.

So Franklin is the archetype Yankee merchant; the successful, though amateur, thinker and inventor; the natural sage, self-taught and unspoiled; and the representative of the poor among the rich courtiers. He is the incarnation of the third son of the märchen. And best of all, unlike Murphy, Allen, or even Revere, one can really emulate him in a forest-bare, megalopolitan world.

* * *

Then here we are—a book on folklore and war, folklore and the American Revolution. Teacher before author, I am compelled to leave

[13] "On the Death of Dr. Benjamin Franklin," Lines 1-2.

you with a few "don't forgets." So don't forget that much, no "most," of the folklore narrated and sung by soldiers has nothing to do with the conflict at hand. Don't forget that when the lore is related to the conflict it has usually been adapted from material already in wide circulation. Don't forget that the tales and songs about war heroes and war situations are most apt to enter oral tradition after the war is over and then for deeply human, certainly not patriotic, reasons.

And don't forget either that mass media is the "oral tradition" of our own concrete society. As education and communication eliminate the genuine folk pockets, fakelore, phoney and pre-packaged, takes over the job of transferring the bulk of our culture from one generation to the next. It is what the mother fox of today turns to when she tells her cubs what it is to be a fox. Thus, there may be places in the United States where the mother foxes yet turn to genuine folk tradition, but they are ethnic, regional, and sometimes occupational pockets, fast vanishing, fast becoming quaint, their lore unable to meet the challenge of urban pap. This is the lesson the demise of a fitting legend like Tim Murphy's teaches us; this is the lesson the fakelore fame of Paul Revere and Ben Franklin teaches us. Lessons we could but repeat were we to study other Continental heroes, other lores or other wars. It is the lesson that forces folklorists to welcome the likes of Revere and Franklin under the aegis of our discipline, not because they gained their share of uncertain glory from the folk in the way Tim Murphy or even Ethan Allen did, but because they serve our society the way Murphy and Allen served the woodland farms and upland villages—when the world was younger and there was no smog to cloud an April day!

Index

Name and Subject Index

Index to Song and Poem Texts

Index to Texts of Folktales